SECOND EDITION

# EVERYMAN IN EUROPE

## ESSAYS IN SOCIAL HISTORY

*Volume 2 — The Industrial Centuries*

ALLAN MITCHELL
*University of California at San Diego*

ISTVAN DEAK
*Columbia University*

PRENTICE-HALL, INC., ENGLEWOOD CLIFFS, NEW JERSEY 07632

**Library of Congress Cataloging in Publication Data**

Mitchell, Allan, comp.
Everyman in Europe.

Includes bibliographies.
CONTENTS: v. 1. The preindustrial millennia.
—v. 2. Social history—Modern, 1500- —Addresses,
essays, lectures—Collected works. I. Deák, István.
HN13.M58 1981 940 80-26438
ISBN 0-13-293613-5 (v. 1)
ISBN 0-13-293621-6 (v. 2)

To Four Women: *Gloria, Catherine, Alexandra, and Eva*

Editorial production/supervision and interior design by Cyrus Veeser
Cover design by A Good Thing, Inc.
Manufacturing buyer: Edmund W. Leone



Printed in the United States of America

10 9 8 7 6 5 4 3 2

Prentice-Hall International, Inc., *London*
Prentice-Hall of Australia Pty. Limited, *Sydney*
Prentice-Hall of Canada, Ltd., *Toronto*
Prentice-Hall of India Private Limited, *New Delhi*
Prentice-Hall of Japan, Inc., *Tokyo*
Prentice-Hall of Southeast Asia Pte. Ltd., *Singapore*
Whitehall Books Limited, Wellington, *New Zealand*

# CONTENTS

# PREFACE

History books ordinarily record major events in a way that we learn not only what happened, and when, but also why. No one would deny that these are important things to know, and few would dispute that it is a necessary and proper function of historians to be concerned with the impact of such events. Yet there has been for some time a realization among professional historians, as well as among students, that history needs to be something more than an analysis of important changes in the conduct of our lives. These changes are brought about by outstanding individuals, by elite groups, or by the faceless masses descending in the streets or marching on the battlefields. If we are really to understand the past, then we ought to know much more about the majority of humankind, about the individuals who make up the faceless masses, about people who endured rather than instigated the events we read about in the books. It is the special concern, then, of this book to learn how most people lived rather than how a few acted.

Most men and women who populate this world have always been poor and uneducated. This is not to say that they have been altogether powerless and inarticulate. What it does mean is that they have tended to express themselves and their interests in social groups, of one sort or another, rather than as individuals. To comprehend their behavior it is therefore more useful to think in terms of social types than of personalities. In the pages that follow, proper names will consequently figure infrequently. As important as they are, it is not Pericles, Julius Caesar, Henry VIII, and Napoleon who stand here in the foreground; rather, it is the peasant, the worker, the woman, and the youth. In short, our chief protagonist is Everyman.

By the careful selection of articles and excerpts we have attempted to trace the changing circumstances and activities of ordinary people from Greek civilization to the present time. Our focus is Europe, and we have attempted to define Europe as broadly as possible, drawing our examples from Ireland to Russia. Too often Europe is conceived largely in terms of what is most familiar to us and to the majority of Western historians: Britain and France. By giving central and eastern Europe their due we hope to redress the balance and to suggest a truer picture of European society.

The attentive reader will quickly perceive that generalizations about Everyman in one area of Europe at a given time are not readily applicable to other areas and other times. Can we nonetheless say that the various social types under consideration have something in common? Is there any constant factor among so many people in such a multitude of times and places? If so, it is certainly *not* that they have been deaf and dumb throughout European history. To the contrary, in their own way they have often and unmistakenly expressed enthusiasm, or dissatisfaction, or just indifference. Even the ostensibly most random forms of violence and deviant modes of behavior have sometimes spoken eloquently as to the character of European society. Yet Everyman has hardly been the master of his own fate, and this has perhaps been the salient characteristic of most people all along: they usually take rather than give orders. They do not command; they obey—or at least they are expected to do so.

Is this, then, a history of the oppressed? That is a question that readers must finally answer for themselves. There is certainly much evidence to support an affirmative reply. Still, readers cannot remain unaware of the relativity of such a notion as "oppression." What degree of consciousness of their deprived social status must oppressed people attain before they want to change it? What degree of liberty is required in order to escape oppression? These are not simple issues, and they are not much clarified by dogmatic assertions of whatever political persuasion. The historian is always on the side of complexity; the dogmatist will therefore find little support here for his terrible simplifications.

We have thus kept two objectives in view: to select essays that are adequate to the difficulty of the subject rather than to choose brief and random fragments, and to achieve a sense of variety by drawing on a broad sample of historical techniques. Readers should gain the altogether legitimate impression that social history is far from becoming a monolithic discipline that represents a fixed consensus of opinion or approach. Only a moribund intellectual enterprise might present such uniformity, and social history, we believe, is still in its adolescence.

The notion that European society was transformed in modern times by an "industrial revolution" need not be accepted without reservation. In the first place, the term "revolution" implies a rapid and thorough change, whereas the development of an industrial society in Europe has been slow, uneven, and incomplete. The transformation was, moreover, not exclusively a matter of industry: one must also take into account demographic, agricultural, and technological innovations of considerable magnitude and complexity. To separate cause from effect, or symptom from correlation, is no simple task.

Another preliminary word of caution: we are perhaps unduly conditioned to believe that history consists of winners and losers. Thus, we may be inclined, without a flicker of protest, to accept the assertion that modern times were marked by the "triumph" of the bourgeoisie. Yet we would do well to recall that the results of a protracted social evolution are seldom to be measured by box scores or body counts, as if history were an athletic contest or a formal military engagement. Even if we could derive a precise definition of "bourgeois"—which would hardly hold for the entire European continent—we cannot be quite certain what "to win" really means in social terms. We know only that industrialization has meant an important alteration in the quality of life for most Europeans. A careful study of the essays in this volume should enrich our understanding of that complex phenomenon.

The preparation of this volume, as well as the preceding one, was greatly facilitated by the superb editorial care of Pieter M. Judson and John S. Micgiel, doctoral candidates in history at Columbia University.

PART

I

# THE AGONY OF INDUSTRIALIZING: 1750-1850

The pace of life noticeably quickened after the middle of the eighteenth century. Not only is that impression common to historians of modern Europe, it was already shared by most of the people who lived at the time. Although the ramifications are, of course, far too complex and numerous to be listed in a few lines, we can nonetheless begin by recalling some of the more salient reasons for that shared perception of increasing speed.

For one thing, the birth rate in Europe started to rise remarkably. A demographic surge meant more births, more children, and also—given the still primitive conditions of hygiene and medicine—more infant deaths. Had all of this activity occurred in scattered rural families, it might have had less impact. But the population growth was simultaneous with a drift toward much greater urbanization. While the expansion of cities was to have some long-term advantages for those who lived in them—they would, for example, have greater access to public education—the immediate experience of urbanites was likely to be crowding, filth, and stress.

This commotion was abetted by improvements in transportation and communication. Roads, canals, and finally railways provided new avenues of movement for goods and for people who dared to venture beyond their agricultural plot or local village. Travel was still relatively slow and uncomfortable, when measured by later standards, but it was feasible and more frequent. Gossip, propaganda, and ideas also percolated more easily in a society that began to develop a taste for pamphlets, cartoons, newspapers, and novels. It is unnecessary to exaggerate the extent to which the Enlightenment directly influenced the thinking of common people—who were ordinarily illiterate—in order to grant that a certain intellectual fermentation was in process during the late eighteenth century. Slogans in print were readily spread by word of mouth. Otherwise the onset and exhilarating shock of the French Revolution would be difficult to comprehend. Politics were no longer confined to royal chambers and became the concern of virtually everyone. The lives of very few Europeans were not in some way disturbed by Napoleon Bonaparte; most of them became infected sooner or later with the booster spirit of nationalism. These were important changes and disruptions that could not fail to agitate the surface of European society.

In this period Britain became the leader, the workshop of Europe, far exceeding the Continent in the earliest development of industrial technology. The social effects there were thus more visible and have been studied more closely than elsewhere. Yet it was already clear that no European nation would remain long untouched and that all would respond in their fashion by bounding ahead or lagging behind. Industry became synonymous with economic progress and "modernization." But there was a heavy social price to pay, and we must now try to count the cost of industrializing.

## CHAPTER I

# THE RURAL REVOLUTION

Without industry, no revolution; without population growth, no industry; without more productive agriculture, no population growth. Probably most historians hold such a concatenation of assumptions to be justified. Stated more cogently, they add up to this: the industrial revolution was necessarily launched from an improved agricultural base. Although this proposition may essentially be correct, it is certainly not as simple as one might suppose. We are still left with the problem of defining what we mean by improvement, and we need to comprehend the interaction of expansion in agriculture and industry.

*E. R. Chamberlin* describes the changing landscape in England during the latter half of the eighteenth century and thereby allows us to grasp what the legal term "enclosure" actually meant to poorer villagers and peasants. For them the confiscation of common lands usually resulted in a personal loss or, at best, a temporary gain. But there is no doubt that the collective effect of the greater rationalization of agriculture was to increase dramatically the supply of available foodstuffs for the entire population of the islands.

*Gwynne Lewis* records the impact of the French Revolution on rural France. The peasantry already owned nearly one third of French land before 1789. While that point is important, several qualifications are in order. The proprietorship of peasants was far from being in proportion to the actual percentage of rural labor in the total population. Also, their lands tended to be poorer and more peripheral as well as smaller than those of the higher estates. And, though few remained serfs, most peasants were still burdened with the galling taxation of the Old Regime. Thus, the complaints, born both of rising expectations and bothersome restrictions, led to the rural violence of the first revolutionary months, for which the climax was the so-called Great Fear. This account considers the many ramifications and ambiguities of the French Revolution in early nineteenth-century France.

*Jerome Blum* draws a contrast between western and eastern Europe. While personal liberty and peasant landholding were spreading in the West, the condition of the Russian peasantry worsened drastically. The onset of new agricultural and industrial techniques brought no commensurate social benefit to the mass of the Russian people mired in serfdom. The consequence was a growing sense of desperation and the exacerbation of long-standing grievances. Until the nineteenth century the only recourse of the peasant was an attempt to escape. But conditions grew so depressing that local insurrections began to occur with increasing frequency. The cumulative effect was to unnerve the tsarist regime and finally to open the way to formal emancipation of the serfs. Not bright ideals but sheer deprivation was, in this case, the motor force of social change.

At least one observation emerges from these discussions: the delicate balance of an old order was everywhere being permanently upset. In some form or other the process of industralization was spreading like an infectious disease. No aspect or area of the European social organism was completely immune. Even the most remote and backward corners of the mainland were bound to feel the repercussions sooner or later. No class and no region could maintain total stability once another was thrown into flux.

E. R. CHAMBERLIN

# CHANGES IN ENGLISH AGRICULTURE

The land through which the black fingers of the railroad were tentatively groping was going through a change as profound as that which affected the towns. It was a change that was, physically, immediately obvious—so much so that a man in his forties at the turn of the eighteenth century would scarcely recognize the village surroundings of his childhood. The ancient nucleus of manor, church and inn remained and would remain: it was the organic, living part of the village that had altered its appearance. Where the village had once stood at—or near—the centre of a huge, treeless, rather bleak field, it was surrounded now with neatly hedged smaller fields. Once, the villager could have walked for miles through the so-called waste or common land that surrounded the village holding. Now, he would be brought to an abrupt halt by a shoulder-high hedge of thorn, pretty enough in spring with its white or pink blossoms, but forming an impassable barrier nevertheless. From the hedges, and the coppices in between, rose hundreds of sturdy young trees—oak and elm for the most part—masking a landscape that once swept unbroken to the horizon.

Enclosure of lands had been going on for centuries, but on an *ad hoc* basis as the important landowners made private arrangements with their smaller neighbours. The pace began to accelerate in the early eighteenth century. There was no one obvious reason for the increase in pace except, perhaps, the self-evident fact that larger units of land were more efficiently farmed than small, isolated strips. From the 1750s Parliament took a hand in the process with the enactment of private Bills of Enclosure. The procedure was, in theory, admirably democratic: a given area could not be enclosed unless the owners of four-fifths of the individual strips assented. In fact, four-fifths of the strips could be owned by two or three wealthy farmers while the remaining one-fifth was split up among scores of men. But once the Bill had been passed, all holders of land in the village had no option but to be included in the scheme. They were not brutally dispossessed: again, in theory, a democratic inquiry was held by parliamentary commissioners whose task was to re-distribute the land and allocate either land or money, in compensation, to the smaller men. In practice, the commissioners were almost invaribly drawn from the ranks of the major

From E. R. Chamberlin, *The Awakening Giant: Britain in the Industrial Revolution* (London: B. T. Batsford Ltd., 1976), pp. 40–44, by permission of the publisher.

landowners, the very men who had promoted the Bill in the first instance and who now had a free hand to adjust the holdings so as best to suit their own convenience.

The pre-enclosure, openfield system had been the last vestige of the ancient system of land tenure which saw the use of soil as essentially the same as the use of air or water. The medieval feudal system had superimposed a social hierarchy upon that ancient fabric, yet even the most absolute feudal lord had hesitated to claim sovereignty over the common lands. The peasant farmer picked up his tiny strips of arable land in exactly the same way as the great man picked up his estates—by purchase or, more usually, by marriage and inheritance. But all had equal right to the common land. The nature of that land varied enormously according to the terrain. It could be meadowland or moorland, marsh, woodland, mountain or downland. The main use of the common land was, for the most part, for grazing, although that seems to have been poor enough under the best of circumstances: "It is painful to observe the very wretched appearance of the animals who have no other dependence but upon the pasture of these commons, and who, in most instances, bear a greater resemblance to living skeletons than anything else," the *Farmer's Magazine* noted as late as 1802.

Time has given the small strip farmers an aura of romance as the last survivors of a sturdy yeomanry. In fact, they seem to have combined to pull each other down to the lowest common level. Long after men like Jethro Tull and Lord Townshend had shown what could be done with systematic farming, the commoners continued with an agricultural system that merely exhausted the soil. It could hardly be otherwise, considering the physical nature of the holdings. Inconsistent in size and shape, dotted erratically over a wide area and, above all, subject to common rights of grazing between harvest and spring, their owners had limited control over them. Most were far too narrow to benefit from Tull's theory of cross-hoeing, and the man who experimented with a winter crop merely saw it devoured by his neighbour's cattle during the open winter season.

Nevertheless, the openfield system did give even the poorest man a stake in the land. This had a great psychological as well as a practical value. The small size of the strips meant that a poor but thrifty man could hope to add a few more to his holding during his life time. The common grazing land reared very poor cattle—but that was better than no cattle at all. The commoner could hope to maintain at least a cow, which would yield some milk for his children. The woodlands could support a few skinny pigs which, slaughtered in autumn, helped tide the family over the long, hungry winter. The common lands also provided wood, or at least dung, for fuel as well as a certain amount of timber and stone for building. In an era of subsistence farming, the meagre pickings provided by communal ownership could mean the difference between survival and starvation. Then, overnight, the commoner found himself dispossessed: some 4,000 Acts were passed between 1760 and 1820 during which five million acres of common land disappeared behind quickset hedges. The soaring food prices created by the Napoleonic Wars gave a powerful economic incentive to more rational farming. The strategic need encouraged Parliament to speed the process even further and a General Enclosure Act was passed, eliminating the tedious business of promoting individual Bills. The rights of the poor man were still, in theory, safeguarded. He did not necessarily lose his stake in the land: his share was rationalized, the scattered strips brought neatly together. All he had to do was pay the charges and put a fence round his new property. He was even given cash compensation for the lands he had lost to the larger landowners. But lawyers' fees were high; so too was the cost of fencing. Even when he went ahead and paid the fees and the cost of fencing, his small poor holding certainly could not support the cow and two or three pigs that were denied their ancient right of access to the common. There was little choice but to sell what little land he had and either hire himself out as a labourer or take the road that led to the industrial towns—the road which promised so much but which, for so many, was merely the path to a living hell.

Some of the dispossessed literally fell by the wayside. These were the ones for whom the cash payment proved a most fatal gift. Never before in their lives had they had so much gold in their pockets. The taverns welcomed them and, for a few weeks—or a few months—they knew the heady delight of dispensing largess, the numbing satisfaction of drinking hour after hour. "Go to an alehouse kitchen on an old enclosed country [county] and there you will see the origin of poverty and the poor rates," wrote Arthur Young. "For whom are they to be sober? For whom are they to save—such are their questions. For the parish? If I am diligent, shall I have leave to build a cottage? If I am sober, shall I have land for a cow? If I am frugal, shall I have half an acre of potatoes? You offer no motives . . . Bring me another pot." Then, at the end, nothing: sometimes not even a home, for their wretched cabin went with the land and the new master might not want such a worker.

This was the debit side—but even the censorious William Cobbett found himself admiring the technical results of enclosure. In one of his Rides, through Huntingdon, he noted that "the fields on the left seem to have been enclosed by Act of Parliament and they certainly are the most beautiful fields that I ever saw . . . exceedingly well planted and raised." Behind those rapidly growing thorn hedges, which separated the landless men from the man of property, there was occurring a revolution that was as profound and far-reaching as the revolution created by steampower. Indeed, in the extraordinary interlocking series of causes and effects that gave birth to a technological civilisation, arguably the greatest single factor upon which all else depended was this immense increase in the supply of food.

GWYNNE LEWIS

# THE IMPACT OF THE REVOLUTION IN RURAL FRANCE

. . . The Revolution destroyed the fabric of village society, undermining the power and prestige of the nobility, questioning the basic assumptions of religious life, sharpening antagonisms within the peasant community itself. As a result of the Revolution vast amounts of property were thrown onto the open market, whetting the already keen appetite of the peasant for land. After a generation of war hundreds of thousands of peasants were never to return to their native fields. Perhaps it was the time and energy devoted to these momentous problems which helps to explain why, in the same period, no great change occurred in the cultivation of the soil.

The peasantry owned about one-third of the land, concentrated, as one might expect, mainly in the poorer and more remote regions. In Flanders, Picardy or the great granaries of the Beauce and the Brie around the capital, peasant property was not extensive. It was in the North West that Arthur Young noted during his travels through France that "the richest scenes of cultivation are to be found." It was in these same regions that the percentage of landless peasants might rise to over seventy percent. In much poorer areas like the Limousin peasant properties might account for over half the land cultivated. It was here that Young was reminded "of the misery of Ireland . . . the country girls and women do without shoes or stockings." Most French peasants were not serfs, tied to the soil and their masters: less than one million fell into this category. The great majority regarded themselves as free men, owning and disposing of their property within traditionally-defined limits. If they owned property on a noble estate, and there were relatively few who did not, the peasants paid the *cens* or *champart,* occasionally both, in recognition of the seigneur's sovereignty, for "the seigneurie represented the corner-stone of the social edifice of France." In addition to [a] multiplicity of feudal dues and services . . . the peasant was also obliged to pay the tithe to the Church and the *taille* to the government, the latter tax being a particularly heavy load on his already overburdened shoulders.

The paradox of regarding themselves as property-owners, and yet paying dues to a lord in order to dispose of their property as they wished, had occasioned only sporadic protests among the peasantry until, in the second half of the eighteenth century, the seigneurs and the bourgeoisie began to exploit their estates more efficiently. Frequently the nobility leased their property to merchants, lawyers or even the wealthier farmers, often endowed with a more developed sense of business acumen. The property was then sublet to sharecroppers or small farmers usually on short leases of four to nine years duration. The existence of a growing number of wealthy peasants, the *laboureurs,* who provided grain for the markets, work for the landless and mortgage facilities for the impoverished, was provoking serious conflicts within the peasant community before 1789. . . .

The above résumé provides a very over-simplified picture of rural life; it reduces the complex system of landholding to its simplest terms; it takes no account of the thousands of village artisans like blacksmiths, carpenters, wheelwrights or of the violent and usually ostracised groups of woodcutters, charcoal-burners, clog-makers, who moved from region to region, often living like animals in forest huts, and frequently crossing the narrow frontier between respectability and rural crime.

One should also emphasise the importance of domestic industry in the French countryside. In Normandy, Alsace, Languedoc, wherever textile industries were based, the peasant usually supplemented his meagre income by finishing-off silk, cloth or woollen goods for a merchant-manufacturer. Arthur Young, travelling from Rouen to Le Havre, found "farmhouses and cottages everywhere and the cotton manufacture in all." In Languedoc, the great majority of peasants, particularly in the Protestant districts, grew raw silk or had a loom upon which the whole family worked during the winter months. The size of domestic industry in France, and the existence of a huge reservoir of labour, helps to explain why the country did not industrialise at the same pace as Britain in the eighteenth century.

In a way it was the conservatism of the French peasantry which swelled the rising tide of discontent in the countryside on the eve of the Revolution. It was not that the vast majority of peasants were becoming poorer; indeed, since agricultural prices rose by 60 percent in the course of the century, many were making increased profits from the sale of grain on the open market. It was the attack upon traditional customs and contracts which provoked the anger of the French peasant. More often than not peasants rioted to protect what they had, not to "revolutionise" the system. The seizure of communal lands by the lords; the revision of old charters laying down the precise nature of feudal obligations; the increasing rapacity of the labourer class; the law of June 1787 which destroyed what remained of the old democratic village assembly, handing over effective control to the notables—all this contributed to a growing sense of unease and dissatisfaction. The disastrous harvest of 1788, occurring as it did when the textile and wine industries were still suffering from a serious slump, exacerbated an already tense situation.

It was in these circumstances that the Government asked the peasants, in February 1789, to draw up lists of grievances which would be presented to the States-General at their meeting in the following May. These lists, or *cahiers de doléances,* reflect the misery and poverty of many small-owners, share-croppers and day-labourers as well as a more general hatred of the tithe, aspects of the feudal system and the inequality of taxation. The very act of meeting to discuss the preparation of the cahiers produced a new sense of purpose and hope. In May, the States-General duly met at Versailles, but as the weeks passed in what appeared to be endless constitutional wrangling, the peasantry began to take matters into their own hands.

During the spring of 1789 there had been many isolated reports of attacks on grain convoys and peasants congregating outside the farm gates of a wealthy labourer demanding grain at "popular prices." In July and August, provoked beyond measure by soaring bread prices and political events in Paris, peasant riots assumed a new and more violent form with the burning and plundering of chateaux and monasteries and the destruction of feudal records and contracts. Some of the worst scenes of violence were enacted in the Northeast, although the repercussions of the movement were felt in many provinces. The forces of order were either too few or too sympathetic to contain the violence with the result that many noble families were obliged to flee or to promise an end to the exaction of feudal payments and service. These widespread disturbances provided an admirable pretext for the settlement of personal feuds, the renunciation of longstanding debts and, particularly in Alsace which had a large Jewish population, a renewed outburst of anti-semitism. Some property-owners organised resistance in the larger towns and villages: at the famous monastery of Cluny in the Maconnais scores of peasants were shot or strung up on hastily-erected gallows as a grim warning of middle-class susceptibilities concerning attacks on property rights.

The eruption of violence, news of the fall of the Bastille in Paris, and the very real misery of many peasants in a period of acute economic shortage, all help to explain the escalation of agrarian revolt into the "Great Fear" of 1789. With the memory of one bad harvest behind them and the wheat ripening in the fields the peasantry tended to be singularly receptive to reports of aristocratic plots and the imminent arrival of "the brigands." A cloud of dust on the horizon made by a passing carriage, exaggerated reports transmitted from village to village by travellers, the sight of a stranger in a local inn, precipitated shock waves of panic and alarm which spread in just over a fortnight from northern France to the Mediterranean. There were of course brigands roaming the countryside: a cahier from the province of Picardy referred to "poor beggars, and strangers who were becoming brigands, thieves and fire-raisers," but the traditional rural trinity of rumour, plot and fear exaggerated the truth out of all proportion. The comte des Echerolles, who owned property in the Nivernais, tells us that in his locality, "The terror was so widespread that we saw bands of peasants arriving from all parts armed with scythes and pitchforks determined to march against the brigands, but demanding to know where they could be found." *"Les brigands"* were not the less important in the spread of the Great Fear for being largely imaginary.

The famous decree passed on "the night of 4 August" 1789, which purported to abolish feudalism in its entirety, was wrung from a reluctant Assembly, partly in response to the above events. Subsequent debates, as well as the definitive decrees published in the spring of 1790, indicated that the National Assembly was determined to defend, if not the right of privilege, then certainly the sanctity of property. All forms of "personal" servitude were in fact abolished, along with the seigneurial courts, the tithe, provincial and municipal privileges. Seigneurial dues, however, were not abolished but, unless the peasant could prove that such dues had been exacted from him by force which, in the great majority of cases he could not, they were declared redeemable by purchase over twenty or twenty-five years. There is no doubt that a deathblow had been struck at the privileged nature of *ancien régime* society; there is equally no doubt that for the majority of peasants, convinced that the seigneurs had seized their lands by violence and usurpation in the irredeemable past, the solution proposed by the government was totally unsatisfactory. The logic of a revolutionary situation clashed with that of lawyers and property-owners. . . .

The peasantry was far less fortunate in satisfying its hunger for land, despite the vast tracts of Church and émigré property placed on the open market after 1789. The decree of 14 May 1790 did provide for the sale of such land in small lots and offered the peasant reasonable time to finance the operation. Peasant syndicates were formed to purchase big estates for later subdivision amongst their members, but six months later the government applied severe restrictions, reducing the time allowed for payment and forbidding division of property into small lots. From 1793 to 1795, a certain amount of émigré property was put up for sale and it appears that in a few areas the peasantry did benefit. In certain regions of the Nord department the amount of land owned by the peasantry rose from 30 to 40 percent between 1789 and 1804. It has been estimated (although it should be stressed that such conclusions are rather tenuous) that the number of peasant small-owners increased by well over a million from 1789 to 1815, although the total amount of land cultivated by the peasantry did not substantially increase. It is true that many other factors, apart from the purchase of National Lands, were operating to produce a nation of peasant small-owners and that, compared with the gains made by the middle classes, the peasantry did not accomplish very much. Nonetheless, for the wealthier peasants at least, the early years of the Revolution had proved quite beneficial.

Only in one respect can it be said that the Revolution "capitalised" the agricultural sector of the economy. This process involved the transformation of village life from a collective to an individualistic basis. Certain laws encouraged the division of communal lands in the village; others made it far easier for the peasant to grow what crops he pleased than to be restricted in his choice by custom. This freedom could only be exercised at the cost of the poorest small-owner and landless labourer; the loss of communal rights proved to be a severe blow for the most miserable section of the peasant community. It is also true that the transformation of village life occurred very slowly. As late as 1892 it was still necessary to introduce legislation giving the municipality the right to decide on the abandonment of collective grazing rights. Revolutionary legislation, however, like the influence of the Enclosure Act on an English village, did mark a decisive stage in the breakup of the village as a community.

Released from the burdens of feudalism, the peasantry, or rather that section of the peasantry which produced food and wine for the towns, was to be imprisoned by the controlled economy of the Terror. Although many made a fortune on the "black market," the machinery of repression devised by the Committee of Public Safety brought government much closer to the peasants than at any time under the *ancien régime.* The Terror meant a detachment of the Revolutionary Army, or a *commissaire des subsistances,* poking about in the barn for hoarded grain supplies, or possibly closing down the local church. The government, faced with a critical wartime situation, did its best to requisition food for the armies and the towns but, lacking a modern bureaucracy, was only partially successful. Imprisoning or executing a farmer for hoarding was not the best way to ensure constant supplies of food and the resistance practised by many local authorities effectively frustrated all but the most energetic of the Government's Representatives-on-Mission.

Once the Government, by the decree of 29 September 1793, had fixed a ceiling, or General Maximum, on basic food supplies, the rich farmer, living on the expectation of higher prices, had the same interest as the poorest day-labourer in ensuring that grain did not leave his village. One of the major tasks of the Revolutionary Army was to break down resistance such as that encountered by the sergeant-major of the Compiègne detachment who reported that one peasant, when asked for wine had replied, "that he had plenty, but it was not for sale at the price fixed by the Maximum . . . he didn't care a damn about the Maximum since those who had thought up the idea had only done so in order to get their hands on his property."

The Terror undoubtedly sharpened antagonisms between the town and the countryside: the Revolutionary Army addressed placards to "the inhabitants of the countryside" from "their brothers in the towns," promising that unless the requisite supplies of grain were forthcoming the guillotine was only too anxious to perform its civic duties. The importance of bread supplies to the urban population is reflected in the following extract from a petition of the 48 Sections of Paris on 12 February 1793: "The people must have bread, because without bread there is no law, no liberty and no Republic." If the towns were not requisitioning grain (paid for by the assignat which the peasant, with every justification, detested) or imposing dechristianisation on the countryside, they were sending out merchants, lawyers or rentiers who were eagerly buying up property which the peasant coveted for himself. In the West, as Professor Tilly has shown, "the bourgeois were the principal beneficiaries of the sales of church property." The identification of the town-dweller with the purchase of National Lands and the propagation of antireligious doctrines was one of the distinguishing features of the revolt of the peasantry against the Republic in the Year II. In the Southeast, as late as 1815, Protestant merchants were being attacked as "purchasers of National Lands at the beginning of the Revolution.

Some groups did benefit from the controlled economy introduced under the Terror: rural consumers like day-labourers, village artisans, and the army of black-marketeers or *revendeurs* waiting a mile or so outside the towns in order to purchase grain from the villages which was then sold, clandestinely, at prices above the Maximum. On the whole, however, the majority of peasants were overjoyed to learn of the fall of Robespierre and the dismantling of the political and economic system of the Terror at the end of 1794. For the richer farmers in particular 1795 was to prove an extremely lucrative year. Freed from the restrictions of the Maximum, benefiting from rising grain prices as a result of a disastrous harvest, the big farmer began to imitate the style of life hitherto associated only with the urban bourgeoisie. In the Pays de Caux district, "their houses are well-furnished . . . their wives and daughters decked with the finest jewellery. The old image of the peasant sitting by the fireside drinking his bowl of thin soup is no longer valid." The bitter hostility between rich and poor in the town aggravated by the worst famine in France since 1709, was not entirely absent in the countryside.

The famine of 1795, for all the immediate suffering it caused, did at least serve one useful purpose: it reminded the Government and the peasantry of their dependence on wheat as the basic unit of food production. The Revolution did not initiate any major changes either in the methods of cultivation or in the type of crops which the peasantry produced. Custom, collective rights and the complicated system of landholding in scattered strips outside the village all proved to be powerful brakes on agricultural improvement.

Marginal advances had been made in the course of the second half of the eighteenth century such as the introduction of root crops and fodder for animal stock, but, despite the prompting of the Physiocrats and the learned discourses delivered in hundreds of Academies, the vast majority of peasants continued to go about their labours in the time-honoured fashion. The shortage of cattle helps to explain why the land was allowed to lie fallow once in every three years, even in alternate years in many regions south of the Loire; few cattle meant little fertilization and lack of fertilization meant fallow land. In 1795, the Government introduced rice and potatoes to alleviate the widespread suffering caused by the shortage of grain, but the people had very little notion of how to prepare rice, and they still regarded the potato as fit only for their pigs.

It was only under Napoleon who, like the Physiocrats, considered agriculture to be the primary source of wealth, that important, although still limited, advances were made. In a few Southeastern departments maize was introduced to offset the traditional dependence on wheat and the potato was seen more frequently, although only reluctantly, on the peasant's table. As a result of Napoleon's continental blockade and the loss of France's colonies, an attempt was made to introduce new crops like chicory, sugar beet, tobacco and cotton. Promoted by the Prefects and various Ministers of Agriculture, the majority of these laudable schemes foundered on the resistance of the soil, the climate and the peasantry. The production of sugar beet, however, might be termed a qualified success: by 1815 there were approximately five hundred sugar-refining plants in France. Artificial fertilizers began to make their appearance on the most efficient farms. Although it is clear that these changes in cultivation and variation of crops only affected a small sector of the agricultural economy there is little doubt that they did mitigate the worst effects of the bad harvest of 1812. It was to be a long time, however, before French agriculture overcame the drawbacks of outmoded techniques, the lack of adequate credit facilities and the absence of a truly national market.

Apart from a relatively small number of affluent farmers, the style of life which characterised peasant society did not undergo any appreciable change during the Revolution and Empire.

—JEROME BLUM

# REFORMERS, REBELS, AND ABOLITIONISTS IN RUSSIA

. . . A paradoxical situation—paradoxical at least to our Western liberal ways of thinking—had developed in Russia in the era from Peter I to Alexander II. On the one hand, commerce made important advances, the factory form of production became increasingly common, and an industrial proletariat was called into being. On the other hand, during these same years the social structure of the empire retrogressed. The nobility emerged as a self-conscious class and established itself as the dominant group in society, while the mass of the people were either reduced to an unfree status, or if already in a servile condition had their positions worsened.

This mixture of modernity and medievalism seemed to provide a workable social organization. The empire expanded enormously in area and population; it became one of the major powers of the world; and it successfully withstood challenges from within and without. But as time went on, some people detected serious faults in the system that made them doubt its continued ability to survive. Above all else, they were concerned about serfdom, the central feature of the entire social order. Sooner or later, all of these people came to the conclusion that unless serfdom was reformed or abolished Russia faced certain disaster.

These critics of the existing order can be divided into three separate groups; the tsars and members of the topmost levels of the bureaucracy, the peasantry, and the intellectuals. . . .

The peasants were the second of the three groups arrayed against serfdom. Their record of opposition, of course, was far older than that of the tsars and the bureaucracy and the intellectuals. They had always been against it. But their servile status, their dispersion, and their lack of leadership, had prevented them from mounting an effective campaign to destroy it. The only way they could manifest their discontent was by flight and by sporadic outbursts of disobedience and violence. Into the nineteenth century these tactics had given the government much trouble, but had not succeeded in persuading the rulers of the empire that reform was necessary. Then, in the reigns of Nicholas and Alexander II rural unrest reached proportions that thoroughly frightened the tsars and their counselors, and convinced them that changes designed to still peasant discontent had to be made.

The peasants themselves never presented a work-out program of reform. Their protests were essentially negative. They fled from or revolted against specific injustices, such as increases in the obligations demanded by their seigniors, cruel treatment, the sale of their fellows for recruit substitutes, seizures by their masters of their personal property, or reductions in the size of their holdings. Nor was their discontent directed against the tsar and the autocracy. On the contrary, they cherished the sovereign and thought him their protector. Their enemies were the seigniors who, they believed, gave the tsar evil counsels, kept a knowledge of the true state of affairs from him, and circumvented the orders he gave to raise the peasantry from their lowly condition.

Flight continued to be the most common form of protest. Just between 1719 and 1727 the far from complete official sources showed around 200,000 fugitives.[1] Not only individuals or families but entire villages took off. Some of the runaways did not go very far, while others travelled great distances to start

1 Pavlenko, "O nekotorykh storonakh," p. 398.

new lives in the Urals, Siberia, along the lower reaches of the Volga, or in New Russia. Many in the western provinces crossed the border into Poland, then still independent. According to complaints voiced by nobles at the Legislative Commission in 1767, 50,000 serfs of both sexes had fled to Poland from Smolensk guberniia alone. The serfowners of these western provinces rejoiced when the partitions of Poland moved the frontiers much farther to the west.[2]

Flight did not always bring freedom. Often the fugitives settled on the land of some other seignior and so gained nothing, except that perhaps the new master demanded less from them. Sometimes they found themselves serfs of their old master from whom they had fled, as did runaways from the Spaso-Evfimev Monastery who settled on empty land in Penza and Simbirsk. The monastery discovered their whereabouts, and instead of bringing back the fugitives preempted the land on which they had settled. Others who went to the Urals and took employment in the industries there, found themselves assigned to the plant in which they worked. Those who got as far as Siberia, however, became state peasants and never reverted to serfdom. Local officials there were supposed to return the runaways to their owners, but the need for colonists outweighed the property rights of the serfowners. In fact, the authorities in Siberia did everything they could to help the fugitives get settled, and even went so far as to hide them when they were in danger of being apprehended and returned to their old homes.[3] Similarly, officials in New Russia, eager to populate that newly won region, protected runaways from the efforts of their masters to recover them. By far the majority of the fugitives followed agricultural pursuits in their new homes, but some took employment in industry and transportation, others became professional vagabonds, and some turned to brigandage.[4]

Nothing the government or the serfowners did seemed able to check the stream of runaways. Scores of decrees, and harsh punishment of captured fugitives and those who sheltered them, had no effect. There were more laws about runaways and their recovery than any other subject—a fact that in itself bears witness to the proportions of peasant flight. Periodically, hunts were organized to track down all the fugitives in a district or town, and return them to their owners.[5]

Peasants did not always leave their old homes at their own volition. Large proprietors continued on into the eighteenth century to abduct serfs from the lands of less powerful seigniors. Peter I tried to end this practice by imposing heavy fines on the abductors, but his efforts proved unsuccessful.[6]

2 Semevskii, *Krest'iane,* I, 337-340.

3 Pavlenko, "O nekotorykh storonakh," pp. 398-399; Treadgold, *The Great Siberian Migration,* p. 25.

4 Sacke, "Adel und Bürgertum," pp. 813-814; Pavlenko, "O nekotorykh storonakh," pp. 399-400; Nolde, *La Formation,* I, 96.

5 Pavlenko, "O nekotorykh storonakh," p. 398.

6 Kliuchevskii, *History,* iv, 333-334.

Flight was a passive mode of protest. Occasionally the peasants' discontent took the more direct form of revolt against their masters. Usually these were restricted to a single property or village, and could be handled by local authorities. But every once in a while whole districts took fire as if by some spontaneous combustion, and then the central government had to use its power to crush the rising. In 1707 a revolt against the government of Peter I broke out among some of the cossacks of the Don under the leadership of Kondratii Bulavin, their hetman or chieftain. In proclamations reminiscent of that earlier Don Cossack rebel, Stenka Razin, Bulavin promised freedom and a better life to all the oppressed. Word of his promises spread to the serfs of neighboring regions of the black earth, and violence directed against seigniors broke out in a number of places. The movement subsided in 1708 when regulars defeated Bulavin's forces and followed up their victory with a cruel repression. During Elizabeth's reign troops had to be used against the peasants on a number of occasions. Unrest seemed endemic on church properties, and in the factories of the Urals. Then Peter III's manifesto of 18 February 1762 that freed the nobles of their service obligation started rumors among the peasants of impending emancipation. They connected the requirement of the dvorianstvo to serve the state with their own enserfment, and reasoned that if the former was abolished then serfdom, too, must end. When their hopes were not realized some of them turned to violence. Official accounts recorded around forty outbreaks between 1762 and 1772 in the great Russian provinces, and it is certain there were many more. Between 1764 and 1769 in Moscow guberniia alone thirty proprietors—nine of them women—were slain by their peasants, and five others had attempts made on their lives.[7]

These risings gained the serfs nothing beyond the momentary exhilaration their acts of violence must have brought them. The seigniors continued to oppress them and the government did nothing on their behalf. The peasants seemed to realize the hopelessness of their position, and the first few years of the seventies were apparently free of open revolt. But the calm proved deceptive. Only a spark was needed to set off a new jacquerie. In 1773 it was provided by Emelian Pugachev, and for a few unbelievable months it seemed possible that rebelling peasants might overthrow the established order.[8]

Pugachev, who was born in 1726, was a Don Cossack. In 1773, after many fantastic adventures, he appeared among the cossacks of the River Iaik as a fugitive from justice. He found these frontiersmen, who roamed the southeast corner of the empire, and their neighbors, who included many Old Believers, full of grievances against the government's efforts to impose new restrictions on them. Pugachev saw a ready-made opportunity to make himself the leader of a mass movement. So he adopted a ruse that was not new to Russian history. He

7 Semevskii, *Krest'iane,* I, 347, 356–357.

8 There is a large literature on this rising. The best work in a Western tongue that I have come across is Portal, "Pugačev: une révolution manquée."

declared himself to be the tsar, namely, Peter III, husband of Catherine and rightful sovereign of Russia. The circumstances of Peter's deposition and murder in 1762 were unknown to the people. Rumors had spread among them that he had been driven from the throne because he had wanted to help the peasants, and that he had miraculously escaped death and was in hiding, waiting the time when he could win back what was rightfully his and carry through the reforms he had originally planned. Several adventurers found it easy to convince ignorant peasants that they were indeed the tsar, but none of the other false Peters enjoyed Pugachev's success, nor, apparently, possessed his qualities of leadership.

The Iaik cossacks took him at his word and put themselves under his command. On 17 September 1773 he issued the first of the proclamations that made his rebellion a genuine social revolution. He promised his followers freedom and the ownership of all the land. The news that "Peter III" had declared a war for liberty spread quickly to the Bashkirs, the nomadic indigenes of the borderland, who had long harbored a hatred of Moscow's domination, and to the harshly exploited workers in the factories of the Urals. These people joined Pugachev. In an incredibly short time nearly all the Eurasian frontier was in revolt.

In October 1773 the central government realized it had a full-scale war on its hands, and launched a major campaign against the rebels. Pugachev suffered reverses and retreated northward. Here he began a new stage in his rising. For the first time he raised his standard in a farming area where the peasants were serfs of private landlords. He arrived outside Kazan and took the city. The road to Moscow lay before him. But once again government forces defeated him and he ordered a withdrawal to the south. On 31 July 1774 he addressed a manifesto to the serfs of the region through which he was passing, emancipating them from their bondage and from all obligations to lord and state, and giving them possession of "the fields, forests, meadows, fisheries, and saltpans without cost and without obrok." He commanded them to seize, punish, and hang the nobles whom he called "the foes of Our rule and the disturbers of the empire and the despoilers of the peasants," and proclaimed that "after the extermination of these enemies, these criminal nobles, everyone will be able to enjoy tranquility and a peaceful life that will endure till the end of time."[9] The serfs responded with wild enthusiasm to this trumpet call. Just at the rumor of his approach thousands of them left their villages to join his columns, and to plunder, burn, and kill.

But Pugachev's odyssey was nearing its end. His rag, tag, and bobtail army of peasants could not stand up against regulars. On 24 August 1774 in a battle not far from Tsaritsyn, where a century before Stenka Razin had first proclaimed his revolt, the army of Pugachev melted away. Pugachev himself fled

9 *Russkaia Starina,* XIII (1875), 441.

into the steppe, was betrayed by his entourage, and executed in Moscow on 10 January 1775.

Official casualty lists revealed that 796 men, 474 women, and 304 children of the dvorianstvo were murdered by the rebels.[10] No records were kept of peasants who were executed in the terrible retribution visited upon the rebellious districts. The gallows put up in the villages did not come down until January 1775, and not until the end of that year was a general amnesty declared. Nor did the rising suggest to the rulers of the empire the need to improve the condition of the peasantry. In fact, in the remaining years of Catherine's reign the government followed an exactly opposite policy.

Catherine tried to stamp out every memory of the *Pugachevshchina*—as the revolt is known in Russian history. She forbade it to be mentioned publicly, and ordered that henceforth the Iaik River and the town of Iaisk should bear the names of the Ural River and Uralsk. Her efforts, of course, were in vain. The government and the nobility never forgot the threat Pugachev had presented to them, and resolved that such a crisis must never rise again. The people remembered him, too, as their only defender against oppression.

After the *Pugachevshchina* official records tell of only twenty risings between 1774 and Catherine's death in 1796, though studies based on local archives and estate records indicate the number was much larger.[11] At Paul's accession a new rash of outbreaks swept across the land. In three years of his reign there were a reported 278 disturbances in 32 different provinces.

In the quarter century of Alexander's rule official sources show a total of 281 risings. During the three decades of Nicholas's reign the frequency of disturbances steadily increased. According to data of the Ministry of Interior there were 556 risings between 1826 and 1854, but this figure included only the most serious outbreaks. A later survey that included data from other official sources showed 712 disturbances in those years and reveals, too, the unbroken upward trend in the number of risings as the years went by. Between 1826 and 1834 there were 148 outbreaks, between 1835 and 1844, 216, and between 1845 and 1854, 348. Then, from 1855, when Alexander II became tsar, to 5 March 1861, the day on which the emancipation decree was published, there were another 474 disturbances. Between 1801 and 1861, then, there were a total of 1,467 peasant risings.[12]

Many of these outbreaks were purely local affairs that were put down by whippings, arrest of ringleaders, and sometimes by soothing words and promises. But some of them took on the character of mass revolts. Out of 261 risings

10 Semevskii, *Krest'iane,* I, 381.

11 Rubinshtein, "K kharakteristike votchinnogo rezhima," pp. 140–141.

12 Liashchenko, *History,* pp. 280, 370; Ignatovich, "Krest'ianskie volneniia," p. 48.

between 1836 and 1854 for which the details of pacification are known, troops were used to quell 132. Sometimes tens, and even hundreds, of thousands of peasants were involved and whole districts affected. Frequently the disturbances were only concerted refusals to obey seigniorial commands or render certain obligations—in short, strikes or collective disobedience. On occasion the serfs beat their lords and estate officials, and burned, looted, and murdered. Between 1835 and 1854 Ministry of Interior reports show that rioting peasants killed 144 seigniors (among them the father of the novelist Dostoevskii) and 29 stewards, and made unsuccessful attempts on the lives of 75 other lords and stewards.[13]

Official studies of the causes of disturbances of 423 properties indicated that rumors of emancipation were as important as the harsh treatment and inordinate demands of seigniors in inciting peasant disturbances. This bore out Tsar Nicholas's conviction that all discussions of reforms should be secret, lest the peasant become impatient and resort to violence. The belief that the tsar had abolished serfdom was found to have been the cause of outbreaks on 210 of the 423 estates. The peasants, understandably excited by the false news, rose when their owners refused to free them. On 95 properties excessive barshchina was responsible for the disturbances, on 26 burdensome obrok, on 9 it was the exacting of arrears, on 30 famine was responsible, on 17 the resettlement of peasants, and on 13 reduction in the size of holdings started troubles.[14]

Peasant unrest was not confined to serfs alone. Nonseigniorial peasants, too, expressed their discontent by open clashes with the authorities. State and appanage peasants protested against demands made of them, and against corrupt and oppressive local officials; the military colonists rebelled against the regimentation of their lives; and peasants assigned to industrial enterprises rose against their compulsory employment and the conditions under which they had to work.[15]

The increase in the number of peasant risings in the first half of the nineteenth century did not mean that peasants no longer ran away. Fugitives left their old homes in a never ending stream that sometimes swelled to huge proportions, especially in the second quarter of the century. A rumor of freedom and land to be had for the asking in some frontier would sweep through a district and suddenly scores and hundreds of peasants would take off. So many runaways arrived in Astrakhan, New Russia, and Bessarabia that the government, interested in colonizing these regions, ordered that if the fugitives had lived in these places for a certain time they did not have to be returned to their owners if apprehended. The owners were to be compensated with a recruit quittance, or by a payment from the person on whose land the runaway had settled. Nor, apparently, were some officials in these colonial areas above issuing false papers to fugitives to protect them from being captured and returned to their old homes.[16]

13 Semevskii, *Krest'ianskii vopros,* II, 583–584, 596; Linkov, *Ocherki,* p. 271.

14 Liashchenko, *History,* p. 372; cf. Semevskii, *Krest'ianskii vopros,* II, 598.

15 Linkov, *Ocherki,* pp. 42–72; Tugan-Baranovskii, *Russkaia fabrika,* I, ch. IV.

16 Engelmann, *Die Leibeigenschaft,* p. 206; cf. Kohl, *Reisen in Südrussland,* II, 24–25.

Peasants also expressed their discontent with their masters by complaints to the government. The law specifically forbade this, and provided for heavy punishments of those who dared to go over the head of their owners. Yet some serfs were willing to take the chance, and a small but steady stream of petitions for protection and relief came to the throne and to the Ministry of Interior. In 1840, for example, the Ministry received three complaints; in 1842 it received seven and the tsar eight. The Ministry also reported in 1842 that local authorities received a large number of complaints from peasants about seigniorial excesses, but "strict investigation" showed these charges to be unfounded. In 1844 the Ministry received 51 complaints, in 1845, 44 and the emperor 3, and so on.[17] Finally, some peasants found the only way of escape from the intolerable condition of their lives was through suicide. These were officially reported as "sudden deaths." After the emancipation a notable decline was reported in the suicide rate.[18]

The increase in rural unrest in the nineteenth century, and especially after 1825, was fearfully watched by the tsars. . . . Nicholas was certain that unless reforms were inaugurated social revolution was inevitable, even though he himself was incapable of introducing them. His successor, Alexander II, equally convinced of the dangers that peasant discontent portended, and possessed of the resolution to command emancipation, justified his act by warning that if serfdom was not abolished by legal methods the peasants would take matters into their own hands. . . .

17 Semevskii, *Krest'ianskii vopros,* II, 571–573.

18 Masaryk, *Spirit,* I, 131 and note.

# CHAPTER 2

# THE FORMATION OF A LABOR FORCE

Although the majority of Europeans remained rural well into the nineteenth century, the city always played a role disproportionate to the number of its inhabitants. This was no less true in antiquity and in medieval times than during more recent eras. Might European civilization therefore be fairly judged according to the ebb and flow of its townlife? This is an intriguing question, as the growing interest in urban history testifies. In any event, the century of early industrialization was a troubled and trying time for the populace huddled in the cities. Between 1750 and 1850 the density of the urban masses noticeably increased and the predictable consequences were material deterioration and social tension.

*E. P. Thompson* records the first stirrings of organized labor in Britain. Incipient class antagonisms were evident, especially in the towns and cities, where a growing population of workers came to resent the imposition of legal restrictions and punishments that they considered unfair. Bread riots were the most common form of popular protest. Thompson warns us, however, to beware of distorting the character of "mobs" that took to the streets. They were often better disciplined and more purposeful than we perhaps imagine. They were, moreover, harbingers of a new laboring class that was increasingly to congregate in mill towns as the nineteenth century progressed. In social terms, the industrial revolution was beginning to take recognizable form.

*E. J. Hobsbawm* starkly poses the alternatives of the urban poor: to imitate the wealthy as best they could, to resign themselves to a degraded and demoralized existence in the slums, or to rebel. Hobsbawm gives a grim view of the impact of early industrialization in terms of urban crowding, disease, crime, alcoholism, prostitution, and pauperism. Consequently, he finds the rationale of rebellion both sensible and self-evident. Nothing was more inevitable, he contends, than the socialist attempts to create a labor movement as a vehicle of organized protest.

*William L. Langer* points out that the huge increase in the European population beginning in the mid-eighteenth century inevitably meant that poverty would be more widespread and would affect country and town alike. For want of reliable statistics, it is impossible to generalize securely about the impact of industrialization on the European standard of living. But an increase in pauperism and the instability of urban employment were manifest facts of life. On the Continent, Langer estimates, well over half of the entire labor force might be left unemployed at certain times. While prices were high, therefore, unskilled labor remained cheap and masses of people were consequently held at a level of bare subsistence.

If there is one impression of mid-nineteenth-century Europe that we are likely to retain from these analyses, it is that of growing confusion. Yet the urban picture is not without certain apparent contours, and we can discern at least three recurrent themes: the social dislocation of the lower classes, the obvious gap between rich and poor, and the tendency toward formal association of the working population. The full consequences could not be clearly foreseen, but it is easy to understand the great expectations of those who anticipated a wave of social revolution.

—E. P. THOMPSON

# THE MAKING OF THE ENGLISH WORKING CLASS

If we are concerned with historical change we must attend to the articulate minorities. But these minorities arise from a less articulate majority whose consciousness may be described as being, at this time, "sub-political"—made up of superstition or passive irreligion, prejudice and patriotism. . . .

From E. P. Thompson, *The Making of the English Working Class* (New York: Random House, Vintage Books, 1966), pp. 55, 59–64, 189–94, by permission of the publisher. *The Making of the English Working Class* © E. P. Thompson, 1963, 1968, 1980. Extracts reprinted by kind permission of Victor Gollancz Ltd., London.

We may isolate two ways in which these "sub-political" traditions affect the early working-class movement: the phenomena of riot and of the mob, and the popular notions of an Englishman's "birthright." For the first, we must realise that there have always persisted popular attitudes towards crime, amounting at times to an unwritten code, quite distinct from the laws of the land. Certain crimes were outlawed by both codes: a wife or child murderer would be pelted and execrated on the way to Tyburn. Highwaymen and pirates belonged to popular ballads, part heroic myth, part admonition to the young. But other crimes were actively condoned by whole communities—coining, poaching, the evasion of taxes (the window tax and tithes) or excise or the press-gang. Smuggling communities lived in a state of constant war with authority, whose unwritten rules were understood by both sides; the authorities might seize a ship or raid the village, and the smugglers might resist arrest—"but it was no part of the smuggling tactics to carry war farther than defence, or at times a rescue, because of the retaliatory measures that were sure to come. . . ."[1] On the other hand, other crimes, which were easily committed and yet which struck at the livelihood of particular communities—sheep-stealing or stealing cloth off the tenters in the open field—excited popular condemnation.[2]

This distinction between the legal code and the unwritten popular code is a commonplace at any time. But rarely have the two codes been more sharply distinguished from each other than in the second half of the 18th century. One may even see these years as ones in which the class war is fought out in terms of Tyburn, the hulks and the Bridewells on the one hand; and crime, riot, and mob action on the other. Professor Radzinowicz's researches into the *History of the English Criminal Law* have added a depressing weight of evidence to the picture long made familiar by Goldsmith:

> Each wanton judge new penal statutes draw,
> Laws grind the poor, and rich men rule the law. . . .

It was not (an important reservation) the judge but the legislature which was responsible for enacting ever more capital punishments for crimes aginst property: in the years between the Restoration and the death of George III the number of capital offences was increased by about 190—or more than one for every year: no less than sixty-three of these were added in the years 1760–1810. Not only petty theft, but primitive forms of industrial rebellion—destroying a silk loom, throwing down fences when commons were enclosed, and firing corn ricks—were to be punished by death. It is true that the police force was totally

1 Serjeant Paul Swanston, *Memoirs of . . . a Soldier's Life* (n.d.).

2 For insight into the unwritten traditions of the transported, see Russel Ward, *The Australian Legend* (Melbourne, 1958), Ch. II.

inadequate and the administration of "justice" haphazard. It is true also that in the latter years of the 18th century, while capital offences multiplied, some juries became reluctant to convict, and the proportion of convicted offenders who were actually brought to execution fell.[3] But the death sentence, if respited, was generally exchanged to the terrible living death of the hulks or to transportation. The procession to Tyburn (later, the scaffold outside Newgate) was a central ceremonial of 18th-century London. The condemned in the carts—the men in gaudy attire, the women in white, with baskets of flowers and oranges which they threw to the crowds—the ballad-singers and hawkers, with their "last speeches" (which were sold even before the victims had given the sign of the dropped handkerchief to the hangman to do his work): all the symbolism of "Tyburn Fair" was the ritual at the heart of London's popular culture. . . .

This second, quasi-insurrectionary, form . . . was a form of direct action which arose in specific conditions, which was often highly organised and under the protection of the local community, and as to which we should be chary of generalisation. The first form is only now beginning to receive the attention of historians. Dr. Rudé, in his study of *The Crowd in the French Revolution,* suggests that "the term 'mobs,' in the sense of hired bands operating on behalf of external interests . . . should be invoked with discretion and only when justified by the particular occasion." Too often historians have used the term lazily, to evade further analysis, or (with the suggestion of criminal elements motivated by the desire for loot) as a gesture of prejudice. And Dr. Rudé suggests that the term "revolutionary crowd" may be more useful when discussing riot in late 18th-century England as well as in revolutionary France.

The distinction is useful. In 18th-century Britain riotous actions assumed two different forms: that of more or less spontaneous popular direct action; and that of the deliberate use of the crowd as an instrument of pressure, by persons "above" or apart from the crowd. The first form has not received the attention which it merits. It rested upon more articulate popular sanctions and was validated by more sophisticated traditions than the word "riot" suggests. The most common example is the bread or food riot, repeated cases of which can be found in almost every town and county until the 1840s.[4] This was rarely a mere uproar which culminated in the breaking open of barns or the looting of shops. It

3 See [L.] Radzinowicz, [*History of the English Criminal Law* (1948–56)], I, Parts 1 and 2. Dr. Radzinowicz shows that of 527 sentenced to death in London and Middlesex between 1749 and 1758,365 were executed; whereas in 1790–9,745 were sentenced and only 220 executed. Thus the ratio of executed to sentenced falls from roughly two in three to one in three: and continues to fall in the 1800s. One the other hand, the majority of executions were for offences against property; e.g., of ninety-seven executions in London and Middlesex in 1785, only one was for murder, forty-three for burglary, and the remainder for offences against property (forgery, horse-stealing, etc.). He concludes that these figures indicate national tendencies, and that "in 1785 the death penalty was inflicted almost exclusively for economic offences."

4 For the incidence of riots, see R. F. W. Wearmouth, *Methodism and the Common People of the Eighteenth Century* (1946).

was legitimised by the assumptions of an older moral economy, which taught the immorality of any unfair method of forcing up the price of provisions by profiteering upon the necessities of the people.

In urban and rural communities alike, a consumer-consciousness preceded other forms of political or industrial antagonism. Not wages, but the cost of bread, was the most sensitive indicator of popular discontent. . . .

Food riots were sometimes uproarious, like the "Great Cheese Riot" at Nottingham's Goose Fair in 1764, when whole cheeses were rolled down the streets; or the riot in the same city, in 1788, caused by the high price of meat, when the doors and shutters of the shambles were torn down and burned together with the butcher's books, in the market-place.[5] But even this violence shows a motive more complex than hunger: retailers were being punished, on account of their prices and the poor quality of the meat. More often the "mobs" showed self-discipline, within a customary pattern of behaviour. Perhaps the only occasion in his life when John Wesley commended a disorderly action was when he noted in his journal the actions of a mob in James' Town, Ireland; the mob—

> had been in motion all the day; but their business was only with the forestallers of the market, who had bought up all the corn far and near, to starve the poor, and load a Dutch ship, which lay at the quay; but the mob brought it all out into the market, and sold it for the owners at the common price. And this they did with all the calmness and composure imaginable, and without striking or hurting anyone.

. . . An aristocratic traveller who visited the Yorkshire Dales in 1792 was alarmed to find a new cotton-mill in the "pastoral vale" of Aysgarth—"why, here now is a great flaring mill, whose back stream has drawn off half the water of the falls above the bridge":

> With the bell ringing, and the clamour of the mill, all the vale is disturb'd; treason and levelling systems are the discourse; and rebellion may be near at hand.

The mill appeared as symbol of social energies which were destroying the very "course of Nature." It embodied a double threat to the settled order. First, from the owners of industrial wealth, those upstarts who enjoyed an unfair advantage over the landowners whose income was tied to their rent-roll:

> If men thus start into riches; or if riches from trade are too easily procured, woe to us men of middling income, and settled revenue; and woe it has been to all the Nappa Halls, and the Yeomanry of the land.

Second, from the industrial working population, which our traveller regarded

5 J. Blackner, *History of Nottingham* (Nottingham, 1815), pp. 383–4.

with an alliterative hostility which betrays a response not far removed from that of the white racialist towards the coloured population today:

> The people, indeed, are employ'd; but they are all abandon'd to vice from the throng. . . . At the times when people work not in the mill, they issue out to poaching, profligacy and plunder. . . .[6]

The equation between the cotton-mill and the new industrial society, and the correspondence between new forms of productive and of social relationship, was a commonplace among observers in the years between 1790 and 1850. Karl Marx was only expressing this with unusual vigour when he declared: "The hand-mill gives you society with the feudal lord: the steam-mill, society with the industrial capitalist." And it was not only the mill-owner but also the working population brought into being within and around the mills which seemed to contemporaries to be "new." "The instant we get near the borders of the manufacturing parts of Lancashire," a rural magistrate wrote in 1808, "we meet a fresh race of beings, both in point of manners, employments and subordination . . ."; while Robert Owen, in 1815, declared that "the general diffusion of manufactures throughout a country generates a new character in its inhabitants . . . an essential change in the general character of the mass of the people."

Observers in the 1830s and 1840s were still exclaiming at the novelty of the "factory system." Peter Gaskell, in 1833, spoke of the manufacturing population as "but a Hercules in the cradle"; it was "only since the introduction of steam as a power that they have acquired their paramount importance." The steam-engine had "drawn together the population into dense masses" and already Gaskell saw in working-class organisations an "'imperium in imperio' of the most obnoxious description."[7] Ten years later Cooke Taylor was writing in similar terms:

> The steam-engine had no precedent, the spinning-jenny is without ancestry, the mule and the power-loom entered on no prepared heritage: they sprang into sudden existence like Minerva from the brain of Jupiter.

But it was the human consequence of these "novelties" which caused this observer most disquiet:

> As a stranger passes through the masses of human beings which have accumulated round the mills and print works . . . he cannot contemplate these "crowded hives" without feelings of anxiety and apprehension almost amounting to dismay. The

6 *The Torrington Diaries,* ed. C. B. Andrews (1936), III, pp. 81–2.

7 P. Gaskell, *The Manufacturing Population of England* (1833), p. 6; Asa Briggs "The Language of 'Class' in Early Nineteenth-century England," in *Essays in Labour History,* ed. Briggs and Saville (1960), p. 63.

> population, like the system to which it belongs, is NEW; but it is hourly increasing in breadth and strength. It is an aggregate of masses, our conceptions of which clothe themselves in terms that express something portentous and fearful . . . as of the slow rising and gradual swelling of an ocean which must, at some future and no distant time, bear all the elements of society aloft upon its bosom, and float them Heaven knows whither. There are mighty energies slumbering in these masses. . . . The manufacturing population is not new in its formation alone: it is new in its habits of thought and action, which have been formed by the circumstances of its condition, with little instruction, and less guidance, from external sources. . . .[8]

For Engels, describing the *Condition of the Working Class in England in 1844* it seemed that "the first proletarians were connected with manufacture, were engendered by it . . . the factory hands, eldest children of the industrial revolution, have from the beginning to the present day formed the nucleus of the Labour Movement."

However different their judgements of value, conservative, radical, and socialist observers suggested the same equation: steam power and the cotton-mill = new working class. The physical instruments of production were seen as giving rise in a direct and more or less compulsive way to new social relationships, institutions, and cultural modes. . . .

. . . And when . . . popular agitation is recalled [during the period 1811–50] alongside the dramatic pace of change in the cotton industry, it is natural to assume a direct causal relationship. The cotton-mill is seen as the agent not only of industrial but also of social revolution, producing not only more goods but also the "Labour Movement" itself. The Industrial Revolution, which commenced as a description, is now invoked as an explanation.

From the time of Arkwright through to the Plug Riots and beyond, it is the image of the "dark, Satanic mill" which dominates our visual reconstruction of the Industrial Revolution. In part, perhaps, because it is a dramatic visual image—the barrack-like buildings, the great mill chimneys, the factory children, the clogs and shawls, the dwellings clustering around the mills as if spawned by them. (It is an image which forces one to think first of the industry, and only secondly of the people connected to it or serving it.) In part, because the cotton-mill and the new mill-town—from the swiftness of its growth, ingenuity of its techniques, and the novelty or harshness of its discipline—seemed to contemporaries to be dramatic and portentous: a more satisfactory symbol for debate on the "condition-of-England" question than those anonymous or sprawling manufacturing *districts* which figure even more often in the Home Office "disturbance books." And from this both a literary and an historical tradition is derived. Nearly all the classic accounts by contemporaries of conditions in the Industrial Revolution are based on the cotton industry—and, in the main, on Lancashire: Owen, Gaskell, Ure, Fielden, Cooke Taylor, Engels, to mention a

8 I. W. Cooke Taylor, *Notes of a Tour in the Manufacturing Districts of Lancashire* (1842), pp. 4–6.

few. Novels such as *Michael Armstrong* or *Mary Barton* or *Hard Times* perpetuate the tradition. And the emphasis is markedly found in the subsequent writing of economic and social history.

But many difficulties remain. Cotton was certainly the pacemaking industry of the Industrial Revolution,[9] and the cotton-mill was the pre-eminent model for the factory-system. Yet we should not assume any automatic, or over-direct, correspondence between the dynamic of economic growth and the dynamic of social or cultural life. For half a century after the "breakthrough" of the cotton-mill (around 1780) the mill workers remained as a minority of the adult labour force in the cotton industry itself. In the early 1830s the cotton hand-loom weavers alone still outnumbered all the men and women in spinning and weaving mills of cotton, wool, and silk combined.[10] Still, in 1830, the adult male cotton-spinner was no more typical of that elusive figure, the "average working man," than is the Coventry motor-worker of the 1960s.

The point is of importance, because too much emphasis upon the newness of the cotton-mills can lead to an underestimation of the continuity of political and cultural traditions in the making of working-class communities. The factory hands, so far from being the "eldest children of the industrial revolution," were late arrivals. Many of their ideas and forms of organisation were anticipated by domestic workers, such as the woollen workers of Norwich and the West Country, or the small-ware weavers of Manchester. And it is questionable whether factory hands—except in the cotton districts—"formed the nucleus of the Labour Movement" at any time before the late 1840s (and, in some northern and Midland towns, the years 1832-4, leading up to the great lock-outs). Jacobinism . . . struck root most deeply among artisans. Luddism was the work of skilled men in small workshops. From 1817 onwards to Chartism, the out-workers in the north and the Midlands were as prominent in every radical agitation as the factory hands. And in many towns the actual nucleus from which the labour movement derived ideas, organisation, and leadership, was made up of such men as shoemakers, weavers, saddlers and harnessmakers, booksellers, printers, building workers, small tradesmen, and the like. The vast area of Radical London between 1815 and 1850 drew its strength from no major heavy industries (shipbuilding was tending to decline, and the engineers only made their impact later in the century) but from the host of smaller trades and occupations. . . .[11]

Nevertheless, when every caution has been made, the outstanding fact of the period between 1790 and 1830 is the formation of "the working class." This is revealed, first, in the growth of class-consciousness: the consciousness of an iden-

9 For an admirable restatement of the reasons for the primacy of the cotton industry in the Industrial Revolution, see E. J. Hobsbawm, *The Age of Revolution* (1962), Ch. 2.

10 Estimates for U.K., 1833. Total adult labour force in all textile mills, 191,671. Number of cotton hand-loom weavers, 213,000.

11 Cf. Hobsbawm, op. cit., Ch. 11.

tity of interests as between all these diverse groups of working people and as against the interests of other classes. And, second, in the growth of corresponding forms of political and industrial organisation. By 1832 there were strongly-based and self-conscious working-class institutions—trade unions, friendly societies, educational and religious movements, political organisations, periodicals—working-class intellectual traditions, working-class community-patterns, and a working-class structure of feeling.

The making of the working class is a fact of political and cultural, as much as of economic, history. It was not the spontaneous generation of the factory-system. Nor should we think of an external force—the "industrial revolution"—working upon some nondescript undifferentiated raw material of humanity, and turning it out at the other end as a "fresh race of beings." The changing productive relations and working conditions of the Industrial Revolution were imposed, not upon raw material, but upon the free-born Englishman—and the free-born Englishman as Paine had left him or as the Methodists had moulded him. The factory hand or stockinger was also the inheritor of Bunyan, of remembered village rights, of notions of equality before the law, of craft traditions. He was the object of massive religious indoctrination and the creator of new political traditions. The working class made itself as much as it was made.

E. J. HOBSBAWM

# THE LABORING POOR

Three possibilities were . . . open to such of the poor as found themselves in the path of bourgeois society, and no longer effectively sheltered in still inaccessible regions of traditional society. They could strive to become bourgeois; they could allow themselves to be ground down; or they could rebel.

The first course . . . was not merely technically difficult for those who lacked the minimum entrance fee of property or education, but profoundly distasteful. The introduction of a purely utilitarian individualist system of social behavior, the theoretically justified jungle anarchy of bourgeois society with its motto "every man for himself and the devil take the hindmost," appeared to men brought up in traditional societies as little better than wanton evil. "In our times," said one of the desperate Silesian handloom linen-weavers who rioted vainly against their fate in 1844,[1] "men have invented excellent arts to weaken and undermine one another's livelihood. But alas, nobody thinks any longer of the Seventh Commandment, which commands and forbids as follows: Thou shalt not steal. Nor do they bear in mind Luther's commentary upon it, in which he says: We shall love and fear the Lord, so that we may not take away our neighbor's property nor money, nor acquire it by false goods and trading, but on the contrary we should help him guard and increase his livelihood and property." Such a man spoke for all who found themselves dragged into an abyss by what were plainly the forces of hell. They did not ask for much. ("The rich used to treat the poor with charity, and the poor lived simply, for in those days the lower orders needed much less for outward show in clothes and other expenses than they do today.") But even that modest place in the social order was now, it seemed, to be taken from them.

Hence their resistance against even the most rational proposals of bourgeois society, married as they were to inhumanity. Country squires introduced and laborers clung to the Speenhamland system, though the economic arguments against it were conclusive. As a means of alleviating poverty, Christian charity was worse than useless, as could be seen in the Papal states, which abounded in it. But it was popular not only among the traditionalist rich, who cherished it as a safeguard against the evil of equal rights (proposed by "those dreamers who maintain that nature has created men with equal rights and that social distinctions should be founded purely on communal utility"[2]) but also among the traditionalist poor, who were profoundly convinced that they had a *right* to crumbs from the rich man's table. In Britain a chasm divided the middle class champions of Friendly Societies, who saw them entirely as a form of individual self-help, and the poor, who treated them also, and often primarily, as *societies,* with convivial meetings, ceremonies, rituals and festivities; to the detriment of their actuarial soundness.

That resistance was only strengthened by the opposition of even the bourgeois to such aspects of pure individual free competition as did not actually benefit him. Nobody was more devoted to individualism than the sturdy American farmer and manufacturer, no Constitution more opposed than theirs—or so their lawyers believed until our own century—to such interferences

1 The weaver Hauffe, born 1807, quoted in Alexander Schneer, *Ueber die Noth der Leinen-Arbeiter in Schlesien . . .* (Berlin 1844), p. 16.

2 The theologian P. D. Michele Augusti, *Della libertà ed eguaglianza degli uomini nell'ordine naturale e civile* (1790), quoted in A. Cherubini, *Dottrine e Metodi Assistenziali dal 1789 al 1848* (Milan 1958), p. 17.

with freedom as federal child labor legislation. But nobody was more firmly committed . . . to "artificial" protection for their businesses. New machinery was one of the chief benefits to be expected from private enterprise and free competition. But not only the laboring Luddites arose to smash it: the smaller businessmen and farmers in their regions sympathized with them, because they also regarded innovators as destroyers of men's livelihood. Farmers actually sometimes left their machines out for rioters to destroy, and the government had to send a sharply worded circular in 1830 to point out that "machines are as entitled to the protection of the law as any other description of property."[3] The very hesitation and doubt with which, outside the strongholds of bourgeois-liberal confidence, the new entrepreneur entered upon his historic task of destroying the social and moral order, strengthened the poor man's conviction.

There were of course laboring men who did their best to join the middle classes, or at least to follow the precepts of thrift, self-help and self-betterment. The moral and didactic literature of middle class radicalism, temperance movements and protestant endeavor is full of the sort of men whose Homer was Samuel Smiles. And indeed such bodies attracted and perhaps encouraged the ambitious young man. The Royton Temperance Seminary, started in 1843 (confined to boys—mostly cotton operatives—who had taken the pledge of abstinence, refused to gamble and were of good moral character), had within twenty years produced five master cotton spinners, one clergyman, two managers of cotton mills in Russia "and many others had obtained respectable positions as managers, overlookers, head mechanics, certified schoolmasters, or had become respectable shopkeepers."[4] Clearly such phenomena were less common outside the Anglo-Saxon world, where the road out of the working class (except by migration) was very much narrower—it was not exceptionally broad even in Britain—and the moral and intellectual influence on the Radical middle class on the skilled worker was less.

On the other hand there were clearly far more who, faced with a social catastrophe they did not understand, impoverished, exploited, herded into slums that combined bleakness and squalor, or into the expanding complexes of small-scale industrial villages, sank into demoralization. Deprived of the traditional institutions and guides to behavior, how could many fail to sink into an abyss of hand-to-mouth expedients, where families pawned their blankets each week until pay-day* and where alcohol was "the quickest way out of Manchester" (or Lille or the Borinage). Mass alcoholism, an almost invariable companion of headlong and uncontrolled industrialization and urbanization, spread "a pestilence of

* In 1855, 60 percent of all pledges with Liverpool pawnbrokers were 5*s*. or less in value, 2 percent 2*s*. 6*d*. or less.

3 E. J. Hobsbawm, The Machine Breakers, *Past and Present,* I, 1952.

4 "About some Lancashire Lads" in *The Leisure Hour* (1881). I owe this reference to Mr. A. Jenkin.

hard liquor"[5] across Europe. Perhaps the numerous contemporaries who deplored the growth of drunkenness, as of prostitution and other forms of sexual promiscuity, were exaggerating. Nevertheless, the sudden upsurge of systematic temperance agitations, both of a middle and working class character, in England, Ireland and Germany around 1840, shows that the worry about demoralization was neither academic nor confined to any single class. Its immediate success was shortlived, but for the rest of the century the hostility to hard liquor remained something which both enlightened employers and labor movements had in common.†

But of course the contemporaries who deplored the demoralization of the new urban and industrialized poor were not exaggerating. Everything combined to maximize it. Towns and industrial areas grew rapidly, without plan or supervision, and the most elementary services of city life utterly failed to keep pace with it: street-cleaning, water-supply, sanitation, not to mention working-class housing.[6] The most obvious consequence of this urban deterioration was the reappearance of mass epidemics of contagious (mainly waterborne) disease, notably of the *cholera,* which reconquered Europe from 1831 and swept the continent from Marseilles to St. Petersburg in 1832 and again later. To take a single example: typhus in Glasgow "did not arrest attention by any epidemic prevalence until 1818."[7] Thereafter it increased. There were two major epidemics (typhus and cholera) in the city in the 1830s, three (typhus, cholera and relapsing fever) in the 1840s, two in the first half of the 1850s, until urban improvement caught up with a generation of neglect. The terrible effects of this neglect were all the greater, because the middle and ruling-classes did not feel it. Urban development in our period was a gigantic process of class segregation, which pushed the new laboring poor into great morasses of misery outside the centers of government and business and the newly specialized residential areas of the bourgeoisie. The almost universal European division into a "good" west end and a "poor" east end of large cities developed in this period.* And what social institutions except the tavern and perhaps the chapel were provided in these new

† This is not true of hostility to beer, wine or other drinks forming part of men's habitual everyday diet. This was largely confined to Anglo-Saxon protestant sectarians.

* "The circumstances which oblige the workers to move out of the center of Paris have generally, it is pointed out, had deplorable effects on their behavior and morality. In the old days they used to live on the higher floors of buildings whose lower floors were occupied by businessmen and other members of the relatively comfortable classes. A sort of solidarity grew up between the tenants of a single building. Neighbors helped each other in little ways. When sick or unemployed the workers might find much assistance within the house, while on the other hand a sort of feeling of human respect imbued working-class habits with a certain regularity." The complacency is that of the Chamber of Commerce and the Police Prefecture from whose Report this is quoted; but the novelty of segregation is well brought out.[8]

5 "die Schnapspest im ersten Drittel des Jahrhunderts," *Handwoerterbuch d. Staatswissenschaften* (Second ed.) art. "Trunksucht."

6 L. Chevalier, *Classes Laborieuses et Classes Dangereuses, passim.*

7 J. B. Russell, *Public Health Administration in Glasgow* (1903), p. 3.

laborers' agglomerations except by the laborers' own initiative? Only after 1848, when the new epidemics sprung from the slums began to kill the rich also, and the desperate masses who grew up in them had frightened the powers-that-be by social revolution, was systematic urban rebuilding and improvement undertaken.

Drink was not the only sign of this demoralization. Infanticide, prostitution, suicide, and mental derangement have all been brought into relation with this social and economic cataclysm, thanks largely to the contemporary pioneering work of what we would today call social medicine.† And so has both the increase in crime and that growing and often purposeless violence which was a sort of blind personal assertion against the forces threatening to engulf the passive. The spread of apocalyptic, mystical or other sects and cults in this period indicates a similar incapacity to deal with the earthquakes of society which were breaking down men's lives. The cholera epidemics, for instance, provoked religious revivals in Catholic Marseilles as well as in Protestant Wales.[8]

All these forms of distortions of social behavior had one thing in common with one another, and incidentally with "self-help." They were attempts to escape the fate of being a poor laboring man, or at best to accept or forget poverty and humiliation. The believer in the second coming, the drunkard, the petty gangster, the lunatic, the tramp or the ambitious small entrepreneur, all averted their eyes from the collective condition and (with the exception of the last) were apathetic about the capacity of collective action. In the history of our period this massive apathy plays a much larger part than is often supposed. It is no accident that the least skilled, least educated, least organized and therefore least hopeful of the poor, then as later, were the most apathetic: at the 1848 elections in the Prussian town of Halle 81 percent of the independent crafts masters and 71 percent of the masons, carpenters and other skilled builders voted; but only 46 percent of the factory and railway workers, the laborers, the domestic workers, etc.[9]

The alternative to escape or defeat was rebellion. And such was the situation of the laboring poor, and especially the industrial proletariat which became their nucleus, that rebellion was not merely possible, but virtually compulsory. Nothing was more inevitable in the first half of the nineteenth century than the appearance of labor and socialist movements, and indeed of mass social revolutionary unrest. The revolution of 1848 was its direct consequence.

That the condition of the laboring poor was appalling between 1815 and

† The long list of doctors to whom we owe so much of our knowledge of the times—and of subsequent improvement—contrast vividly with the general complacency and hardness of bourgeois opinion. Villermé and the contributors to the *Annales d'Hygiène Publique,* which he founded in 1829, Kay, Thackrah, Simon, Gaskell and Farr in Britain, and several in Germany, deserve to be remembered more widely than in fact they are.

8 Chevalier op. cit. pp. 233–4.

9 E. Neuss, *Entstehung u. Entwicklung d. Klasse d. besitzlosen Lohnarbeiter in Halle* (Berlin 1958), p. 283.

1848 was not denied by any reasonable observer, and by 1840 there were a good many of these. That it was actually deteriorating was widely assumed. In Britain the Malthusian population theory, which held that the growth of population must inevitably outrun that of the means of subsistence, was based on such an assumption, and reinforced by the arguments of Ricardian economists. Those who took a rosier view of working-class prospects were less numerous and less talented than those who took the gloomy view. In Germany in the 1830s the increasing pauperization of the people was the specific subject of at least fourteen different publications, and the question whether "the complaints about increasing pauperization and food shortage" were justified was set for academic prize essays. (Ten of sixteen competitors thought they were and only two that they were not.)[10] The very prevalence of such opinions is itself evidence of the universal and apparently hopeless misery of the poor.

No doubt actual poverty was worst in the countryside, and especially among landless wage-laborers, rural domestic workers, and, of course, land-poor peasants, or those who lived on infertile land. A bad harvest, such as in 1789, 1795, 1817, 1832, 1847, still brought actual famine, even without the intervention of additional catastrophes such as the competition of British cotton goods, which destroyed the foundation of the Silesian cottage linen industry. After the ruined crop of 1813 in Lombardy many kept alive only by eating manure and hay, bread made from the leaves of bean plants and wild berries.[11] A bad year such as 1817 could, even in tranquil Switzerland, produce an actual excess of deaths over births.[12] The European hunger of 1846–8 pales beside the cataclysm of the Irish famine, but it was real enough. In East and West Prussia (1847) one-third of the population had ceased to eat bread, and relied only on potatoes.[13] In the austere, respectable, pauperized manufacturing villages of the middle German mountains, where men and women sat on logs and benches, owned few curtains or house-linen, and drank from earthenware or tin mugs for want of glass, the population had sometimes become so used to a diet of potatoes and thin coffee, that during famine-times the relief-workers had to teach it to eat the peas and porridge they supplied.[14] Hunger-typhus ravaged the countrysides of Flanders and Silesia, where the village linen-weaver fought his doomed battle against modern industry.

But in fact the misery—the increasing misery as so many thought—which attracted most attention, short of total catastrophe such as the Irish, was that of

10 J. Kuczynski, *Geschichte der Lage der Arbeiter* (Berlin 1960), Vol. 9, p. 264 ff; Vol. 8 (1960), p. 109 ff.

11 R. J. Rath, The Habsburgs and the Great Depression in Lombardo Venetia 1814–18, *Journal of Modern History,* XIII, p. 311.

12 M. C. Muehlemann, Les prix des vivres et le mouvement de la population dans le canton de Berne 1782–1881. *IV Congrès International d'Hygiène* (1883).

13 F. J. Neumann, Zur Lehre von d Lohngesetzen, *Jb.f.Nat.Oek* 3d ser. IV, 1892, p. 374 ff.

14 R. Scheer, *Entwicklung d. Annaberger Posamentierindustrie im 19. Jahrhundert* (Leipzig 1909), pp. 27–8, 33.

the cities and industrial areas where the poor starved less passively and less unseen. Whether their real incomes fell is still a matter of historical debate, though, as we have seen, there can be no doubt that the general situation of the poor in cities deteriorated. Variations between one region and another, between different types of workers and between different economic periods, as well as the deficiency of statistics, make such questions difficult to answer decisively, though any significant absolute general improvement can be excluded before 1848 (or in Britain perhaps 1844), and the gap between the rich and the poor certainly grew wider and more visible. The time when Baroness Rothschild wore one and a half million francs worth of jewelry at the Duke of Orléans' masked ball (1842) was the time when John Bright described the women of Rochdale: "2,000 women and girls passed through the streets singing hymns—it was a very singular and striking spectacle—approaching the sublime—they are dreadfully hungry—a loaf is devoured with greediness indescribable and if the bread is nearly covered with mud it is eagerly devoured."[15]

It is in fact probable that there was some general deterioration over wide areas of Europe, for not only (as we have seen) urban institutions and social services failed to keep pace with headlong and unplanned expansion, and money (and often real) wages tended to fall after 1815, the production and transport of foodstuffs probably also fell behind in many large cities until the railway age.[16] It was on lags such as this that the contemporary Malthusians based their pessimism. But quite apart from such a lag, the mere change from the traditional diet of the preindustrial man to the ignorant as well as impoverished free purchase of the urbanized and industrial one was likely to lead to worse feeding, just as the conditions of urban life and work were likely to lead to worse health. The extraordinary difference in health and physical fitness between the industrial and agricultural population (and of course between the upper, middle and working classes), on which the French and English statisticians fixed their attention, was clearly due to this. The average expectation of life at birth in the 1840s was twice as high for the laborers of rural Wiltshire and Rutland (hardly a pampered class) than for those of Manchester or Liverpool. But then—to take merely one example— "till steam-power was introduced into the trade, towards the end of the last century, the grinder's disease was scarcely known in the Sheffield cutlery trades." But in 1842, 50 percent of all razor-grinders in their thirties, 79 percent of all in their forties, and 100 percent of all razor-grinders over the age of fifty retched out their lungs with it.[17]

Moreover, the change in the economy shifted and displaced vast strata of

15 N. McCord, *The Anti-Corn Law League* (1958), p. 127.

16 "Par contre, il est sûr que la situation alimentaire, à Paris, s'est deteriorée peu à peu avec le XIX siècle, sans doute jusqu'au voisinage des années 50 ou 60." R. Philippe in *Annales* 16, 3, 1961, 567. For analogous calculations for London, cf. E. J. Hobsbawm, The British Standard of Living, *Economic History Review,* X, 1, 1957. The total per capita meat consumption of France appears to have remained virtually unchanged from 1812 to 1840 (*Congrès Internationale d'Hygiène Paris 1878* (1880), vol. I, p. 432).

17 S. Pollard, *A History of Labour in Sheffield* (1960), pp. 62–3.

laborers, sometimes to their benefit, but more often to their sorrow. Great masses of the population remained as yet unabsorbed by the new industries or cities as a permanent substratum of the pauperized and helpless, and even great masses were periodically hurled into unemployment by crises which were barely yet recognized as being temporary as well as recurrent. Two-thirds of the textile workers in Bolton (1842) or Roubaix (1847) would be thrown totally out of work by such a slump.[18] Twenty percent of Nottingham, one-third of Paisley might be actually destitute.[19] A movement like Chartism in Britain would collapse, time and again, under its political weakness. Time and again sheer hunger—the intolerable burden which rested on millions of the laboring poor—would revive it.

In addition to these general storms, special catastrophes burst over the heads of particular kinds of the laboring poor. The initial phase of industrial revolution did not, as we have seen, push all laborers into mechanized factories. On the contrary, round the few mechanized and large-scale sectors of production, it multiplied the numbers of preindustrial artisans, of certain types of skilled workers, and of the army of domestic and cottage labor, and often improved their condition, especially during the long years of labor shortage in the wars. In the 1820s and 1830s the iron and impersonal advance of machine and market began to throw them aside. At its mildest this turned independent men into dependent ones, persons into mere "hands." At its frequent harshest, it produced those multitudes of the declassed, the pauperized and the famished—handloom weavers, framework knitters, etc.—whose condition froze the blood of even the most flinty economist. These were not unskilled and ignorant riff-raff. Such communities as those of the Norwich and the Dunfermline weavers which were broken and scattered in the 1830s, the London furniture-makers whose old-established negotiated "price-lists" became scraps of paper as they sank into the morass of sweatshops, the continental journeymen who became itinerant proletarians, the artisans who lost their independence: these had been the most skilled, the most educated, the most self-reliant, the flower of the laboring people.* They did not know what was happening to them. It was natural that they should seek to find out, even more natural that they should protest.†

* Of 195 Gloucestershire adult weavers in 1840 only fifteen could neither read nor write; but of the rioters arrested in the manufacturing areas of Lancashire, Cheshire and Staffordshire in 1842 only 13 percent could read and write well, 32 percent imperfectly.

† "About one-third of our working population . . . consists of weavers and laborers, whose average earnings do not amount to a sum sufficient to bring up and maintain their families without parochial assistance. It is this portion of the community, for the most part decent and respectable in their lives, which is suffering most from the depression of wages, and the hardships of the times. It is to this class of my poor fellow-creatures in particular, that I desire to recommend the system of co-operation." (F. Baker, *First Lecture on Co-operation,* Bolton 1830.)

18 H. Ashworth in *Journal Stat. Soc.* V (1842), p. 74; E. Labrousse, ed. *Aspects de la Crise . . . 1846–51* (1956), p. 107.

19 *Statistical Committee appointed by the Anti-Corn Law Conference . . . March 1842* (n.d.), p. 45.

WILLIAM L. LANGER

# THE SOCIAL QUESTION

In the decades preceding 1848 Europe was deluged with literature discussing the "social question" or, as it was called in Britain, the "condition of England question." Everywhere thoughtful people were appalled not so much by the existence of poverty, hunger and disease, for they had been familiar social afflictions since the beginning of time, as by the alarming increase of what came to be known as "pauperism" and by what seemed like the further deterioration of the lower classes. "Such is now the accumulation of misery endured by thousands of skilled and industrious laborers, that no conceivable alteration for the worse can take place," wrote an English journal in 1826, while Thomas Carlyle, in his *Past and Present* (1843), could declare: "I venture to believe that in no time since the beginnings of society, was the lot of those same dumb millions of toilers so entirely unbearable as it is even in the days now passing over us."[1]

Since the deterioration in the condition of the working classes was most striking in the cities, it was natural that it should have been linked by many contemporary writers to the concurrent progress of industrialization. The question was often raised whether the price being paid for greater and cheaper production of goods was not, in terms of human suffering, disproportionately high. Goethe, among others, saw industrialization as a slowly gathering storm, soon to break over the land, bringing with it, along with obvious benefits, social calamity.[2]

Actually it was a mistake to attribute the greater woes of mankind to the coming of the machine, for the frightening growth of pauperism was fully as great in nonindustrialized areas as in the new manufacturing centers. The basic fact, increasingly so recognized by modern scholars, was the unprecedented growth of the European population after 1760. This led to overpopulation, "that condition of a country in which part of the inhabitants, although able-bodied and capable of labor, are permanently unable to earn a sufficiency of the necessaries of life."[3] There were, according to Edward Gibbon Wakefield, simply "too many competitors for a limited fund of enjoyment."[4] Everywhere, on the Conti-



1 Sidney Pollard: "Nineteenth Century Coöperation" (in Asa Briggs and John Saville, eds.: *Essays in Labour History,* London, 1960, 74–112); David Daiches: *Carlyle and the Victorian Dilemma* (Edinburgh, 1963).

2 *Wilhelm Meisters Wanderjahre* (1829).

3 William A. Thornton: *Overpopulation and its Remedy* (London, 1846), I.

4 *A View of the Art of Colonization* (London, 1848), 66.

nent as in Britain, there were just too many people for the available jobs, and the surplus (or "redundant") population was the great ulcer of European nations, "the master evil," to borrow Francis Place's description.[5]

It was inevitable that so great and sudden an increase in the population should have entailed major dislocations in European society. Agrarian laborers unable to find work were reduced to utmost destitution or forced to migrate to the nearest towns in the hope of finding employment, if possible in the new factories, or at any rate in some menial occupation. In the cities many of them were no better off than they had been before, to put it mildly. The new machine industry provided a precarious existence for some, but at the same time proved ruinous for many engaged in the traditional home industries, which were unable to compete with the new methods of production. Taken all in all, it would seem that in Europe the lowest classes, the "poor," those who lived on the brink of starvation and who in the sixteenth century had comprised about one-fifth of the population, had come in the nineteenth to number a third or more.[6]

Among present-day British writers there has existed for some time a school of so-called "optimists," who hold that industrialization brought at least some rise in the standard of living; in other words, that the workers shared to some extent, however modest, in the benefits of the new economy. This was certainly not the impression of contemporary writers and indeed it is a view that has been vigorously challenged by adherents of the "pessimist" school, who think that the lower classes were for a time worse off than they had ever been. The question is obviously one of prime importance, but unfortunately one that can never be "solved," for lack of adequate statistical data. The debate has been complicated by the fact that different students have taken different periods for their analyses, and that the term *workingman* has frequently been loosely used. In the cities as in the country there were endless gradations of labor, from skilled technicians and specialized craftsmen, through artisans, journeymen and apprentices, to the homeworkers of the putting-out system and factory workers, among whom again there were gradations from foremen to the younger child workers. Lowest of all was what Karl Marx was to term the *Lumpenproletariat,* the riffraff consisting of nondescript workers, mostly unemployed and often driven by desperation to vice and crime.

Although the standard-of-living debate has proved inconclusive, it has brought at least some measure of agreement. There was undoubtedly an aggregate rise in real wages, but this benefited the skilled, well-paid worker rather

5 Quoted by James A. Field: *Essays on Population* (Chicago, 1931), chap. iii.

6 Wolfram Fischer: "Soziale Unterschichten im Zeitalter der Frühindustrialisierung" (*International Review of Social History,* VIII, 1963, 414–435). In 1844 Friedrich Harkort estimated that one-third of the Prussian population was hardly able to earn a living, and it has been asserted that in the 1840s fully a third of the Paris population lived in a "precarious condition." See Max Quarck: *Die erste deutsche Arbeiterbewegung* (Leipzig, 1924), 11; Adeline Daumard: *La bourgeoisie parisienne de 1815 à 1848* (Paris, 1963), 8–9.

than the lowest class. It may be that even the poorest element experienced some improvement, for while wages remained fairly unchanged, prices declined. However, all seem to be agreed that if there was a change in the standard of living, it was not a significant one. Furthermore, the actual condition of the poorest class depended at any time largely on the availability of work, about which reliable data are meager and unsystematic.[7]

While it is true that aggregate prices declined in this period, food prices remained high, reflecting the pressure of population, and fluctuated greatly according to the state of the harvest and the general economic situation. Meanwhile, wages certainly did not rise substantially, if at all, until after the depression of 1841–1842. The matter is one difficult to generalize about, for the data, which are abundant, are often contradictory or at least widely divergent. Regional differences were important. Wages were markedly higher in Britain than on the Continent and might vary greatly within any country. Furthermore, wages differed according to the type of work and might fluctuate significantly according to the supply and demand for labor. Finally, any discussion of actual wages must take account of the changing values of money, of the fact that family income was more important than that of the individual male worker, and that the extent of unemployment was often the crucial factor in deciding the fate of the worker and his family.

Certain general statements can, however, be ventured. Everywhere in Europe workers in the traditional skilled handicrafts and trades, as also foundrymen and the new mechanics, ordinarily earned a wage that enabled them to live in relative comfort, with decent lodgings and an adequate diet that might include meat two or three times a week. In England such workers might earn thirty shillings to two pounds a week, and in France twenty-five to thirty francs. British coal miners could earn fifteen to twenty shillings and so could the average cotton mill "operative." The French journeymen or factory workers had about the same wage, but the rate was distinctly lower in Belgium, Switzerland and Italy. In Germany the average worker had a money wage of about nine to ten marks a week, which was somewhat more than he could earn in Austria. Everywhere in Europe, in Britain as on the Continent, the hardest hit were the

7 The literature on the standard of living in England is so rich that it cannot be listed here. Among important recent items are the debate between R. M. Hartwell and E. J. Hobsbawm: "The Standard of Living during the Industrial Revolution" (*Economic History Review,* Ser. 2, XVI, 1963 119–149); E.J. Hobsbawm: "The Standard of Living Debate: a Postscript" (in his *Labouring Men,* London, 1964,120–125); J. E. Williams: "The British Standard of Living, 1750–1850" (*Economic History Review,* Ser. 2, XIX, 1966, 581–589); Phyllis Deane: *The First Industrial Revolution* (Cambridge, 1965), chap. xv; E. P. Thompson: *The Making of the English Working Class* (London, 1963); Sydney G. Checkland: *The Rise of Industrial Society in England, 1815–1885* (London, 1965), 225 ff.; and, on the general problem: W. Woodruff: "Capitalism and the Historians" (*Journal of Economic History,* XVI, 1956, 1–17), A. J. Taylor: "Progress and Poverty in Britain, 1780–1850" (*History,* XLV, 1960, 16–31); J. Potter: "'Optimism' and 'Pessimism' in Interpreting the Industrial Revolution" (*Scandinavian Economic History Review,* X, 1962, 245–261).

handloom weavers, particularly in the cotton industry. In their case the population pressure made itself keenly felt, for the handloom weavers were not exposed to the competition of the machine until the 1830s in Britain and the 1840s elsewhere. Their problem derived from the fact that ever more unskilled and unwanted laborers resorted to the handloom in the hope of earning at least a pittance, with the result that they achieved that and nothing more. While in 1815 they were still earning thirteen shillings and sixpence a week, their wages had fallen to six shillings in 1833 and never again rose much above that figure. In Germany, where handloom weaving was still the most important industry, the wages had fallen to two and a half marks per week and in Silesia even to one and a half marks. The position of framework knitters and ribbon makers was hardly better.[8]

The figures in themselves are fairly meaningless unless taken in conjunction with the cost of living. The evidence is quite conclusive that the average worker (for example, the millhand) could barely earn enough to support a family with three children when he was fully employed. It was estimated that in London in 1841 a family could live in reasonable comfort on thirty shillings a week; that it led a tight existence on twenty-one shillings; and that it could barely survive on fifteen shillings. Another study demonstrates that in Switzerland a textile worker could earn only a little more than half of what was required to support a family, while in the mountainous region of Saxony, one of the poorest sections of home industry in Europe, most families could not make a living and were therefore dependent on relief or charity.[9]

This consideration if no other explains the widespread employment of women and children, who were welcomed in the textile mills because they could do the work as well as men, were far more tractable, and required respectively only one-half or one-quarter of the man's wage. To be sure, women and children had always been employed in home industries, but now they were subjected, even at tender ages, to the long unbroken hours and strict discipline of

8 The movement of wages is, of course, discussed in all economic histories. Thornton: *Overpopulation,* 26 ff., gives a useful contemporary survey, based largely on government reports. For the Continent, see Carl von Tyska: *Löhne und Lebenskosten in West Europa im 19. Jahrhundert* (Munich, 1914); Paul Louis: *Histoire de la classe ouvrière en France* (Paris, 1927), 58 ff.; Ernest Labrousse: *Aspects de la crise de l'économie française, 1846–1851* (Paris, 1956), 93–141; Jürgen Kuczynski: *Darstellung der Lage der Arbeiter in Deutschland von 1800 bis in die Gegenwart* (6 ed., Berlin, 1954); P. H. Noyes: *Organization and Revolution* (Princeton, 1966), chaps. i and ii; M. Peeters: "L'évolution des salaires en Belgique de 1831 à 1913" (*Bulletin de l'Institut de Recherches Economiques et Sociales,* X, 1939, 389–420); Antonio Fossati: *Lavoro e produzione in Italia* (Turin, 1951), 135 ff.; Luigi Bulferetti and Raimondo Luraghi: *Agricoltura, Industria e Commercio in Piemonte dal 1814 al 1848* (Turin, 1966), 118 ff.; and in general, John Burnett: *Plenty and Want* (London, 1966), chap. iii.

9 Burnett: *Plenty and Want,* 45; Jürg Siegenthaler: "Zum Lebensstandard schweizerischer Arbeiter im 19. Jahrhundert" (*Schweizerische Zeitschrift für Volkswirtschaft und Statistik,* CI, 1965, 423–444); Heinrich Bodemer: *Die industrielle Revolution mit besonderer Berücksichtigung der Erzgebirgischen Erwerbsverhältnisse* (Dresden, 1856), 99.

the factories. Besides, during the first half of the nineteenth century there was a vast increase in this type of labor, so that in most mills less than half the employees (sometimes only one-quarter) were adult men, while another half consisted of boys and girls under eighteen. The same was true of the industrial labor force in France, Belgium and Germany.[10]

European workers had been accustomed, long before the Industrial Revolution, to stay at their tasks from dawn till dusk. This traditional workday, long in summer and shorter in winter, was taken over by the factories, though there was soon a tendency to extend it as gaslighting became available. Everywhere in Europe the normal workday was twelve to fourteen or fifteen hours, with about an hour and a half out for lunch and afternoon refreshment. This stiff regimen applied not only to women as well as men but also to the children, many of whom tended to doze off unless prodded to continue at their task. The factory system, unlike that of home industry, did not permit variations in the work tempo. The inexorable demands of the machine therefore taxed the endurance of mankind to the very utmost.

The worst feature of the new industrial system was its instability, no doubt natural under the circumstances but nonetheless puzzling, even to the economists. Good and bad times alternated every four or five years, the depressions coming with great suddenness and the periods of recovery tending to be long and unsteady. This meant that the factory workers were liable at any time and without warning to find themselves without work, while the home-industry workers likewise could not dispose of their product. If the crisis continued for several years, like that of 1838–1842, all business would stagnate to the point where even skilled workers were obliged to accept any kind of work, with miserably low wages. At Bolton in 1842 the earnings of handloom weavers were down to three shillings and sevenpence hapenny a week. Masons, who ordinarily made thirty-four shillings a week, were lucky to earn ten shillings and sixpence. In Bath 150 skilled workers were obliged to content themselves with five shillings and eightpence per week.[11]

It is unfortunate that statistics on unemployment in this period are lacking in all countries, but British government reports and private analyses provide enough evidence to indicate that it was extensive and that its consequences were

10 For contemporary accounts, see Peter Gaskell: *The Manufacturing Population of England* (London, 1833), chap. vii; John Fielden: *The Curse of the Factory System* (London, 1836), 2 ff., 40; Edouard Ducpétiaux: *De la condition physique et morale des jeunes ouvriers, etc.* (Brussels, 1843). Further, I. Pinchbeck: *Women Workers in the Industrial Revolution* (Chicago, 1959); Jürgen Kuczynski: *Geschichte der Kinderarbeit in Deutschland* (Berlin, 1958); Gustav Otruba: "Zur Geschichte der Frauen und Kinderarbeit im Gewerbe . . . von Niederoesterreich" (*Jahrbücher für Landeskunde von Niederoesterreich,* n.s. XXXIV, 1958–1960); Karl-Heinz Ludwig: "Die Fabrikarbeit von Kindern im 19. Jahrhundert" (*Vierteljahrschrift für Sozial- und Wirtschaftsgeschichte,* LII, 1965, 63–85); Valerie Castronovo: *L'Industria coloniera in Piemonte nel secolo XIX* (Turin, 1965), chap. iv.

11 Thornton: *Overpopulation,* 30 ff.; R. S. Neale: "The Standard of Living, 1780–1844: a Regional and Class Study" (*Economic History Review,* Ser. 2, XIX, 1966, 590–606).

often disastrous. Karl Marx estimated in 1845 that one in ten of the European population was a pauper, that is, dependent on relief. This figure was probably too high for the Continent and too low for Britain, where at times one in six was destitute. Reliable investigations showed that in Manchester 50 to 75 percent of all workers were idle in 1841–1842. In Stockport, out of a population of 15,823, only 4,070 were even partially employed, while the remainder were totally unemployed or unemployable.[12]

On the Continent as many as 60 or 70 percent of the workers might be idle at certain periods. In the large cities they made a pathetic sight as in winter they stood around in the public squares, shivering and hungry, hoping for something to turn up. Many were dependent on public relief (which was meager) or on private charity (which was hard to come by). In Paris 85,000 were on relief in 1840; in all Belgium 400,000, the figure rising to 530,000 in 1845 and to 691,000 in 1847. In one district of Silesia, where destitution reached unprecedented dimensions, 30,000 were in need for relief in 1844 out of a population of 40,000. In many parts of Europe the problem of relief had become so formidable that local authorities were unable to cope with it.[13]

Under the circumstances, the food consumption of the workers was absolutely minimal. Their diet consisted of bread, potatoes, a little milk or cheese, an occasional turnip or cabbage, and very rarely a bit of bacon or meat. In some places bread was reported to be a luxury, the population subsisting almost entirely on potatoes, like the Irish peasants. The evidence is conclusive that the lower classes were obliged to spend 60 to 70 percent of their income on food and drink, this in itself an indication of a very low standard of living. Careful studies leave little doubt that the worker in 1850 could buy far less food for his wages than he could in the year 1500. The decline was most striking in the item of meat consumption. In 1500 the per capita meat consumption in Germany was in the neighborhood of 200 pounds per annum; in the early nineteenth century, in both Germany and England, it was thirty-five to forty pounds.

Budgets of workers' families are hard to come by. In 1825 an English family of five required per week twenty-four pounds of grain stuffs (at three shillings and sixpence); roughly two pecks of potatoes (one shilling and twopence); six pounds of animal food (two shillings and three-pence); and coal (one shilling and

12 W. Cooke Taylor: *Tour in the Manufacturing District of Lancashire* (2 ed., London, 1842), 38, 113, 220; Friedrich Engels: *The Condition of the Working Class in England* (1845, new ed. by W. O. Henderson and W. H. Chaloner, Oxford, 1958), chap. iv; Thornton: *Overpopulation,* 30 ff.; Hans Stein: "Pauperismus und Assoziation" (*International Review for Social History,* I, 1936, 1–120).

13 Ferdinand Dreyfus: *L'assistance sous la Séconde République* (Paris, 1907), 13 ff.; Ernest Labrousse: *Aspects de la crise . . . de l'économie française, 1846–1851* (Paris, 1956), 104 ff.; Laurent Dechesne: *Histoire économique et sociale de la Belgique* (Paris, 1932), 411 ff.; J. Dhondt: "De sociale kwestie in Belgie" (in *Algemene Geschiedenis de Nederlanden,* Utrecht, 1955, X, 314–349); Kuczynski: *Lage der deutschen Arbeiter,* 233 ff.; Karl Obermann: *Die deutschen Arbeiter in der Revolution von 1848* (2 ed., Berlin, 1953), 40.

ninepence). Three shillings and sixpence were spent on clothing and two shillings and threepence on rent. In Paris a carpenter's family of four, of which the father could earn 1,200 francs a year if he had 300 days of work, required 1,050 to 1,300 francs to live decently. In Belgium a poor linen weaver, together with his wife and two children, could earn only 12.90 francs a week, while his living expenses (including two younger children) required 14.20 francs. Fortunately, in this case the deficit could be met by cultivating a little home garden.[14] Obviously, wages and cost of living were such as to leave the worker without a margin even in good times. When out of work he was reduced to relief and even to starvation. It was the plight of the urban workers that inspired Thomas Carlyle to write his impassioned *Past and Present* (1843) and produced throughout Europe a landslide of literature on the shocking social question.[15]

14 There is some discussion of workers' budgets in Gaskell: *Manufacturing Population,* chaps. iv and v, and in Edouard Ducpétiaux: *Budgets économiques des classes ouvrières en Belgique* (Brussels, 1855). See also Frances Collier: *The Family Economy of the Working Classes in the Cotton Industry, 1784–1833* (Manchester, 1964), 49 ff.; Burnett: *Plenty and Want,* 42; E. H. P. Brown and Sheila V. Hopkins: "Seven Centuries of Prices of Consumables Compared with Builders' Wage-rates" (*Economica,* n.s., XXIII, 1956, 296–314); Wilhelm Abel: *Der Pauperismus in Deutschland am Vorabend der industriellen Revolution* (Dortmund, 1966), 17 ff.

15 On the voluminous German literature, see Jürgen Kuczynski: *Bürgerliche und halbfeudale Literatur aus den Jahren 1840 bis 1847 zur Lage der Arbeiter* (Berlin, 1960). Carl Jantke and Dietrich Hilger: *Die Eigentumslosen* (Munich, 1965) is an admirable anthology of these writings.

CHAPTER 3

# THE CYCLE OF LIFE

From birth to death the life of the urban poor was bleak during the early stages of industrialization. Even when there was plenty of food it was poorly distributed, and even where there was ostensibly enough housing it was crowded and unsanitary. Among those to suffer most, of course, were women and children. They were the most vulnerable and the least able to defend themselves in a struggle for survival that was everywhere inescapable.

*Olwen Hufton* reconstructs what she gloomily calls a "hierarchy of wretchedness." It is encouraging to note that the eighteenth century was somewhat less distressed than the seventeenth: the population was better protected from plague and famine than before. But if a minimum of subsistence became more certain after 1700, the hardships of everyday life were little diminished. The squalid conditions that Hufton describes were all the more keenly felt by those who endured them because of the ostentatious wealth of the few who knew no deprivation. All in all, it is a pitiless tale of unrelieved labor, shared alike by men, women, and children from early childhood to the crippling humiliations of disease or advanced age.

*Elise Boulding* concentrates on the plight of working-class women, who were usually forced either to compete with men for strenuous factory jobs or to fall into a life of prostitution. In France, since many women were used to marching in the bread riots of the eighteenth century, their participation in the revolutionary events of 1789 was not surprising. If political life was still entirely dominated by men, women were slowly becoming a social force with which to reckon.

*Louise A. Tilly* and *Joan W. Scott* examine the institution of marriage as a vehicle, even among the laboring populace, to convey status and property. At the lowest edge of society, however, there was little or nothing to be joined in holy matrimony except two propertyless souls, who were therefore free to marry at a younger age or not at all. Most marriages produced children, despite the increasing use of birth control in the nineteenth century. The rate of infant mortality remained high among working people, and few poor families escaped the tragedy of losing one of their members by disease, accident, or starvation. Medical practice was often unprofessional or unavailable, and the life expectancy of Europeans was accordingly low by comparison with that of the twentieth century.

The only possible comfort that one might derive from reading such a lamentable record is the thought that sometimes things must get worse before they get better. While this view may mollify our own feelings, it would have been of precious little value to the generations of humanity who lived through the beginning phases of industrialization. We can never know, of course, just how much of the misery described here was in some sense necessary and how much was simply the consequence of negligence or insensitivity. But it is small wonder that some of those who lived through these times asked themselves whether it was all worthwhile.

OLWEN HUFTON

# LIFE AND DEATH AMONG THE VERY POOR

The economist Malthus, concerned in the nineteenth century with the problem of maintaining the precarious balance between population and supply, saw as the only answer the two natural checks, famine and disease, which rising at intervals applied a ruthless shears to a growing populace whose demands were rapidly outstripping food production. He might well have chosen the latter half of the seventeenth century and the first decade of the eighteenth as classic crises of the type he delineated. Indeed, so general was harvest failure in almost all the countries of Europe that historians have conjectured a change in climate, have noted the growth of glaciers—a little ice age—and attributed the hardship to a meteorological upheaval. The debate remains undecided but certainly the closing years of the century did see an extraordinary run of disasters for European food supplies from Castile and Sicily in the south to Finland in the north; striking alike Alpine villages, the cornlands of Poland and even the chestnut crop of the Tarn. In the north the enemy was damp—rain which caused the corn to rot in the fields before it reached fruition or which brought the grain weevil, the *hanneton* of Normandy, to consume the crop; in the Mediterranean lands the enemy was drought, which—ironically—produced a bumper wine harvest but which reduced corn production to one of the lowest recorded levels and brought with it to Spain and France plagues of grasshoppers which descended like locusts and stripped the fields. In the train of famine came disease. It is almost a truism to point out the enhanced susceptibility of an undernourished population to epidemics, to typhus, enteric fevers, influenza and so on; but as well as these, the food crisis of the late seventeenth century was accompanied by the killer of all killers, the bubonic plague, a disease which could strike the nourished as well as the undernourished and which had a devastating effect upon town populations in particular. The coincidence of serious plague outbreaks with protracted harvest failure leaves no doubt that these two events were in some way associated. But whether this was because at such times the rat hosts of the fleas which carried the plague migrated to towns and granaries in search of food, or whether the plague fleas multiplied most rapidly in the same climatic conditions which caused harvest failure is still not known. Great Britain was last struck by plague in 1665 and though the years immediately after 1693 were known as the "seven ill years" because of the heavy death toll from typhus, France and Spain suffered far more from plague in the 'nineties. Then in 1708 came the outbreak in Poland which spread through Silesia, Brandenburg, the Baltic countries and Scandinavia, halving the population of Danzig, fractionalizing those of Copenhagen, Königsberg, Prague, Cracow, Stockholm and Helsinki, leaving eleven thousand vacant farms in East Prussia alone and pressing west through northwest Germany in 1712, to Austria, Bohemia and Bavaria in 1713 and there petering out mysteriously before making its route southwards to Italy.

The combined effects of dearth and disease arrested population growth and in some areas led to decline. The impact was nowhere quite the same. Most probably the population of Europe was slightly higher at the end of the seventeenth century than it was at the beginning though it was differently distributed. By 1700 Spain had 932 *despoblados*—deserted villages—mostly gathered in the arid interior whilst the littoral, healthier and better watered, bore a relatively prosperous air. After 1640 the population of England either remained static or experienced an increase, slight in comparison to the estimated growth of the previous century, and the same could be said of Italy and France though that tentatively in the light of very defective figures. But beyond doubt, the food shortage and the great epidemics both checked population growth and caused a severe dislocation in the economic life of Europe.

## A CENTURY OF SUFFERING

One can do scant justice in a few sentences to the effects of famine and epidemic upon the lives of the European populace. The small landowner was forced to consume seed needed for the next sowing and to borrow in order to plant the next crop; his mounting indebtedness to the large landowner from whom he had to borrow corn at interest until repayment of the debt might even force him to part with his land. This is only one aspect. Women rendered infertile by starvation, an increase in the number of still births, and family units cut down by quite minor diseases in face of lowered resistance are others. Nor did the countryside alone suffer, for local industries were seriously affected by the shrinkage of rural markets in times of dearth when the small peasants, forced to spend their entire income on food, simply ceased to buy other goods. Small towns in affected areas found themselves flooded with the starving and destitute from the surrounding countryside who came hoping to draw attention to their plight. The towns of the plain of Languedoc, for example, became the burial ground of the mountain dwellers of the Massif Central who, disease ridden and weak from lack of food, swarmed out of the barren hills and perished, mere names and a date in a death register.

The effects of plague or virulent epidemic were no less terrifying—indeed perhaps they were more so for no one knew where and who they would strike, the flea being no respecter of persons—and if the rat-ridden hovels of the poor rendered them the most susceptible, the rich were not guaranteed immunity. The best account of the psychological aspects of an outbreak remains Defoe's imaginative *Journal of the Plague Year.* It depicts the rich fleeing, panic stricken, from the scene of the outbreak, the suspension of trade, the inadequacy of the attempts to seal off the victims, the carelessness of the poor who did not hesitate to invade abandoned houses for loot and deal in old clothes and objects which may well have been contaminated. He also touches on another point of relevance—the revival of religious intensity in face of impending death. One of the strange ironies about the late seventeenth century is that at a time when intellectuals were taking their first tentative steps along a road that was to lead them to disbelief, the larger part of the populace was moving in the opposite direction. Processions of penitent sinners, barefoot and sometimes indulging in self-flagellation, led by bishops and clerics, were designed to wring mercy from the deity; and when the plague had passed, splendid ceremonies brought together dignitaries of the Church, town officials and magistrates in flowing robes, with *Te Deums* and orations to offer humble thanks for delivery.

It is certainly not surprising that every country in Europe between 1660 and 1685 found it necessary to reconstitute its methods of according poor relief . . . and that it is from this period that dates the foundation of many of the great European *hospices,* for example of Dijon and Lyons, whilst in Spain the Hospital de la Caridad in Seville serves as a good instance, decorated by Murillo with scenes to recall the love of God for the destitute, his infinite mercy towards the poor and afflicted and the shelter offered by the Church to those in need. Splendid buildings, founded on private philanthropy yet insufficient to cope with the extent of the misery with which they were designed to contend, remain as the expression of yet another paradox—that for all its magnificence, at root *le grand siècle* was a century of poverty, human suffering and squalor.

## THE PLAGUE RELENTS

The eighteenth century proper presents a different picture. The hardship of the late seventeenth century and the first decade of the eighteenth is without parallel thereafter in western Europe. There were, it is true, occasional years of shortage scattered at intervals through the period but the cumulative effect of year after year of scanty harvests had vanished forever. This factor provides the single most cogent explanation of the sudden upward movement of population in the eighteenth century. Throughout Europe the mortality rates declined rapidly not in normal years but because of the abatement of the great crises: "the peaks rather than the plateau of mortality were lowered." Secondly, with the mysterious dying out of the plague—the last outbreaks were in Marseilles and Provence in 1721–22 and Messina in 1743 and both were strictly localized—the greatest killer of adults and children alike had vanished. Other epidemics struck with less virulence and were predominantly infantile, often leaving the family unit reduced but essentially capable of repairing the breach.

One would wish to create the impression of a population that breathed more easily for its liberation from famine and plague without overstressing the extent of that liberation. The population of Europe and especially the poorest sections remained a prey to typhus, enteric fevers (typhoid in particular), smallpox, measles and diphtheria; the first two reigned perennially in all large European cities—indeed in London they killed a minimum of one thousand people a year and perhaps only a small proportion of those afflicted died: and in Sweden ten to twelve thousand people of a population of under two million perished annually from typhus and smallpox. Known as putrid, malignant or intermittent fever, depending on the severity of the outbreak, typhus, transmitted by the bite of a body louse, was predominantly the disease of the poor and associated with the depths of human misery, undernourishment and infestation with body lice. Gracious as doubtless were the public buildings of the great European cities, the streets remained filthy with refuse, and drainage was totally inadequate. Berlin could be smelt six miles away: Linnaeus compared the stench of Hamburg to an open sewer. In Stockholm, Amsterdam and Venice stagnant water and damp dwelling houses offered an open invitation to typhoid and malaria. Every city had its share of ramshackle dwellings, cramped together in medieval confusion, sometimes spilling over the still present medieval town walls. In continental Europe all except the rich let out the upper parts and the cellars of their houses to the poor. Whole families lived within the confines of one room, sleeping on straw, their only possessions a few blankets and battered cooking pots. Hygiene in rural areas was if anything even less apparent. Dwelling in one-roomed cottages where light and air were secondary considerations to warmth, and huddled together often with their animals for the heat their bodies afforded, the laboring poor lived in habitations that were an abnegation of all standards of cleanliness. To read Bishop Berkeley on the cabin of the Irish peasant filled with pigs, stinking children and animal excrement, or Doctor Bagot on the odors that issued from the Breton farm laborer's cottage, is to understand why if the winters were in any way prolonged and the family longer confined than usual the death toll was heavy, for these tiny dwellings were breeding grounds for disease. But though perhaps more perished from typhus than ever before, and though mortality rates in many large cities exceeded the birth rate, in no way did they approach the numbers annihilated in the previous century. Only one French province, Brittany, suffered a demographic setback from *la maladie de Brest,* typhus, which originated in the ports and spread rapidly through the hinterland of chronically underfed beings, whilst in England only the great towns were seriously affected.

## A DEMOGRAPHIC PUSH

Indeed, to explore the conditions of extreme misery in which the population expansion of the eighteenth century took place is to render yet more horrible the demographic stagnation of the late seventeenth. Every child that was born jeopardized the life of its mother, and the female relatives or the village wise woman who assisted at the labor, were powerless to save her if the presentation of the fetus was in any way abnormal. The entry for ''accouchement'' in the *Encyclopédie Méthodique de la Jurisprudence* gives at least one explanation for the larger number of crippled and deformed who counted among the poor in the eighteenth century:

> One sees men who are blind, crippled or physically handicapped from birth owing to the ignorance of the midwife who pulled or pressed too hard bones still soft and membraneous with the result that many are mentally or physically damaged for life.

French doctors, given the opportunity in the 1770s, inveighed against midwives who were in fact well-meaning murderesses of mother and child, their only knowledge based on observations, their only implements farm tools. Small wonder that hazards of birth and infantile proneness to disease caused the young baby to be regarded with a singularly dispassionate eye by its parents who reserved affection for the older children who had survived the rigors of infancy.

If disease and conditions of reproduction make the phenomenon of expansion remarkable, the quality of the diet in the eighteenth century makes it more so. In spite of the improvements in agriculture the Lancashire cotton worker and the Yorkshire woolen worker lived largely on a monotonous diet of potatoes and oatcake, and could count themselves amongst the best fed in Europe. Even if meat and protein foods were conspicuously lacking from their food they lived substantially better than the peasant farmer of central France who lived largely on boiled chestnuts or the Breton with his *bouillie*—a form of gruel made largely from buckwheat, a cereal now reserved for feeding poultry—or the Spaniard on his grease-soaked rye bread. In any country meat appeared only on the table of the relatively wealthy.

Yet in spite of the circumstances, the population growth of the eighteenth century was unprecedented not so much because of the rate of increase as for the fact that the upward movement started from a higher level and that this was *maintained.* It was also markedly uneven. To point out that Europe as a whole sustained a growth of 20 percent between 1700 and 1750 and 30 percent between 1750 and the end of the century is to overlook a variety of regional changes. Broadly speaking the demographic push showed itself first in southern not northern Europe, in Spain, Italy and the Mediterranean littoral of France, west of Marseilles—Catalonia, for example, doubled its population between 1718 and 1788—but the growth had slackened by the 1780s when that of northern Europe was accelerating and indeed was very rapidly to overtake it. From 1750 to 1800 Scandinavia, the Low Countries, Russia, England and Wales, Ireland and Germany underwent an annual growth of about one percent (higher in Russia and Ireland) whilst Spain, Italy and France sustained one of less than one-half percent per annum. By the end of the century the population of Britain had risen from about 5,500,000 in 1700 to 9,200,000 and that of France from 18,000,000 in 1715 to over 26,000,000, to quote only two examples. But population figures alone are meaningless; the significant question to ask is how European society responded to this protracted growth.

## *THE DEMAND FOR FOOD*

Very evidently the fate of Europe hinged upon the two basic factors of feeding and employing this rapidly growing population. For unless the supply of food could be increased sufficiently then the periodic devastation caused by famine would eventually be replaced by long term malnutrition and even before that stage had been reached the price of food would have risen in view of the greater demand. If potentialities of employment were not enlarged, either by bringing under cultivation new land or by developing new industrial resources, then the result would be underemployment, a ridiculous subdivision of existing holdings, and a surplus labor force whose wages would not rise to counteract the rise in prices. Put another way, the population explosion made more efficient and intensive farming essential everywhere and, in many cases, industrialization crucial to the well-being of the state concerned.

Moreover, though one should perhaps not overstress this, even in those countries which were developing most rapidly and which could provide a solution to the problems presented by population growth, economic gains were often secured at the expense of those displaced in the course of change—the artisan in an industry rendered uncompetitive or redundant in a world of larger scale industries and the rural worker, both male and female, when domestic industry dried up, or those turned off the land by enclosure in the pursuit of agrarian progress. In Great Britain especially, this period might be regarded simply as one of painful adjustment to changing circumstances: the gradual transition, for example, from the family as the basic unit of production to larger scale manufacturing which took production out of the home and hence disrupted the whole pattern of the family economy. Moreover each country had special problem areas: those which were chronically overpopulated in relation to their resources and disgorged their excess into adjoining areas—often with the effect of universalizing poverty. The Irish, for example, refugees from misery, were already beginning to pour into London and the larger English cities to infest the cellars and attics with their tubercular lice-covered bodies, creating their own ghettos of poverty where the rich never set foot.

France had the problem nearer to hand. The north and northeast, the wealthy cornlands of the Beauce, the great areas of viticulture of which Bordeaux and Marseilles were the ports must be balanced against the infertile Massif Central, the Alps and the Pyrenees, all of them reservoirs of men and human suffering where available land was only too readily saturated by increased demand. Something under a fifth of the destitute of the Mediterranean littoral were actually indigenous: the rest were drawn from the desolate hills to the north. In Marseilles it has been estimated that a settled population of 106,000 supported a floating population of 30,000 who reserved the profits of their efforts to buttress a minute holding more likely than not in the barren Dauphiné.

## "THE COMMON SORT"

Such circumstances make more readily understandable an apparent contradiction: that it was fully possible for progress and relative emancipation from famine and plague to produce a greater number of poor than ever before. A starving population generally speaking cannot reproduce itself, an undernourished one has no difficulty in so doing. In the hierarchy of wretchedness there is a world of difference between the man who is literally starving—even for a short period—and he who is merely undernourished all the year round. To understand this particular subtlety of the problem of poverty is to understand something of the difference in many European countries between the early eighteenth century and the end. For if by the end of the period the number of those fitting into the first category had almost vanished, the other had multiplied beyond all proportion. Indeed, the most significant consequence of the population explosion was the broadening of the base of the social pyramid more widely than ever before and this was to endow the eighteenth century with its most distinctive feature: proliferation of those whom contemporaries referred to in a vocabulary of distaste as "the meaner kind," "the common sort," the "mob," "rabble" or *canaille.* They were in reality the laboring poor but with a crucial difference for not only were they now scattered throughout the countryside, docile peasants whose occasional *jacqueries* burnt themselves out beyond the pale of civilization, but increasingly they were gathered in towns. All European societies, both at the beginning and end of this period, were predominantly agrarian and moreover in every country the population expansion, as far as it has been analyzed, appears to have been a rural phenomenon. Certainly in the large cities, and often in the less considerable towns, mortality rates continued to be higher than the birth rates but if urban growth was not self-generated it occurred notwithstanding because of the heavy rural influx. London perhaps provides an extreme case: there the number of deaths seems to have surpassed that of births annually until 1790, yet the population rose from about 674,500 in 1700 to 900,000 in 1801. Nevertheless smaller cities like Strasbourg, Montpellier, Nottingham or Leghorn would provide equally good examples. Flooded by immigrants from the surrounding rural area and often almost totally without the means to employ them, they were impotent to arrest the process. Driven thither in a search for employment, attention, relief or because of the enhanced possibilities of criminal pursuits, the intensely mobile poor swarmed into the cities and small towns; teeming humanity gathered together, depressed, emotionally unstable, volatile, potentially dangerous, something for governments to fear or repress. Between the peasant risings of distress in the wake of the great famine of the later seventeenth century and the vicious vindictiveness of the Gordon Riots lies something of the difference. It is expressed eloquently in the works of the Le Nain brothers on the one hand and Hogarth on the other. The first, in the 1640s, saw the poverty of the small French peasant and painted exactly what they saw, without pausing to moralize: they saw suffering and patient resignation, acceptance of starvation, pain and deprivation. The other, unparalleled as the painter of the urban poor, caught an element of the times. He depicted the poor as vicious, cruel and immoral: his subjects were alive struggling beings responding vigorously to the hardship of their surroundings, anaesthetizing themselves to the ugliness of their lives with cheap alcohol or eking out a pitiful income with prostitution or pilfering or both. Often what he saw as the causes of poverty were perhaps the results, but no one conveyed better than he the conglomeration of human misery that made up the back streets of London, "the great wen." That in Europe in the eighteenth century the working classes became the dangerous classes in a meaningful juxtaposition, and 1848, when urban revolutions shook Europe and brought down governments, is perhaps the most natural corollary of events started in our period. Nor is it insignificant that Hogarth's harlot like Cleland's Fanny or Restif's *La Paysanne Pervertie* is a country girl corrupted by the evil influences of the city—a common enough literary device but one which became increasingly frequent in works of this period—for to begin to discuss the condition of the people in the eighteenth century one must inevitably begin with the victims of changing conditions in the countryside: with the subsistence farmer, those of whom Arthur Young remarked in his "Travels in France" they "marry on the *idea* of an inheritance," a tiny unit fractionalized by each generation; and with the even commoner figure, the day laborer looking for work in an overcrowded market; and with their wives and sons and daughters and perhaps even their grandchildren. However else one sees the problems of the eighteenth century one must see them as family problems and begin with the recognition that the family economy of the working classes was their natural economy—the family needed the work of each of its component members to support the whole. Hence, broadly speaking, the man who had sufficient land to provide for the wants of his family had sufficient means to employ that family. In the event of his not having enough, he or his family or both must seek an alternative source of income. In the case of the day laborer or the wage earner this was doubly true for nowhere in Europe could the wage earner expect to earn more than he needed for his own personal maintenance. Indeed, at the beginning of our period this factor was an integral part of current economic theory, an aspect of mercantilism in which the wage was allied with the costs of production and hence must be kept low if goods were to remain competitive. But laying theory aside, one does not need to look any further than the state of the labor market, overcrowded to an unprecedented extent, to appreciate that one did not need to pay the laborer more than a minimal personal subsistence rate and that he was lucky if he could command even that. To do so he had perhaps uprooted himself, travelled vast distances, possibly leaving his family behind to fend for themselves and his situation became less and less tenable as more and more joined his ranks.

Indeed, one can almost make the generalization that nowhere in Europe did any section of the working class stand a chance of bettering their condition in their lifetime and in southern Europe at least an actual deterioration in living standards took place between 1750 and the end of the century. The remark must be qualified, however, because in certain industries at certain times—good instances would be the English weavers in the period immediately following improvements which accelerated spinning output, and the building workers of expanding Barcelona who could command the best salaries of their kind in Spain—temporary demand made an exception to this rule.

## WOMEN AND CHILDREN

If one takes as a point of departure the limited earning capacity of the working man, one must then consider not only his potentialities for employment but also those of his wife and children. In most societies the young unmarried man was not a real problem for poor law administrators, he could make out—perhaps not with ease—but he was one of the most mobile sections of the population in his search for work, and he was the one whom uprooting caused the least trouble and who had the least to restrain him. The same could not be said of the married man or of the wives and daughters of laboring men. Marriage and procreation brought a whole series of new problems; there was certainly no spirit of academic dispassion behind the demand, reiterated throughout the French *cahiers* of grievances of 1789, that extra taxes should be placed on bachelors for the support of the children of large families.

In any society in the eighteenth century, women of the working classes were expected to work to support themselves both when single and married: "Consider, my dear girl," runs *A Present for a Serving Maid* (1743), "that you have no portions and endeavor to supply the deficiencies of fortune by mind. You cannot expect to marry in such a manner as neither of you shall have occasion to work and none but a fool will take a wife whose bread must be earned solely by his labor and who will contribute nothing towards it herself." In fact they had no option but to do so. Generally speaking female employment fitted into three main categories. The first, restricted to the unmarried, was domestic service, perhaps the most highly sought after employment by the unmarried girl because it made her independent of the family and she needed little skill or tuition—though Irish women in London and the Savoyardes in Paris were considered too barbaric to perform even the most menial tasks in the home.

Secondly, domestic industry of several kinds which could be carried out either by the unmarried or the married but which, in the latter case especially, was of crucial significance to the family economy. The commonest forms of this were, of course, spinning wool or cotton and the manufacture of lace. The first might or might not form part of an integrated family manufacture—the children helping in the initial stages of washing and carding the raw material, the women in spinning, the men in weaving. In this case the woman was not paid a wage as such: rather was the whole family awarded a single sum for the completed cloth and the family, it should be remembered, was up to the end of the period the commonest unit of production.

Elsewhere domestic industry formed a useful supplement to work in the fields for the women of the household. To textile spinning should be added the production of lace which in northern France, Belgium, Holland and parts of southern England came a very close second to spinning in the numbers it occupied. The value of the lace lay almost entirely in the handiwork, for the quantity of linen or silk thread involved was slight. Sometimes this was a skill taught by religious orders with the express purpose of making the wives and daughters of the poor self-supporting, and in France and Belgium often the profits from the sale of the work went in large part to the religious who used it to train more workers whilst the lacemaker herself earned a pittance for her labors. Domestic industry was essentially for women *at home* and herein lay much of its value. The baby could lie in the cradle and the smallest children play on the floor whilst the mother kept to her wheel or attended to her lace bobbins. If she fell behind in her tasks they could be completed late into the night, whilst the children slept. But changes were taking place which were to threaten the continuance of this situation—at least as far as spinning was concerned. For the distribution of the raw material and collection of the finished product an elaborate network of travelling merchants was involved, a lengthy and irregular process. Little wonder that spinning was the first process to be subject to industrial change, an important point for no changes were to disrupt more the family economy. They were to take the spinner out of the house and destroy the family as a unit of production and hence to render employment in some cases very difficult for married women. Early town factories in England in fact accorded preference to the unmarried.

By far the commonest kind of female labor throughout the world at this time was simply the worst kind of heavy and distasteful tasks such as load carrying. Nothing in fact was too menial. They carried soil, heavy vegetables to market, water, coal—anything. The terraces cut into the steep mountain hillsides of Spain, France and Italy were kept watered by thousands of women who daily made the steep ascent with buckets—in the Auvergne it was estimated that the climb could take anything up to three hours and often they performed as many as three a day. The Scottish miners employed their wives as "fremd bearers" to carry coal from the face. The mines at this period had no winding gear and the women had to climb with their burden up a spiral staircase winding around the walls of the shaft. Sometimes the return journey could take up to four hours. The man was of course paid a single wage and if unmarried, had to find a girl to act as his beast of burden to whom he paid a part of his earnings. Irish women, unable to sew or clean who found their way to London acted as load carriers or helped their husbands work as navvies. Elsewhere women found employment as rag sorters, cinder sifters, refuse collectors, assistants to masons and bricklayers and so on.

Easily the most mobile section of the population in their search for work, women, especially unmarried ones, would travel many miles in the hope of finding employment. Annually women from North Wales left their homes to work on the fruit harvest in Middlesex, carrying a load on their backs into the London markets and sometimes walking anything up to fifteen miles a day during the fruit season. Moreover they had walked from Wales. One must imagine the wives and daughters of the poor condemned to a lifetime of drudgery in an attempt to keep themselves and their offspring fed. Women enclosed in tiny airless rooms, poring over lace bobbins, working late into the night by the light of candles until their eyes would serve them no more. Blindness was the likeliest fate of the lacemaker. Even those who worked at home and delivered the fruit of their labors to a wandering merchant could not afford to be irregular in their production of work. Washing and mending, cooking and cleaning had to be done afterwards and childbirth had to be accomplished with the minimum of disruption. It is not surprising that they were old women by their late twenties.

The question of child labor was perhaps of even greater importance than that of female labor. The wage of the average working man was enough for his personal upkeep and perhaps, if his wife was employed, for that of two young children. Keen social observers were quick to point out that real trouble started for families with the advent of the third child. This consideration alone entitled the silk and diamond workers of Antwerp to some slight relief, but the situation was too common for the funds of public assistance to allow help to every man in this state.

The advent of child labor has often been depicted as the outstanding evil of the factory system and of the tragic plight of many children in the early factories there can be no doubt. But to approach the question from this angle is to view it with twentieth century eyes, for life was hard for the children of laboring men in all European countries in the eighteenth century. They were expected to become self-supporting *as soon as possible* so as to relieve the strain on the family budget. Indeed, the children of the poor were committed as soon as they left the cradle to an unremitting struggle for survival in a hostile world. It is possible that children in areas of domestic industry were singularly privileged. The tasks they performed were unskilled and demanded little physical strength. In manufacturing areas of England and Belgium and Normandy children of seven and upwards were relatively self-supporting. Even four-year-olds were capable of certain jobs. Samuel Crompton's eldest son, George, has left a telling account of the kind of work performed by weavers' children.

> I recollect that soon after I was able to walk I was employed in the cotton manufacture. My mother used to bat the cotton wool on a wire riddle. It was then put into a deep brown mug with a strong ley of soap suds. My mother then tucked up my petticoats about my waist and put me into the tub to tread upon the cotton at the bottom. When a second riddleful was batted I was lifted out, it was placed in the mug and I again trod it down. This process was continued until the mug became so full that I could no longer safely stand in it when a chair was placed besides it and I held on by the back.

The cotton was then dried and carded by the grandmother and mother.

In Belgium children earned enough to support themselves after the age of seven by emptying silk cocoons. But in most communities and especially heavily agrarian communities child employment was almost totally lacking. Bishop Berkeley might fulminate against the Irish peasant who left his eight-year-old child idle in his nakedness and poverty and point out the glowing example of the Protestant Dutch who were held to make a child self-supporting at the age of five, but unless rural industry was in any way developed or the family holding large, there was little to employ women and children apart from a few days' work at hay-making and harvest. When such circumstances prevailed the question of how the family eked out a living assumes complex proportions, unanswerable in simple terms and demanding recourse to hosts of specific examples. . . .

The lesson of the eighteenth century was that there was no quick or simple solution to the problem of poverty; that appeals to "submission" and "contentment" were of little avail and that pity and *noblesse oblige* were outworn attitudes. But the poor remained stranded somewhere between two concepts: as the children of God and the test of a Christian State on the one hand and as the enemies of society on the other. They were left an amorphous, ill-defined mass of men, women and children, old and young, able-bodied and sick and as such they were destined to remain until, caught up in the momentum of a rapidly industrializing economy, economic progress carried sufficient of them above the most precarious subsistence level. That achieved, the problem of poverty was reduced to such manageable dimensions that gradually an eighteenth-century ideal could be realized and the poor indeed legislated away.

But this is to look far into the future. The student of social history is drawn to the eighteenth century in part at least because of its infinite variety. The elegant town houses and public buildings . . . bear witness to the refined tastes and new wealth of substantial sections of the community but they are only one side of the coin. It is hoped that these pages have shown something of the other. Whilst the merchants of Liverpool grew rich on an amalgam of slaves and cotton, Irish immigrants perished in the cellars of the city; whilst the profits of the wine trade built a new and beautiful Bordeaux, the garrets of the old town were crammed with the influx from the Pyrenees.

Our period is *par excellence* one of contrasts in which, to an unprecedented extent, European society was sharply divided into rich and poor, a dichotomy which became more and more apparent as urbanization intensified and the two dwelt closer together—indeed we are not far from the day when Disraeli would speak of the "two nations" between whom there was no contact and even less understanding. The road from the conquest of plague to the welfare State and social security was long, circuitous, uncharted and if by 1800 a way-stage had already been passed, for the most part the journey was still only beginning

—ELISE BOULDING

# WOMEN WORKING AND DEMONSTRATING

The situation of laboring women in [the eighteenth] century was very hard, as the references to rioting suggest. In the countryside, women were pushed more and more into competing with men for the heaviest and hardest jobs because of dwindling employment opportunities except at harvest time. The family work gangs, migrant and local, continued. Opportunities for craftwork at home had dwindled substantially, though some village factories, such as pin factories, gave out piecework to be done at home. Cottage industry never totally disappeared, even by the twentieth century, since there were always women willing to add extra hours to their working day at home to increase meager incomes, and there was always some demand for products that could be produced in this way. Women cottagers who could get at land to raise food were lucky; many could not because of the reduced amount of common land. Women who had regular skilled work such as dairying were not much better off than the irregularly employed, because the working conditions were so bad. Working on cheeses that weighed up to 140 pounds destroyed the health of dairymaids and made plowing look like easy work.

The hardest hit by unemployment were widows, partnerless women with children, and young singles. Parish records frequently refer to "vagrant women"; these helpless unemployed women, along with vagrant children, were put in institutions that were increasingly indistinguishable as to whether they were poorhouse, workhouse, or penal institution. In the labor force women got half or less of male earnings, children much less than that.

Many of these women emigrated to the city, but ignorant and ill fed as they were, they had few employment opportunities there. The women already in the cities were being pushed out of occupations they formerly had through pressures from male unemployment—a process that had already been going on for a long time. What apprenticeship and skill-training opportunities they had were similarly dwindling through pressure from male workers. The new immigants

From Elise Boulding, *The Underside of History: A View of Women through Time* (Boulder, Colo.: Westview Press, 1976), pp. 583–85, 587–90, by permission of the publisher.

from the countryside took anything they could get, usually odd jobs at starvation wages. If they were lucky they might get jobs as maids to upwardly mobile women who were leaving the labor force, but the latter shrank from taking in rough laboring types of women as domestics.

Shallow-pit mining, working in blast furnaces for twenty-four-hour spells at a time, and other types of industry-related heavy labor gave rise to inhuman working conditions and high casualty rates for women. A hard day's work was not new for women. Rather, the severe suffering of laboring women in the eighteenth and nineteenth centuries was due to the lengthening workday, the low wages, and the complete dependence of poor women on shops for food. The bit of food grown or scrounged in the country, a standby for centuries for the poorest of rural day laborers, was totally unavailable for urban women. It was increasingly so for poor villagers as well. Sixteen- to eighteen-hour workdays left no energy for home or child care, obviously, and contributed further to the problems of the children.

Public exposés of these working conditions began in 1793, but it took another fifty years for governmental notice to be taken. There were easier occupations for women at this time, such as jobs in village smithies and metal shops, making nails, locks, and tools, as well as relatively "light" work in the new industrial textile factories. Even in these factories, however, the work load was heavy and the hours long.

The women most vulnerable of all to the evils of industrialism were the urban employed. Many sold sexual services for food under the grimmest of conditions. Prostitution in this century changed character with the increase in poverty . . . there was a vast difference between the wealthy courtesan and the underemployed proletarian prostitute. The development of urban destitution vastly widened that gap, and created the class of streetwalkers that represent the very bottom of the pit of social suffering for women. The poorer women were, the more liable they were to be picked up and imprisoned, and they made up a goodly number of the ten thousand convicts that were shipped from the Old Bailey alone to the North American colonies between 1717 and 1775. This practice of dumping prisoners in the colonies, increasingly protested by the colonists themselves, was only brought to a halt by the American Revolution. . . .

The long period of relative prosperity in France came to an end by 1778 with falling prices and unemployment, and strikes and riots increased in frequency and intensity. The issues of the French Revolution are far too complex to be explicated here, but by the '70s all the unsolved issues of the previous century exploded at once for the monarchy. The administrative divisions of France no longer reflected social, economic, and political realities. The fiscal system was an absurdity and the country was bankrupt. The king and queen, and the four thousand families of the Great Nobility who controlled one-fourth of the national budget, were trying to hang onto the old absolute monarchy. The minor nobility and the bankers (who had money) were trying for a limited monarchy. The middle class and the artisans were more or less manipulated by the minor nobility and the bankers, and the poor peasants and unskilled workers (the three million illiterate poor of France) were squeezed out entirely. Women fought hard in the first, second, and third groups during the revolution (and fought against each other too), but in the end all but the nobility and the bankers' daughters were dumped and disqualified from every kind of participation, sharing the lot of the poorest of the men. Whoever "won" the revolution, the women of France lost it.

What was the role of women in the time of the revolution? Starting at the top, Queen Marie Antoinette by the early 1780s was busy mobilizing the resources available to the French monarchy through the alliance Empress Maria Theresa had created back in 1756. Poor Queen Marie—she is not usually thought of as a victim of the social expectation that women should remain quiet and demure, but she was. Her well-meaning husband was a do-nothing, so her efforts came to nothing. By 1792 she was writing to a friend

> As for myself I could do anything, and appear on horseback were it needed; but that would be furnishing weapons to the king's enemies throughout all France a cry against the Austrian and the rule of a woman would be raised instantly. By coming forward I should, moreover, reduce the king to a humiliating and inferior position. A queen who, like me, is nothing in her own right—who is not even regent has but one part to act—to wait the event silently, and prepare to die (Kavanagh, 1893: 94).

She died with dignity. In fact, all the women who went to the guillotine, nobility, middle class, and working class, died with such quiet bravery that Kavanagh (1893) suggests this alone prolonged the Reign of Terror. A few hysterical scenes by women at the scaffold might have shocked the men of the Terror sooner into realizing what they were doing. Only poor old Madame DuBarry, the king's former mistress, gave way to hysterics on the scaffold—embarrassing everyone terribly.

The bankers' daughters went scot-free. They moved right through every phase of the revolution without being touched. Madame de Pompadour was the first banker's daughter to play politics, well before the revolutionary decade. As a young girl she had been a adopted by one banker, later married another, and as Louis XV's mistress ruled France (according to one school of historical thought) for the bankers. She was the coarchitect with Maria Theresa of the French-Austrian alliance. Her foreign policy was terrible for France, and her secret police were everywhere. She died before the revolution.

Madame Necker, the wife of a Swiss banker, and her daughter Germaine, who became Madame de Staël, ran salons that brought together bankers, literati, and political leaders in clever conversation in an atmosphere of "liberalism." They closed down their salons in the Reign of Terror, but not their activities. Mme de Staël ran a newspaper chain and survived not only the revolution but also the enmity of Napoleon. Another banker's daughter, Therése de Fontenay, recreated a court atmosphere in her Paris home after the revolution, and was acknowledged as "uncrowned queen of Paris." Her friend Rose de Beauharnais, not a banker's daughter but a bourgeois adventuress friend of bankers' daughters, survived the revolution by her wits and then, as Josephine, married Napoleon.

Not all salons were run by bankers' daughters, and not all women of the upper class insulated themselves from concern for the deeper issues of the revolution and from the poverty of the masses. Madame de Condorcet and her husband, one of the few genuine husband-wife teams in the salon world, championed the equality of women and the rights of the working class when very few of their social class were interested in these subjects. Their salon has been called "the command center for thinking Europe." It was the most international of all the salons, anticipating by a century the internationalism of later political movements. Condorcet was the only Frenchman who spoke out strongly in the National Assembly for the political participation of women. He lived in hiding, protected and supported by his wife for the last months of his life, only to be discovered in the end and guillotined. Mme de Condorcet, a former canoness and a pupil of Rousseau, survived and brought up their only child in retirement.

Mme Roland was another woman who did not insulate herself from the issues of the revolution, though she was strictly a "limited monarchy" advocate. An engraver's daughter who married into the upper class, she never moved in salon circles. Because of her own keen interest in the liberal politics of the upper-middle-class-minor-nobility alliance, however, she created a kind of political salon under cover of helping her husband (at one point finance minister to the king) in his work. She appears as a kind of *eminence grise,* for she never spoke in public, hardly spoke even to the political visitors in her own house, and yet was generally recognized in her time as the authoress both of the ideas and of the documents that issued from the gatherings of highly placed political personages that took place in her modest home. She was both hated and admired in her day, and both positive and negative pictures of her have come down to us through the history books. She wrote many letters to political leaders, and both her style and her sentiments today seem sententious. She had courage, however, and went to the guillotine (sedately) for continuing to support the limited-monarchy idea after the revolution had swept past that point.

The heroines of the French Revolution were other kinds of women entirely. Shopworkers, fish vendors, laundresses, seamstresses, journalists, actresses, street women—they were a real medley of lower-middle-class and laboring women. Their participation in the revolution is somewhat unique in the annals of European history, both because they were so visible and well mobilized during certain crucial events, and because they were so completely excluded from all civic participation even before the revolution was over.

Their effectiveness was founded in the preceding decades of experience with bread riots and protest demonstrations. Though each of the previous demonstrations had been spontaneous, the women who participated in them gained a certain sense of the patterning of demonstrations, and of their value, which they could now draw on. Women on the whole succeeded in keeping the price of bread within bounds; because the authorities could not afford to be dealing continually with riots, they sometimes went to great lengths to control the price of bread. The women who were present at the storming of the Bastille were not neophytes. They had been there before.

The decision of women to march to Versailles three months after the storming of the Bastille, and to bring the king to Paris, was also a direct outcome of their previous experience. When bread prices were lowered it was usually done in the name of the king, so in their view the king was the source of rectification of injustice. If he could be brought to Paris to see how bad things were, he would do something about it. Members of the bourgeoisie-minor-nobility alliance were not hungry, so this item was not on their political agenda. But the unemployed women of Paris, and the poorest of the employed, *were* hungry. And their children were hungry. Their slogan reflected their concerns: "Bring back the Baker, and the Baker's wife, and the Baker's little boy, to Paris."

The women who marched to Versailles (it is a fairly long walk—twenty miles) were of all kinds, and historians have described the crowd differently depending on their political sympathies. "Poor but honest" working women led the way. Women like Madelaine ("Louison") Chabray, a seventeen-year-old unemployed sculptress who was now making a living as a flower girl, walked side by side with the market women and porteresses of the city. The unemployed who picked up what pennies they could by prostitution followed. These poverty-stricken women are the ones who have been described as an obscene drunken mob. Well-wishers (and there were many) gave them wine on the road, not thinking what wine would do to malnourished women with empty stomachs. Some of the walkers were reeling by the time they got to Versailles, but the reeling was as much from hiking twenty miles on empty stomachs, as from wine. Louison, the flower girl, was appointed spokesperson. When she stood before the king she was so overcome with emotion and hunger that she fainted. The king picked her up and embraced her, and she came stumbling out crying *"Vive le roi!"* Much fun has been made of this scene, but the women did march back to Paris with grain decrees from the king, and with the Declaration of Rights from the National Assembly. They had used the tactics familiar to them, and they had gotten results.

LOUISE A. TILLY AND JOAN W. SCOTT

# BIRTH, MARRIAGE, AND DEATH

The demographic patterns of early modern England and France reflected the need to balance people and resources. Death frequently influenced these patterns. Perhaps the most sensitive indicator of the relationship between resources and population was the age at which couples married. The precise age at marriage varied from city to country and from region to region depending on inheritance laws and on specific conditions. Yet among the popular classes the crucial differences were between the propertied and the propertyless.

Marriage was, among other things, an economic arrangement, the establishment of a family economy. It required that couples have some means of supporting themselves and, eventually, their children. For peasant children this meant the availability of land; for artisans, the mastery of a skill and the acquisition of tools and perhaps a workshop. Wives must have a dowry or a means of contributing to the household. Among families with property these resources most often were passed on from generation to generation.

In England, inheritance by the eldest son prevailed. In France this custom of primogeniture was not universal. In some areas of France, particularly in the west, an heir and his wife lived with his parents, in a stem family arrangement. In northern France, on the other hand, a young man had to postpone marriage until a house was vacant. This meant until the death of one or both parents. Land was passed to one child—usually, though not necessarily, the oldest son. He paid his siblings a cash settlement which represented their share of the family land. A brother could use his money to buy some land of his own or to set himself up in a trade. A sister used her money as a dowry. Often the heir had to mortgage the property to pay off his sisters and brothers. Sometimes, too, the money was not available. Then the heir's siblings might remain on the family farm as unmarried laborers in the brother's household, working in exchange for room and board. "A peasant reckons this way; my farm can feed no more than one, at most two, sons; the others may have to remain unmarried or seek their fortune elsewhere."[1]

Among artisans, trade regulations prevented early marriage. Apprentices and journeymen were not allowed to marry until they had completed their training. In some cases, the duration of apprenticeship was as much a function of the artisans' desire to control workers' access to their trade as it was of the difficulty of the skills taught. Apprentices' and journeymen's associations reinforced the control by expelling from their ranks anyone who married. A young man was ready to marry only when he had an established niche in the system of production.

The need for a dowry meant that young women, too, often had to wait for the death of their parents to receive a settlement. In the weaving center of Manchester, for example, in the period 1654–57, more than half of the girls marrying for the first time had recently lost their fathers. Other girls, those who worked to accumulate savings for a dowry, had to spend many years gathering a small sum.[2]

The result of these requirements was a relatively late age at marriage in both England and France; women were generally twenty-four or twenty-five years old, men twenty-seven. The late age at marriage of women meant that couples had fewer children than they would have had if the woman had been nineteen or twenty at marriage. If she married at twenty-five, the woman was actively engaged in childbearing for only a portion of her fertile years. (There was little sexual intercourse outside of marriage, very low rates of illegitimacy. During the eighteenth century in France, the illegitimacy rate increased from 1.2 to 2.7 percent of all births.) Thus relatively late marriage functioned as a kind of birth control, in the sense that it limited the size of the completed family.[3]

Among the propertyless, there were no resources to inherit. When a young man and woman were able to earn wages, they could marry. Not only must an individual be able to work, however, but work which paid wages must be available. (Servants, for example, could not marry since a requirement of their jobs was that they live in the household they served, that they remain unmar-

1 Rudolph Braun, "The Impact of Cottage Industry on an Agricultural Population," in David Landes, ed., *The Rise of Capitalism* (New York: Macmillan, 1966), p. 56; see also [Jean-Louis Flandrin, *Familles, parenté, maison, sexualité dans l'ancienne societé* (Paris: Hachette, 1976)], pp. 180–181.

2 André Armengaud, *La famille et l'enfant en France et en Angleterre du XVIe au XVIIIe siècle. Aspects démographiques* (Paris: Société d'édition d'enseignement supérieur, 1975), p. 145.

3 Pierre Goubert, "Recent Theories and Research on French Population between 1500 and 1700," in D. V. Glass and D. E. C. Eversley, eds., *Population in History: Essays in Historical Demography* (Chicago: Aldine, 1965); Louis Henry, "The Population of France in the Eighteenth Century," in Glass and Eversley; John Hajnal, "European Marriage Patterns in Perspective," in Glass and Eversley; E. A. Wrigley, "Family Limitation in Pre-Industrial England," *Economic History Review,* 2nd Series, 19 (April 1966): 89–109.

ried, and that they receive much of their payment in room and board, not cash.) One study has shown that in Shepshed, England, during the seventeenth century, the coming of domestic industry provided jobs and cash wages and led to a lowered age of marriage[4] In other areas, the growth of commercial agriculture, and the consequent demand for agricultural laborers, may have had the same effect.

Among the poorest, marriage sometimes did not take place at all. The absence of property and the lack of any expectation that it would be acquired, made legalization of sexual relationships unnecessary. From seventeenth-century Aix comes this comment on the urban poor: "They almost never know the sanctity of marriage and live together in shameful fashion."[5] These people, however, were exceptions. In general, those without property did marry. They married younger than their peasant and artisan counterparts, and as a result, their wives bore more children over the course of the marriage. But most expected to be able to live on the fruits of their labor. A couple marrying in Amiens in 1780 acknowledged their poverty, but wrote a contract anyway, agreeing that if they did manage to make some money, the future bride would have "by preciput 150 livres of the estate and the survivor would have the bed and bedclothes, . . . his or her clothes, arms, rings and jewels."[6]

Some people never married, of course. In general, permanent celibacy was more common in cities than in the country. There were examples of unmarried brothers or sisters remaining sometimes on farms with a married sibling. More commonly, however, these individuals migrated to a city in search of work. The occupational structure of particular cities often determined the marital fate of many of its migrants. In Lyons, for example, the women who came to work in the silk industry greatly outnumbered the men. As a result, during the eighteenth century, some 40 percent of adult women were still single at age fifty in that city. (In towns where men outnumbered women, more women were married.) In Amiens, with its mixed occupational structure, 20 percent of the women over forty in one wealthy parish were single at death. The rate was 13 percent in two poorer parishes. Domestic servants in the wealthy parish account for the difference. Cities housed most people whose occupations by definition precluded marriage—members of religious orders, soldiers, servants, and prostitutes were typically urban residents.[7]

4 David Levine, "The Demographic Implications of Rural Industrialization; A Family Reconstitution Study of Shepshed, Leicestershire, 1600–1851," *Social History* (May 1976), pp. 177–196; see also Braun, "Impact of Cottage Industry."

5 [Cissie Fairchilds, *Poverty and Charity in Aix-en-Provence, 1640–1789* (Baltimore: Johns Hopkins University Press, 1976)], p. 33.

6 [Pierre Deyon, *Amiens, capitale provinciale. Étude sur la société urbaine au 17e siècle* (Paris-The Hague: Mouton, 1967)], p. 254.

7 Armengaud, *La famille et l'enfant,* p. 30; Deyon, p. 42; see also John Knodel and Mary Jo Maynes, "Urban and Rural Marriage Patterns in Imperial Germany," *Journal of Family History* 1 (Winter 1976).

Once a couple married, at whatever age, they began to have children. About half of all first babies were born less than a year after their parents' marriage. Studies of French villages indicatea that subsequent children were then born about twenty-five to thirty months apart. This interval was apparently the result of two factors, post partum abstinence from intercourse, and nursing, which postpones the onset of ovulation. Among working-class families in cities, birth intervals were shorter because mothers sent their children to wet-nurses rather than nursing them themselves and because infant mortality was high. In both cases, women became fertile sooner than they would have if they had nursed an infant. In Amiens, for example, in a parish of small shopkeepers, artisans and workers, children were born about two years apart. In Lyons, where work in the silk industry demanded a great deal of a mother's time and where children were regularly sent to wet-nurses, birth intervals were even shorter: births occurred there at the rate of one per year.[8]

There is some evidence to indicate that couples sometimes practiced deliberate birth control. One study, of the English village of Colyton in Devon in the seventeenth century, seems to show that couples were deliberately limiting the size of their families. It author, E. A. Wrigley, suggests that a longer than usual interval between the next-to-last and last birth is an indicator of attempted fertility control. This first attempt of couples to avoid conception failed, of course, but the longer birth interval is evidence of their effort. Such control as there was was probably achieved by means of coitus interruptus, or withdrawal, the most widely known and widely practiced technique.[9] Most other studies, however, using the same kinds of data and the same method of family reconstitution, do not point to deliberate family limitation before the late eighteenth century. Yet completed families were not large: four or five children at most, more often only two or three who lived to adulthood. Why?

First, standards of nutrition and health were very low. Analyses of the diet of the popular classes in this period show consistent evidence of malnutrition, a factor which inhibited conception and which promoted miscarriage. Poor nutrition of a mother increased the likelihood that her infant would be stillborn or weak. And it affected the supply of milk she had to nurse it. In addition, poor nutrition made many women infertile before forty or forty-five—the usual age of menopause.[10]

Second, mortality rates were very high. If infants did not die at birth because of unsanitary or crude childbirth procedures, they died within the first year of life. Young children, too, died in large numbers. Finally, many mar-

8 Armengaud, *La famille et l'enfant,* p. 52; E. A. Wrigley, *Population and History,* p. 124; Flandrin, p. 197.

9 Wrigley, "Family Limitation in Pre-Industrial England," p. 123.

10 Emmanuel Le Roy Ladurie, "L'Amenorrhée de famine (XVIIIe–XXe siècles)," *Annales: ESC,* 24e Année (November-December 1969), pp. 1589–1601; Jean Meuvret, "Demographic Crisis in France from the Sixteenth to the Eighteenth Century," in Glass and Eversley.

riages were shortened by the death of one of the spouses. Childbirth resulted in a high incidence of maternal death. In one fishing village in France, one-third of all marriages were broken by death within fifteen years. Men's opportunities for remarriage were usually greater than those of women. As a result, women did not engage in intercourse during all of their fertile years and hence did not bear children. Given the odds that death would strike a young child or a spouse, there was little need to employ birth control.[11] Death was the natural regulator of family size in early modern England and France.

Premature death was a frequent experience of family life in this period. Death rates nearly matched birth rates, producing a very slow growth of population. The crude birth rate was about 35 per thousand; the death rate 30 per thousand. Moreover, until around 1730, there were years with dramatically high death rates, reaching 150, 300, and even 500 per thousand in some localities. These deaths were the result of widespread crop failures and consequent starvation, or of epidemics of diseases like the plague. The last plague epidemic struck in southern France in 1720–22,[12] but new diseases caused killing epidemics well into the twentieth century. Demographers usually place the end of extreme and widespread mortality due to disease and starvation in the early eighteenth century.

Yet even in relatively stable times, death rates were very high by modern standards—a rate of 30 per thousand is more than triple the present-day rate in Western Europe. Studies of French villages show that about one-quarter of all infants born alive died during their first year of life, another quarter died before they reached the age of twenty. Urban death rates were even higher. In Amiens, for example, during the seventeenth century, 60 to 70 percent of all burials were of persons under twenty-five. Although rates varied from parish to parish and among villages, the overall situation was similar in England and France. Goubert aptly summarized the mortality experience of preindustrial families: "It took two births to produce one adult."[13]

The life expectancy at birth for people in this period was thirty years. Of course, that figure included infant and child mortality. If a person lived to age twenty-five, the likelihood was much greater than at birth that she or he would live to fifty or sixty. Yet, although systematic evidence is hard to accumulate, it is clear that adult mortality was also quite high. The figures on orphans and widows are revealing in this connection. Laslett's analysis of the English village of Clayworth found that during the period 1676–88, "32 percent of all resident children [under 14] had lost one or both of their parents." A study of all children in households in nineteen English communities from 1599 to 1811 indicates that

11 Armengaud, *La famille et l'enfant,* p. 53.

12 Carlo Cipolla, *The Economic History of World Population,* rev. ed. (Baltimore: Penguin, 1964), p. 77; and L. A. Clarkson, *The Pre-Industrial Economy in England, 1500–1750* (London: Batsford, 1971), pp. 28–29.

13 Goubert, "Recent Theories," p. 468.

some 20 percent were orphans. For France, Jean Fourastié has drawn a hypothetical portrait of family life, for a man at the end of the seventeenth century. In that situation marriage would be broken by the death of a spouse after an average of twenty years. The average age of a child orphaned in this way would be fourteen years.[14]

Many children were left orphans when their mothers died in childbirth. Ignorance of the need for sanitary conditions, the crude attempts of midwives to force a baby from the womb, and the general poor health of pregnant women made for high rates of maternal mortality. Age-specific mortality tables drawn for small seventeenth- and eighteenth-century villages show women dying in larger numbers than men between ages of twenty-four and forty—the childbearing years. In Amiens, in the parish of Saint-Rémy in 1674–76, fifty-three women and forty men aged fifteen to forty-five died. In another parish in 1665–68, deaths were recorded for ninety-one women and only fifty-two men in that age range.[15]

The death of a parent left not only orphans, but widows or widowers. The existence of these people is attested to by notices of second marriage, particularly of men, and by charity rolls and tax lists, on which widows' names predominated. Fourastié's calculations show that of 1,000 men married at age twenty-seven and surviving to age fifty, nearly half would have lost their wives. Many of these men would have remarried and would have also lost a second wife. (The calculations for women would be similar except that fewer widows remarried.) Overall, in eighteenth-century France "at least 30 percent of all marriages were second weddings for one of the partners." Most parishes had many widows in them. In Châteaudun, at least half of the seamstresses and spinners listed on tax rolls in 1696 were widows. In eighteenth-century Bayeux, over 46 percent of all textile workers in the linen and woolen trades were widows.[16] The poor widow, struggling to support her children, was a familiar figure in the towns and villages of the period.

Early modern populations could do little medically to control mortality. Nutrition was poor, little was known about hygiene, and medical science had not developed. In 1778, a French demographer noted that "it is still a problem

14 Armengaud, *La famille et l'enfant,* pp. 74–77; Peter Laslett, "Parental Deprivation in the Past: A Note on the History of Orphans in England," *Local Population Studies* 13 (Autumn 1974): 11–18; Jean Fourastié, "De la vie traditionnelle à la vie 'tertiare,'" *Population* 14 (1959): 427.

15 Deyon, p. 39.

16 Mohammed El Kordi, *Bayeux au XVIIe et XVIIIe siècles* (Paris, The Hague: Mouton, 1970), p. 64. See also Fourastié, p. 425; Micheline Baulant, "The Scattered Family: Another Aspect of Seventeenth-Century Demography," in Robert Forster and Orest Ranum, eds., *Family and Society* (Baltimore: Johns Hopkins, 1976), p. 105; Marcel Couturier, *Recherches sur les structures sociales de Châteaudun, 1525–1789* (Paris: S.E.V.P.E.N., 1969), p. 64; [Olwen] Hufton, *The Poor in Eighteenth Century France,* [1750–1789 (Oxford: Clarendon Press, 1974)] p. 116; François Lebrun, *Les Hommes et la mort en Anjou aux 17e et 18e siècles* (Paris-The Hague: Mouton, 1971), p. 190.

whether medicine kills or saves more men.''[17] The result was that every person who survived to adulthood experienced the loss of close relatives: a father, mother, sisters, and brothers. Few children knew their grandparents, few grandparents lived to see the birth of a first grandchild. Orphanhood, widowhood, and the loss of children were common experiences. In calculations about family size, about fertility and household labor supply, the expectation of death played an important part.

17 Armengaud, *La famille et l'enfant,* p. 79. For an overview of the demographic history of this period see Jacques Dupaquier, ''Les caractères originaux de l'histoire démographique française au XVIIIe siècle,'' *Revue d'histoire moderne et contemporaine* 23 (April–June 1976).

PART 2

# ACCELERATION AND SOCIAL CONFLICT: 1850-1914

We usually think of the latter half of the nineteenth century as the heyday of European nationalism and imperialism, the Victorian and Wilhelmian age, or as a prelude to the First World War. These textbook labels have some validity, of course, but they tell us little of the shared experience of millions of ordinary people as they conducted their lives from day to day. The readings that follow should supply that missing perspective.

From the standpoint of social history, what were the distinctive characteristics of the years after 1850? One is tempted to reply simply: more of the same. The increased movement, already apparent in the previous century, continued, and an even greater impact of industrialization was felt on the Continent as well as in Britain. But such a response would fail to account for important qualitative differences between the early and later stages of industrial development. To cite an obvious example, the railroad finally came into its own. Railways extended throughout nearly every section of western and central Europe, connecting countryside to city as never before. It was not the invention of the steam engine or the introduction of a few connector lines before 1850 that changed the face of Europe, but rather the completion of railway networks thereafter. This made possible the creation of national economic markets and the linkage of one to another in an international commercial system. For common people it meant that manufactured goods and agricultural produce became more abundant and more available.

The great pockets of poverty that had been generated by industrialization persisted, and in many cities they were expanded. Although the real wages of most workers were rising throughout late century, slum streets and tenement buildings—not the Crystal Palace or the Eiffel Tower—were the truly typical monuments of the age. One explanation is clear. The sustained population growth of the nineteenth century was more than the cities could absorb. The specter haunting Europe was urbanization. Everywhere the old walls were being outgrown, brought down, or broken through. The notion of city limits was defined only by law or by surveyors, and was frequently revised. The tempo of life was becoming more hectic in a society where production was being mechanized and rationalized. The era of the assembly line was beginning.

Europeans did not necessarily require a Karl Marx or a Charles Darwin to point out that competition and conflict were inevitable consequences for individuals, classes, and nations. That had long been apparent. In earlier phases of the industrial revolution social protests had often been the result of fearful artisans being confronted for the first time with the effects or implications of machine production. But the late nineteenth century brought another day, when industrialized workers began to organize into larger groups in order to secure a better share of their own work. Socialism and trade unionism thus acquired recognizable profiles, and millions of ordinary citizens formed the habit not only of voting but of associating their hopes with labor organizations. If democracy was highly imperfect, participation was at least more frequent than in the past.

We cannot altogether neglect politics. The basic administrative unit of European society, after all, was the nation. Everyone was subject to state bureaucracy, exposed to appeals for national patriotism, and expected to conform to laws and decrees from the national government, whatever its form. After the Franco-Prussian War of 1870, the growing industrial and military power of a unified Germany was particularly upsetting for Europeans. No major armed conflict took place on the Continent for nearly half a century, yet repeated international crises raised public emotions and created sentiments of mass loyalty to one side or another. In the end, it was untrue that workers had no country, as so many of them proved heroically but often futilely in the First World War. No other event in European history has inflicted such heavy casualties on the populace or called more obviously into question the belief in progress through industrialization.

CHAPTER 4

# OLD AND NEW SOCIAL TYPES

One of the most significant results of industrialization was to deepen the fissure between western and eastern Europe. This gap was already apparent long before the industrial era began; by the end of the nineteenth century it was very pronounced. Reduced to its simplest terms the difference was that in the West the common people had, in the majority, become urban dwellers while in the East they remained peasants. Yet the simplicity of this proposition is deceptive. Industrialization did not immediately elevate the life of the common man in the West. Even in Britain it was still far from eliminating poverty and misery, which were often all the more degrading in city life. Russian society, on the other hand, despite its oppressive backwardness, was by no means completely agrarian or static. Thus, everywhere in Europe the new was mingled with the old.

*Peter Laslett* treats the unique case of England, the single fully industrialized society in Europe by the year 1900. Although farm labor may still have busied more persons than any other single occupation, most Britons had by then become urbanites with a salaried income. For the first time in history, it was appropriate to posit the existence of an urban proletariat that was conscious of its social disadvantages. Yet the course that Britain would take was uncertain, since the welfare state was only a glint in the eye of a few reformers. One thing was clear: here was an emerging society that was different from any the world had ever seen.

*Peter N. Stearns* considers the other most rapidly industrialized European society, that of imperial Germany. There the real wages of labor were advancing, but their distribution was inequitable and the effect was often a serious social dislocation. The march of industry, spurred on by credit banking and the formation of joint-stock companies, forced a progressive breakdown of traditional artisanry and required an adaptation of workers' skills to new tasks. Stearns provides illustrations of the transition from countryside to city: shifting family patterns, the creation of entirely new trades, participation in union and wildcat strikes, changing styles of consumption and fashion. In these and other ways the factory system extracted a price from those who were drawn into the demanding pace of industrial life.

*Lazar Volin* explains why formal emancipation from serfdom provided no drastic solution to the social problems of the Russian peasantry. One obvious factor was the retardation of industry and hence the absence of any major outlet from the countryside. This outer fringe of European society remained overwhelmingly rural. It is impossible, in fact, to overlook the similarities between the lot of the Russian peasants in this period and that of the French before the Revolution of 1789. One important difference, however, was the *mir,* that communal organization of the peasants that was peculiarly Russian. As Volin demonstrates, a "chronic rural distress" was still the primary fact of Russian history, and it afforded a somber backdrop for the revolutions of 1905 and 1917.

Benjamin Disraeli was moved to write of the "two nations," by which he meant the upper and lower classes. It would seem equally appropriate to speak of the two Europes, one rapidly advancing to an industrial society and the other only gradually yielding the coveted terrain of tradition. Yet, for reasons amply explained, such conceptions are largely rhetorical. In its social structure Europe was developing toward complexity rather than simplicity. The geographical bifurcation, quite apart from exceptions and qualifications, had nothing immutable about it. In hindsight we know that the twentieth century was to provide much different circumstances than one might have imagined on the eve of the First World War.

—PETER LASLETT—

# THE TRANSFORMATION OF ENGLISH SOCIETY

## *THE WORKING CLASS SINCE 1901*

Rattle his bones, over the stones
He's only a pauper whom nobody owns

When Queen Victoria died at the very outset of the twentieth century one person in five could expect to come to this, a solitary burial from the workhouse, the poor-law hospital, the lunatic asylum. On the whole the first year of our century, 1901, was a prosperous time for the English, one of the twenty good years not marked by depression or by war to the death which they were to have in the fifty which followed. There was a war going on, it is true, the South African War, which, if men had but known it, was the beginning of the end of the English as a people of commanding world-wide power, but its social effects at the time did not go very deep. The huge coalfields of Yorkshire and Lancashire, the great shipbuilding towns, the acres and acres of factory floor given over to textiles, were made busier by the demand for armaments and uniforms and machinery. Nevertheless something like a quarter of the whole population was in poverty.

Poverty, we must notice, was no vague condition then, nothing like as uncertain as the state of "decreasing wealth of the kingdom" has to be for the historian looking back to England in 1688 through the eyes of Gregory King. Families were in poverty "whose total earnings were insufficient to obtain the minimum necessary for the maintenance of mere physical efficiency."

Those precise syllables come from Seebohm Rowntree's book called *Poverty* which appeared in 1901 and which published the somber results of a house-to-house survey carried out with monumental thoroughness in his native city of York, a railway center, where the family firm of Rowntree manufactured chocolates as it has ever since. Confectionery is perhaps as representative a light industry of the twentieth century type, as railways were of the heavy industry of nineteenth century, which had given England and especially the north of England her world-wide manufacturing supremacy. Young Mr. Rowntree had done his work in order to find out whether a reasonably typical provincial city was like London. He had discovered that 27.84 percent of the citizens of York were living in poverty according to his definition. In London 30.7 percent of the people were in poverty as his predecessor and mentor, Charles Booth, had already shown. London, which was the richest city in the world and a fifth of the whole kingdom!

Englishmen in 1901 had to face the disconcerting fact that destitution was still an outstanding feature of fully industrial society, a working class perpetually liable to social and material degradation. More than half of all the children of working men were in this dreadful condition, which meant 40 percent of all the children in the country.

There were the scrawny, dirty, hungry, ragged, verminous boys and girls who were to grow up into the working class of twentieth-century England. This was the generation which was to man the armies of the First World War, although they were inches shorter and pounds lighter than they would have been if they had been properly fed and cared for. Those who were left of them became the fathers and mothers of the working people who endured the Depression of the 1920s and the Great Depression of the 1930s, and who saw at last the squalid streets in which they made their homes luridly lighted up by Hitler's bombs. They were also the men and women who nurtured the Labor Party, the working-man's party, and brought it to maturity in the 1920s, and to overwhelming, if somewhat short-lived, political victory in 1945. They are still, it could be claimed, the most easily neglected element in English political and historical consciousness even today.

We might take a very well-known example to demonstrate this fact, though the tenacious memory of labor politicians and labor voters for the terrible days of not so long ago might seem to prove it straightaway. Young Beatrice Potter was an assistant in Booth's survey, as gifted and extraordinary a member of the governing minority as ever took to "Social Reform" as the Edwardians called it. But she did not go as far as a year or two with the Charity Organization Society, and then marry one of her own set, compounding for a series of subscriptions to worthy causes as so many of her fellows seem to have done. She became the wife of Mr. Sidney Webb, of the London County Council and the Fabian Society, and the two of them founded the London School of Economics as well as the New Statesman. As Lord Passfield and Mrs. Webb—for the aristocratic Beatrice would have nothing to do with Sidney's silly title—they visited Russia in the early 1930s. Hence the title of their final book, the last of a long series, *Soviet Communism, a New Civilization*. Irreducible poverty, that of London in the 1890s and of all the English unemployed forty years later, had helped to turn them from liberal socialism and the most successful movement of gradual reform that the world perhaps has ever seen, into prophets of communism.

In this final mood, and perhaps only then, they ceased to be typical of the attitude taken up by their countrymen to what was ordinarily known in their youth as the "condition of England question," one question amongst the many others that the eminent English political leaders had to deal with. The exact percentages in Booth's and Rowntree's figures make uneasy reading in our generation, when statistics are so much more cautiously handled that two places of decimals almost never appear in sociological percentages. An attempt at a scientific, a physiological definition of poverty, one graduated in terms of the biological needs of an ordinary man in performing his day's physical work, would never be attempted today. It will, therefore, perhaps be doubted whether the shift from 1688 to 1901, from counts of parishioners and Gregory King, to house-to-house surveys, Mr. Booth and Mr. Rowntree, makes much difference as to reliability. Can we really be so certain that the problem of poverty was still so urgent after a century and more of miraculous economic growth and change? Our traditional picture of England in 1901, the first year of the golden Edwardian age, is altogether lighter than this.

What about the countryside, and the country towns? What about the really prosperous manufacturing areas, which were to make the England of Edward VII more expansive economically than it ever was to be again until George VI was on the throne and Mr. Attlee became his Prime Minister? The actual condition of the population as a whole of course will never be known, though in the succeeding two generations many cities were submitted to the treatment given to London and York, using an ever more realistic criterion of prosperity and poverty. But Rowntree had thought of agricultural England.

Some years were to pass before his analysis of agriculture was to be completed, but in his book on York he pointed out that in 1899 over three-quarters of the population of England lived in "urban areas." The time in fact had already almost arrived which we talked of when discussing the village community of the traditional world, when the balance between town and country would be completely reversed, and the typical Englishman would be brought up amongst bricks and mortar, and only the exceptional amongst trees and fields. Moreover Rowntree was probably right to assume that those who had remained in the country after three or four generations of steady emigration from it lived rather below the standards endured by their grandchildren, great-nephews and cousins in the city streets.

In 1903 the little village of Ridgmont in Bedfordshire, over the wall from the great park at Woburn, the seat of the Duke of Bedford, was investigated according to the principles of Booth and Rowntree. The Dukes of Bedford were doing very well in that year, with income tax at elevenpence in the pound and death duties at a maximum of 11 percent. Like most noble families they had urban as well as rural property, industrial and commercial wealth as well as landed. In fact the Fabian Society alleged that the Bedford Estate was receiving £15,000 a year from Covent Garden at the time that Professor Higgins met Eliza Doolittle outside the Royal Opera House. Still the estate was managed in an exemplary way and Ridgmont was being rebuilt cottage by cottage; the tall red-brick roofs of that time of expansive if cumbersome domestic architecture are still to be seen in the village. Yet the investigator found that 41 percent of the population living there were in poverty, the sort of poverty which left biological need unsatisfied.

We cannot linger long in Ridgmont, though the facts about countryside and town, about inequality in income and about the persistence of the country house as the political instrument of a very different society are all very important to our subject. In October, 1900, the Marquess of Salisbury submitted the name of the Duke of Bedford to Queen Victoria when he was reconstructing the Cabinet, and his Grace declined because of his interest in estate-management; Woburn remained a center of political power nevertheless. Perhaps the annual income of this great noble family was some £100,000 and it must have ranked with the largest in the country, even with the huge industrial and commercial fortunes, though an English duke might already find it advantageous to marry an American heiress, as the Duke of Marlborough had done in 1895. Here was a splendid contrast with an income of about £50 which was what was earned by a farm laborer in Ridgmont. In Gregory King's time the average nobleman had £3,000 a year and a laborer, £15, which was a similar disproportion if a Duke then possessed double the ordinary noble income.

But though agricultural labor was still the biggest occupation in England in the early 1900s, it cannot have been any longer true that the country could be divided, as King divided it, into a large minority receiving six times the income of the bare majority. We cannot tell how the £6 10*s*. a year which King reckoned to be the resources of that quarter of the people in his day whom he called cottagers and paupers compared with Rowntree's £100 a year, or rather less, which he reckoned to be what a family needed to be above the poverty line in 1899. Still it is clear that the traditional, agricultural society as it had survived in Ridgmont was not more prosperous than the commercial and manufacturing society of the city of York. Nothing went on in this part of Bedfordshire except the tilling of the soil and the keeping of beasts; rural industry was already almost entirely dead. A few cottagers still plaited straw, but lacemaking had disappeared completely. The making of hats had gone off to the factories of Bedford and Luton. Not so much as a loaf of bread was baked in the village; it all came in the horse vans from the towns. And every single village child was living in poverty.

To the historian of an earlier England it is a gross and telling contrast that Ridgmont should have belonged in 1901 to a residual area of rural society within an expanding industrial whole, an area already not much more than a fifth and still getting smaller. This made English society different in order from anything which had ever gone before, in Europe or in the whole world. It means that the process of social and economic transformation which we call *industrial revolution* was already virtually complete in our country. This distinguishes the society of England as it now is, very sharply from other societies. English social experience since the death of Victoria is the only lengthy experience any country has ever had of really mature industrialization.

It has been in fact experience not of a state of things exactly, but of a perpetual tendency towards continuous change. For industrialization is not a once-for-all process and it is an English error to suppose that it is. Since 1901 our country has tended to fall somewhat behind others in the race to reindustrialize with every new technique, but our history since 1901 has been a history of successive transformation all the same. The question of importance for the contrast we are trying to draw in this essay is the question of welfare. In so far as the industrializing process is to be described above all as a change in the scale of living, . . . only in England does it seem to have been virtually complete by 1901. What has happened since then has been a matter of the levelling up of standards, the lengthening of life, the diminution of poverty, the universalization of education. This may not have been the result of what became so suddenly and shockingly apparent after Booth and Rowntree had done their work. But since that time, intentionally or not, the spread of the benefits has gone on both by political compulsion and perhaps also of itself.

PETER N. STEARNS

# THE ADAPTATION TO INDUSTRIALIZATION IN GERMANY

. . . The issue that has dominated historical consideration of working classes—material conditions and their trend—need not delay the student of German workers too long. Real wages rose fairly steadily for factory workers from the beginning of industrialization. They certainly were rising between 1890 and 1914, despite rapid inflation, though the rate of their increase diminished.[1]

Peter N. Stearns, "Adaptation to Industrialization: German Workers as a Test Case," in *Central European History,* III, no. 4 (December, 1970), 304–312, 314–323.

1 Jürgen Kuczynski, *Darstellung der Lage der Arbeiter in Deutschland von 1871 bis 1900* (Berlin, 1962), and *Darstellung der Lage der Arbeiter in Deutschland von 1900 bis 1917–18* (Berlin, 1967); these volumes chart a substantial increase in real wages between the 1880s and 1900, though more limited for craftsmen than for factory and building trades workers, and a slower rise after 1900. Ashok V. Desai, *Real Wages in Germany 1871–1913* (Oxford, 1968), is more detailed but not contradictory.

Conditions were still bad, far worse than in France or Britain. Housing was cramped, diet still rather meager. Yet there was improvement in most consumption items. This being reasonably well established for the 1890–1914 period, we can more readily turn to questions of adaptation to industrial life which many historians, in their preoccupation with material conditions, have only touched in passing. We must in fact broaden the scope of "material conditions" to include pace of work or transportation time from home to job. For material conditions were obviously part and parcel of adaptation. German workers' adaptation may have been facilitated, vis-à-vis Britain at least, by the improvement in living standards over accustomed levels; but we must be sure that the quality of material life did in fact improve, that modest gains in consumption do in fact allow us to judge this quality.

Many aspects of German manufacturing suggest the transitional character of the labor force even after 1900. Of course, given the constant change which industrialization imposes, a social group is always in transition. And a comparative framework for the German economy needs to be more carefully worked out than has been done heretofore. Nevertheless, it can be suggested that from the standpoint of the working class the German economy was not so uniformly advanced as national production figures imply and that some categories of workers were touched by traditions that had long been forgotten not only in Britain but also in France.

Take, for example, the German merchant marine. A large percentage of the sailors were still from sea villages and owned land there. Sailors were given holidays for harvest work—and this was true not only in small ports like Flensburg, but in Bremen as well. It is true that the peasant-sailor type was giving way to the thoroughly urban, propertyless worker, particularly in Hamburg. But the German merchant marine cannot yet be compared to the floating port population of Britain or the semiconscripted, professional marine in France. Relatedly, it was far less prone to agitation.[2]

The factory labor force was also less urbanized than its counterparts in the older industrial countries. Only 7 percent of the workers in one concern in the center of Magdeburg lived in the city; the rest were scattered in suburbs and villages up to 23 kilometers away. Metal workers commuted from the countryside and did occasional agricultural work in many areas.[3] Obviously, the railroad in Germany tended to retard the complete separation of workers from the country in comparison with France as well as Britain.

The character of many German firms themselves reflected the relative newness of industrialization. Leave aside the fact that there were still four

2 E. Fitzer, *Die wirtschaftliche und technische Entwicklung der Seeschiffsfahrt* (Leipzig, 1902), and M. Pappenheim *et al.*, *Die Lage der in der Seeschiffsfahrt beschäftigten Arbeiter* (2 vols., Leipzig, 1902). On France, André Sayous, *Des Grèves Maritimes* (Paris, 1910).

3 Hermann Beck, *Lohn- und Arbeitsverhältnisse in der deutschen Maschinenindustrie* (Dresden, 1902); Otto Homme, *Die Entstehung und Tätigkeit des Deutschen Metallarbeiterverbandes* (Berlin, 1912).

million workers in the rural putting-out system.[4] The typical unit of factory employment was still not overwhelmingly large. The average mining company had 163.5 workers in 1907 and was only a fifth the size of its French counterpart. The average metal firm had six workers, the average textile company eighteen. These figures admittedly conceal the existence of some huge units, but they usefully point to a vast manufacturing economy beneath that level.[5] Nor was German mechanization invariably at the forefront. By 1914, 3 percent of German coal output was produced by the new mining machines, compared to 10 percent in Britain. German printing and shoe manufacture lagged behind French technology. Most important, for understanding German workers and the labor movement, workers in urban industries dominated by small units and fairly traditional methods vastly outnumbered those in factory employment. There were, in 1907, 221,679 metallurgical workers, compared to almost a million metal workers. There were a million and a half construction workers, but only 700,184 workers in the engineering trades. There were almost as many wood workers (571,549) as miners (649,277).[6]

Within this framework, two types of adaptation were being forced on or offered to workers in the decades before the War. The first was within the crafts. It was not new—there are signs of it before 1848—but it reached new levels in this period. This was an adjustment by artisans to employee status and a substantial increase in the size of unit of production. The average construction concern employed 2.3 workers in 1895, 7.5 in 1907, a rate of increase nine times that of mining and several times more shocking to the workers involved. Everywhere there are signs of disruption of artisanal traditions. Bakers—over 47 percent still housed and fed by their employers—began to be forced out of their dependence by employers and simultaneously to grow restive under it.[7] Overlying all of this was the introduction of new machinery and materials, from kneading machines to metal scaffolding. Similar developments were occurring in other industrial countries, but there artisans had made more of a previous transition to new ways. German artisans were unusually accustomed to small units of employment, to contact with the countryside—over one-half of German masons lived in villages and many did some agricultural work, continuing traditions of apprenticeship and *Wanderzeit*.[8] And any changes forced on German artisans were

4 W. H. Dawson, *Industrial Germany* (London, 1912), p. 204; see also his *The Evolution of Modern Germany* (London, 1908).

5 Georg Neuhaus, *Die deutsche Volkswirtschaft und ihre Wandlungen im letzten Vierteljahrhundert,* II (Berlin, 1913). On France, Office du travail, *Résultats statistiques du recensement général . . . de 1911* (Paris, 1914).

6 Kaiserliches Statistisches Amt, *Berufsstatistik,* 1907.

7 Verband der Bäcker und Berufsgenossen Deutschlands, *Jahrbuch,* 1906.

8 Franz Habersbrunner, *Die Lohn-, Arbeits- und Organisations-Verhältnisse im deutschen Baugewerbe* (Leipzig, 1903); Bernhard Adeling, *Sein und Werden* (Offenbach, 1952). The wandering of German artisans, both informally from east to west in the summertime, and formally through the two-years' travel that followed apprenticeship in many trades, is comparable to the situation in Britain in the mid-nineteenth century. See E. J. Hobsbawm, *Laboring Men* (New York, 1964).

automatically important because of their predominance in the manufacturing labor force.

The majority of factory workers were first- or second-generation even in 1914. Census figures reveal this clearly. Between 1895 and 1907 the mining labor force almost doubled, as did that in metallurgy. Textiles grew more slowly and chemicals advanced only 60 percent, but the machine-building industry almost tripled its employment. More specific studies confirm this pattern. In the wool hat industry in Luckewalde, where the industry began in the 1870s and grew only modestly, only 30 percent of the workers had had fathers in the textile industry and only 24 percent had had grandfathers who were factory workers of any sort. Of the fathers 23 percent had been artisans, 9 percent peasants, 11 percent members of the higher professions; of the grandfathers 38 percent had been peasants.[9] In the Ruhr mines in the mid-nineties only 37 percent of the workers were children of miners, and a few years later only 40 percent of the miners' children of working age were in the mines—and this in an industry where stability was usually high aside from outright increments to the labor force.[10] In one Mönchen-Gladbach textile firm only 14 percent of the workers had peasant fathers, though in the city as a whole large numbers of the new semiskilled workers came directly from the countryside.[11] In clearer contrast, a Berlin machine-building giant had only a small core of workers whose fathers had been in the industry; a large number of the new workers were from East Prussia while many of the unskilled had previously been handworkers in textile or shoe manufacturing, many of the skilled former smiths. Everywhere machine building,[12] including automobile production, drew in massive numbers of locksmiths from the villages and small towns.

Despite Germany's ranking as an industrial power, industrialization in the literal sense was new to most of its workers around the turn of the century. It was drawing in peasants. It attracted servant girls, following a common pattern in relatively early industrialization in which servant status constituted a transition from rural life to factory life.[13] It attracted many small-town artisans, even though none of the large artisanal groupings was declining in size. This, too, reminds us of an important aspect of early industrialization which had largely ceased in Britain.[14] . . .

9 Elise Hermann, *Auslese und Anpassung der Arbeiterschaft in der Wollhutindustrie* (Munich, 1912).

10 Franz Schulze, *Die polnische Zuwanderung im Ruhrrevier und ihre Wirkungen* (Munich, 1909).

11 Ernst Bernhard, "Auslese und Anpassung der Arbeiterschaft," *Jahrbuch für Gesetzgebung, Verwaltung und Volkswirtschaft im Deutschen Reich* (1911), p. 1407; Marie Bernays, *Auslese und Anpassung der Arbeiterschaft der geschlossenen Grossindustrie* (Leipzig, 1910); Max Morgenstern *et al.*, *Auslese und Anpassung der Arbeiterschaft* (Leipzig, 1912).

12 Heinz Reichelt, *Die Arbeitsverhältnisse in einem Berliner Grossbetrieb der Maschinenindustrie* (Berlin, 1906).

13 Bernays, *Auslese,* p. 166, and *passim.*

14 Artisans were still being displaced in Britain, of course, but there is no significant trace of the village smithy in the composition of the engineering labor force by 1900.

Unskilled workers who came into the factories from the countryside worked hard without complaint. There is overwhelming evidence on this point. Silesian miners who came to the Ruhr thought it was evil to miss a shift. Amazed at the laxness of the Ruhr miners, they thought, "We Silesians are better than this crummy crew."[15] In metallurgical factories in Hanover Poles and Germans of rural origin were noted as zealous workers. In a Mönchen-Gladbach textile plant workers from small towns and the countryside earned up to 12 percent above the company's average because of their high production.[16] Key groups of workers were loath to strike for a reduction of hours. Dockers did not mount the pressure for a limitation of their long workday that their counterparts in French ports began in the 1890s. Many were proud of their ability to work round the clock periodically, if only because their extra earnings contributed to their family's well-being. German miners rarely raised questions of hours of work in their strikes, though their working day was two hours longer than in France and Britain. Their docility in this matter was due to the fact that over half of them were freshly in from the countryside.

There were several reasons for the new arrivals' zeal for work. They were grateful for regular employment. German unemployment rates were quite low for unskilled workers according to official figures, but there was substantial seasonal unemployment, at the least, in the countryside and the small towns.[17] Satisfaction with what seemed to them high pay was another obvious factor. Miners from eastern Germany thought that pay in the Ruhr was splendid. They delighted in daily meat and butter and were happy to be allowed to work hard, accepting overtime on top of their long shifts.[18] Accustomed to hard work anyway, many of them found nonmaterial satisfactions in working with machines. Some were entranced by the sheer power of machines.[19] Others were lured by the prestige of a big company; a worker took pride when it could be said of him, "He is with Daimler." Perhaps most important, they found factory work exciting or at least not boring. Women were particularly pleased with the bustle and camaraderie of factory work, when contrasted to their rural traditions or their work as servants.

How much did the ardor for work mean beyond the willingness to put in long hours? In the one study of the Mönchen-Gladbach textile factory, the above average production of workers from the countryside contrasted with the up to 30

15 Leo Uhen, *Gruppenbewusstsein und informelle Gruppenbildungen bei deutschen Arbeitern im Zeitalter der Industrialisierung* (Berlin, 1963).

16 Walter Timmerman, *Die Entlohnungsmethoden in der Hannoverschen Eisenindustrie* (Berlin, 1906); Beck, *op. cit.*

17 Zentralverband der Maurer Deutschlands, *Jahrbuch,* 1909; *Der Arbeitsmarkt,* 1912 and 1913. In 1913 1.1 percent of the total work force was unemployed; Germany was remarkable for its low unemployment rate among groups like dock workers.

18 George Werner, *Ein Kempel. Erzählung aus dem Leben der Bergarbeiter* (Berlin, 1930).

19 Waldemar Zimmerman, *Die soziale Verhältnisse der Angestellten im preussischen Staatsbahnbetriebe* (Altenburg, 1902); Heinrich Herkner, *Probleme der Arbeiterpsychologie* (Leipzig, 1912).

percent below average production of city-bred workers. Rural masons and bricklayers also seem to have outproduced their urban counterparts.[20] But in general it seems likely that the rural workers accepted long hours in part because their pace was rather leisurely. They were not usually highly skilled and therefore were not subjected to the most intense pressure to produce at maximum. Comparative studies revealed that German workers despite their longer hours were less productive than British; textile workers, for example, handled only a half to two-thirds the machinery per worker that their British counterparts managed. There is some indication that German workers took more breaks during the day than workers in France and Britain. The unusually high ratio of foremen to workers in Germany reflects the leisurely pace that many workers sought to adopt. Production fluctuated more during the week in Germany than was common elsewhere, with productivity on Mondays particularly low.[21] And workers, including some of rural origin, had habits of job-changing that reduced both their productivity and the work they actually put in during a given year. Much of this evidence admittedly is hard to apply to the newly arrived workers specifically. But it does suggest that the zeal for work had yet to be harnessed to an industrial pace, that it consisted mainly of plodding through a long day.

German workers generally had a different view. Some of the contrast has already been suggested. Big-city workers and miners established in the Ruhr did not seem to work as hard as the new arrivals. Skilled workers found the *Arbeitsfreude* of the unskilled proof of their unintelligence. Adolf Levenstein's survey gives us a statistical picture of sorts. In textiles, 75 percent of the workers found no joy in their work; 60 percent of the miners agreed, while 15 percent enjoyed the work if the pay was good, and 18 percent professed indifference.[22] Of the metal workers surveyed, 57 percent found no pleasure in their work. Levenstein probably had a biased sample, for he elicited responses from an unusual number of convinced socialists. A survey of workers in Mönchen-Gladbach textile plants, while not focusing on attitudes toward work specifically, revealed that 44 to 50 percent of the workers were "satisfied" with their position, though only 29 percent said that they really wanted to be textile workers.[23]

There were workers, then, who enjoyed their work. A weaver wrote that he could get through the day quite pleasantly thinking about other things, par-

20 Beck, *op. cit.;* B. Quantz, "Uber die Arbeitsleistung und das Verhältnis von Arbeitslohn und Arbeitszeit im Maurergewerbe," *Jahrbücher für Nationalökonomie* (1912), p. 644.

21 E. D. Howard, *Causes and Extent of the Industrial Progress of Germany* (London, 1907); Richard Ehrenburg, *Regenerativ-Ofen und Arbeiterbewegung in der deutschen und englischen Grünglas-Industrie,* in *Thünen-Archiv* (1909), pp. 18–139; R. M. R. Dehn, *The German Cotton Industry* (Manchester, 1913); Marie Bernays, *Untersuchungen über die Schwankungen der Arbeitsintensität während der Arbeitswoche und während des Arbeitstages* (Leipzig, 1912).

22 Adolf Levenstein, *Aus der Tiefe. Arbeiterbriefe* (Berlin, 1905), p. 120 and *passim;* Adolf Levenstein, *Die Arbeiterfrage* (Munich, 1912).

23 Bernays, *Auslese, passim.*

ticularly astronomy. A miner said, "There is no work so interesting as that of the miner."[24] Many skilled workers remained proud of their work, even when new machines were introduced. Printers who switched to the new composing machines resisted any return to manual labor, partly because this involved longer hours but partly because, though the skill required on the machines was reduced, they were able to read more manuscripts.[25] Still other workers took pleasure in working for a piece rate, because it increased their freedom and made the job more interesting. This was particularly true of the highly skilled, including some who had been artisanally trained in small towns.[26]

But majority sentiment was against these positions, even if some groups of workers, in metals particularly, had to surrender their opposition to piece work. Textile workers complained of exhaustion: "My eyes burn so—if I could only sleep."[27] Metal workers worried more explicitly about their health. Both complained of noise and boredom, one noting that his work was so dull that "wild longings" tormented him.[28] A miner in the Ruhr, Max Lotz, wrote an impassioned lament about the dangers and hardships of his work, which he found beneath human dignity. Even in the mines he found that "The work is becoming increasingly mechanical. No more incentive, no more haste, we muddle along wearily, we are worn out and mindless."[29] . . .

The reaction to factory work was unquestionably intensified by the speed-up devices manufacturers everywhere were introducing around 1900—such as the *Kalkulationsbüros* which appraised piece rates—and by the relatively advanced technology. Even so, the German workers' reaction may tell us something of the difficulties new workers experienced in comparable stages of industrialization elsewhere. We can speculate about English workers' first exposure to the din and pace of factory labor, but we know that many German workers were appalled. It took a generation for unskilled workers to shake off their rural-bred resignation, but the workers born in the cities *and* the large contingent of artisans entering factories or larger craft units for the first time had real problems of adjustment. Their vigorous resistance may have alleviated the problems, of course, as hours of work declined and in some cases as productivity itself leveled off. At the same time it can be suggested that this stage in the adjustment to industrialization was just that, that contentment with work might grow as experience increased and job conditions improved. A survey of German workers in the 1920s revealed that

24 Levenstein, *Arbeiterfrage,* p. 154.

25 J. Zitzhoff, *Arbeitsgliederung in Maschinenbau-Unternehmungen* (Jena, 1913); Hans Hinke, *Auslese und Anpassung der Arbeiter im Buchdruckgewerbe* (Berlin, 1910).

26 Reichelt, *op. cit.;* Paul Göhre, *Drei Monate Fabrikarbeiter* (Leipzig, 1913); Carl Fischer, *Denkwürdigkeiten und Erinnerungen eines Arbeiters* (Leipzig, 1904).

27 R. Broda and Julius Deutsch, *Das moderne Proletariat* (Berlin, 1906), p. 173.

28 Levenstein, *Arbeiterfrage,* p. 50.

29 Levenstein, *Tiefe,* p. 57 and *passim.*

67 percent of the skilled workers and 44 percent of the unskilled felt more pleasure than distaste for work.[30]

Even before 1914 the labor force was deeply divided in its reactions to work. Probably very few felt as strongly as Max Lotz. How many, at the other extreme, agreed with the miner who thought his work the most interesting in the world? We cannot know precisely, but the existence of strong minority enthusiasm for work and the piece rate is undeniable. Differences in personality and health from one worker to the next make any generalization suspect. One can discern certain industrial patterns. Variations in discontent with work among textiles, mining, and metals were considerable even in Levenstein's poll. Textile workers, at least males, were least happy with their work because they were physically weak—their rate of military rejections was extremely high—and because their pay was low. Metal workers worried about the intensity of their labor but they found some interest in it. And they were better-fed and healthier to begin with. Metallurgical workers were more satisfied still, despite the fact they worked twelve-hour shifts. Their piece rates were rarely altered, partly because labor costs were a low percentage of the total, and so they could earn more as they worked harder or more skillfully. In machine building piece rates fluctuated, if only because the nature of the work changed so often; this created a tension in which the worker could easily feel unfairly paid and therefore overworked.[31]

Variations of this sort could be endlessly refined. I think that, for general purposes, three sets of reactions to industrial labor can be marked off. The first is of course the traditionalist approach brought in by the unskilled, to work long hours but not usually very intensely; traditionalism was sometimes abetted, particularly among women, by a sense that the factory was a diverting place. The second reaction was one of shock and resistance, as with male textile workers. The third embraced workers who found some genuine interest in their job, or whose resistance paid off sufficiently, in shorter hours for example, to remove any fundamental grievance, or who learned to compensate for unpleasant work by other enjoyments. The second group set much of the tone for the period, as was reflected in the polls that were taken. But we cannot determine the importance of each group by reaction to work alone. The outlook toward wages varied widely also, exacerbating the despair of some of those who detested their work—like Max Lotz, who could scarcely imagine being paid enough to compensate for his arduous labor—but aiding the adjustment of others to new methods and a new pace.

The outlook of the new, unskilled workers toward the wage has already been

30 H. De Man, *Joy in Work* (London, 1928). This would qualify the conclusion in [John H.] Goldthorpe *et al.*, [*The Making of the English Working Class* (New York, 1963)], that modern workers take no pleasure in their work, though the comparison with the extent of middle-class pleasure would still stand. I must agree with Hobsbawm, *op. cit.*, p. 411, that workers' enjoyment of their work is commoner than outsiders may imagine.

31 Otto Jeidel, *Die Methoden der Arbeiterentlöhnung in der rheinischwestfälischen Eisenindustrie* (Berlin, 1907); Morgenstern *et al.*, *op cit.*, Timmerman, *op. cit.*

suggested. They seemed content, even delighted with the pay and living standards they won in the factories. As a skilled worker noted scornfully, they were "satisfied when they are able to buy cigarettes."[32] They concentrated particularly on improving their diets, recalling a rural childhood of potatoes and milk. Silesian workers in the Ruhr, particularly the women, adopted local styles, but in most factories a hierarchy of dress persisted in that the unskilled wore simple garb. In Stuttgart factories the unskilled wore no overcoats and professed to find this appropriate. Perhaps the key was the attitude of the women, who were used to plain clothes and did much of the family sewing.[33] Housing—which was quite exiguous in the cities—seemed satisfactory. The unskilled complained of rents but not of housing directly. Here, obviously, the bad quality of rural housing set low expectations. The unskilled were generally satisfied with two rooms. They were not the ones who pressed out to surrounding villages to seek their housing; what they found in the cities sufficed.[34] There was little interest in other items of expense. Medical care was feared. As one East Prussian woman said, "God is the best doctor. If he wishes, I'm healthy; otherwise not . . . I would rather die than let them cut."[35] It is, I admit, always presumptuous to talk of satisfaction among poor people, but this seems to be accurate here. Traditionally low standards which factory work exceeded in terms both of pay and of regularity of work, plus the hope of some that factory life was only temporary, a basis for a return to the countryside with enough money to buy land, make this outlook understandable.

The traditionalists were a large group, but probably not a majority of the labor force. What of the rest: the textile workers and others who hated their work, the skilled workers in factories and shops who faced changing conditions on the job?

To what extent were German workers eager to improve their wages? As the outlook of the traditionalists indicates, such eagerness cannot automatically be assumed. The question can be further refined. To what extent did workers become aware of the wages as a market item, as an incentive which should be increased when production increased?[36] Did they transfer some of their dissatisfac-

32 Levenstein, *Tiefe,* p. 120.

33 Göhre, *op cit.;* W. J. Ashley, *The Progress of the German Working Classes* (London, 1904); Schulze, *op. cit.;* Fritz Schumann, *Auslese und Anpassung der Arbeiterschaft in der Automobilenindustrie* (Leipzig, 1911).

34 Oskar Mulert, *Vierundzwanzig ostpreussische Arbeiter und Arbeiterfamilien* (Jena, 1908); Eugen Jaeger, *Die Wohnungsfrage,* 1 (Berlin, 1902); Kurt Seidl, *Das Arbeiterwohnungswesen in der Oberschlesichen Montanindustrie* (Kattowitz, 1913). The preference for small housing units was not only a matter of tradition; it also saved on heat, which was understandably of great concern in Germany.

35 C. Moszeck, ed., *Aus der Gedankenwelt einer Arbeiterfrau* (Berlin, 1909), pp. 44, 111.

36 Hobsbawm, *op. cit.,* pp. 406–13. Hobsbawm implies a rather sophisticated notion of the relation between work and the wage, without considering the wage from the consumer's viewpoint; yet in traditional labor protest workers more often seized on consumption (price) grievances than on pay grievances—and they were likely to make the transition to a new view of the wage through this same channel.

tion with their work to the wage? Or did they view the wage more as consumers, in which case the question is less involved in the work situation, more in the degree to which improvements in the standard of living were sought? Both of these approaches are useful, but I find the latter more applicable to the situation of most German workers in this period.

Again, even aside from the traditionalists, German workers were divided in wage matters, but let us begin with some general points. Compared to workers in older industrial countries, German workers were not avid for wage gains. It is true that their real wages continued to increase, though slowly, in contrast to trends in Britain and France after 1900. It is also true that one must not exaggerate French and British eagerness for material progress. But there is a difference, clearly related to the stage of industrialization.

If German workers were able to transfer their grievances about changing work conditions to wage demands, one would expect a massive wave of strikes in this period. Such was not the case. Despite Germany's much larger labor force, fewer German than French workers went on strike between 1899 and 1914—25 percent fewer in absolute terms, over 100 percent fewer per capita of the manufacturing labor force. Relatedly, the average strike—with 119 workers—was unusually small. Wage strikes were still smaller than this average, the reverse of the pattern in more advanced industrial countries. Few German workers could be roused over this issue, and often those who were found themselves a minority among their immediate colleagues. Hence a French manufacturing worker was almost two and half times more likely to strike over wage issues than his German counterpart.[37]

It is true that 71 percent of all German strikes did raise pay demands, a percentage higher than that in France (where the figure was under 65 percent) and much higher than that in Britain. Without doubt, a minority of workers were capable of seeking wage gains. But a surprising number of major wage strikes were actually defensive, against a reduction of pay. Unfortunately it is difficult to be very precise in comparisons. Between 1899 and 1914, 8 percent of all German wage strikes were listed as defensive—about the same figure as in France. Even here, it is noteworthy that the French defensive strikes were much smaller than average and that they were bunched around the 1901–1902 slump, declining sharply thereafter. In contrast German defensive strikes were of about average size and their rate increased. Furthermore, the official figures underrepresented defensive wage strikes. Metal workers had to strike repeatedly against price-rate reductions that cut their take-home pay. So did shoe workers and textile workers—like the Cunewalde weavers who struck against an 18 percent cut in 1901.[38] Again, essentially defensive strikes were far more important

37 Kaiserliches Statistiches Amt, *Statistik über Streiks und Aussperrungen*, 1899–1914; Office du travail, *Statistique des grèves*.

38 Münster Staatsarchiv, Regierung Arnsberg I 76 (police reports); Generalkommission der deutschen Gewerkschaften, *Correspondenzblatt*, 1904.

in other countries than official figures convey,[39] but they were less common than in Germany and usually less direct reactions to a pay cut. In many of their wage strikes, German workers argued simply in terms of poverty. Masons in Gelsenkirchen asked for a raise so that they could earn enough "that we can regularly feed our families."[40] Arguments of this sort almost never appeared among workers in older industrial countries.[41] They suggest that many German wage strikes and the high rate of wage strikes overall reflected no new attitude toward the wage but rather the marginal conditions in which many German workers lived. . . .

Only in clothing were there signs of hopes for rather rapid improvement, as Ruhr miners and others awakened to possibilities of new fashions. Correspondingly this was the only nonfood budget category where German workers led those of the older industrial countries. The interest in clothing is characteristic of workers in many early industrial situations. Possession of respectable clothing for walking about the city on Sundays was extremely important. Along with some improvements in diet it seems to be the first new consumption interest to emerge. Why? Obviously clothes are cheap; perhaps an interest in them is naturally human, an extension of the skin as Marshall McLuhan would have it. But students of consumption habits can beware of calling anything "natural." Only by indirection were many workers led to want better housing; as we shall see, changes in family life rather than a virgin birth of the modern economic man were often involved. The early interest in clothing was a reaction to change, a desire to prove one's place in fairly well known terms, for even in the countryside differences in dress were known marks of status. For some of the small-town artisans and others who had status anxieties as well as a general sense of uneasiness in the factories stylish clothes may have been particularly important. By the same token the interest in clothes was not immediately part of a desire for more material goods generally. Workers could be satisfied with better dress. And clothing was cheap enough that it did not prompt elaborate wage demands.[42]

Three factors add to this impression of limited expectations; at least two of them, like the limited expectations themselves, flowed naturally from the early industrial setting. German workers were filled with a longing for the coun-

39 [Peter N.] Stearns, [*Revolutionary Syndicalism and French Labor: A Cause without Rebels* (New Brunswick, 1971)].

40 Münster Staatsarchiv, Regierung Arnsberg I 76.

41 The poorest workers who struck in France, for example, generally referred to past wage rates or to inflation, but not to absolute poverty. See, for an example, Léon de Seilhac, *Les grèves du tissage de Lille* (Paris, 1910), and *Le Lock-out de Fougères* (Paris, 1907).

42 Deutsche Metallarbeiter-Verband, *320 Haushaltsrechnungen von Metallarbeitern* (Stuttgart, 1909); Carl von Tyszka, *Die Lebenshaltung der arbeitenden Klassen* (Jena, 1912), p. 42; (British) Board of Trade, *Report of an Enquiry into Working Class Rents, Housing, and Retail Prices* (London, 1908); Board of Trade, *Report of an Enquiry into Working Class Rents, Housing and Retail Prices . . . in the Principal Industrial Towns of France* (London, 1909) and . . . *of Germany* (London, 1908); Elisabeth Gottheimer, *Studien über die Wuppertaler Textilindustrie und ihre Arbeiter* (Leipzig, 1903).

tryside. "I believe that every city resident, as soon as time permits, should go to the countryside, go to nature, and fill his lungs with pure, unspoiled air."[43] Workers acted on this sentiment. An overwhelming majority listed walks in the country and gardening as their favorite recreations; pastimes that cost more money and might have induced higher expectations—including books and education—could not compete. Miners and then textile workers particularly relied on nature and gardening, but the interest was general. Longing for nature reflected the rural origins of many workers and the grievances about work that many felt. One may speculate that the walks and gardening not only inhibited material expectations but also, for the millions of workers who still could enjoy them, provided some genuine satisfaction.[44]

Drink was another carry-over from tradition that was also fed by discontent with work while inhibiting higher expectations. Many German workers were frequently drunk. They spent 6 to 11 percent of their budget on alcohol—an allocation that was not matched by higher segments of German society until the level of university professors. Articulate miners deplored their fellows' penchant for drink, which retarded their education and limited their goals. When polled, a fifth of the miners admitted their dependence on drink. Less than a tenth of textile and metal workers made a similar admission, but their budgets too revealed high rates of spending on alcohol which tended to rise as incomes went up.[45]

Skilled German workers showed a marked interest in cleanliness. (The unskilled did not, so I think we can dismiss sheer Germanness as a cause of the characteristic.) They carefully washed and changed clothes before leaving the worksite and they often struck for improved wash facilities. Their concern stands out among workers of other industrial countries. It suggests some of the tension and status anxieties of workers from small-town and craft environments. It is related, obviously, to the interest in clothing.[46] It may also have distracted workers from more elaborate consumption expectations because so many German companies provided excellent wash facilities and because agitation for further improvements took up energies that might otherwise have been used for wage gains. As one group of Ruhr workers noted when they won new rules on bathroom conditions in their factory, "These rules are worth much more to us than a pay raise."[47]

43 [Clemens] Heiss [*Auslese und Anpassung der Arbeiter in der Berliner Feinmechanik* (Leipzig, 1910)], p. 222.

44 Lewenstein, *Arbeiterfrage*.

45 [Ernst] Dückerstoff, [*How the English Workman Lives*, trans. C. H. Leppington (London, 1899)]; L. Rexhäuser, *Haushaltungs-Rechnungen Nürnberger Arbeiter* (Nuremberg, 1901); Levenstein, *Arbeiterfrage*. On the university professors, see Kaiserliches Statistisches Amt, Abteilung für Arbeiter Statistik, *Zwei Wirtschaftsrechnungen von Familien höherer Beamten* (Berlin, 1911).

46 Franz Schulte, *Die Entlöhnungsmethoden in der Berliner Maschinenindustrie* (Berlin, 1906); Schumann, *op cit.*

47 Gerhard Adelman, *Die soziale Betriebsverfassung des Ruhrbergbaus vom Anfang des 19. Jahrhunderts bis zum Ersten Weltkrieg* (Bonn, 1962), 1, 247.

In contrast to the general hesitancy about advancing wages, a minority of workers were committed to expanding prosperity. Some were in factories, like the metallurgical workers who shunned company housing and moved into towns distant from concentrations of lower-paid workers. Far more were still in the crafts. At an extreme, artisans like printers adopted an essentially bourgeois consumption pattern, even though their wages might be in the middling range. They cut the percentage they devoted to food—down to 39 percent in one case. They drank little and sometimes had their wives make their clothes. But they valued housing, spending up to 28 percent on rent, and they saved for the education of their children.[48] Still more workers kept a rather proletarian expenditure pattern but strove for steadily advancing wages. Skilled construction workers led the way. Their wage strikes resembled those in France and Britain in frequency and in the arguments used, which means they sharply departed from the norm in Germany. They conducted 32 percent of all strikes between 1899 and 1914, though they numbered only 18 percent of the manufacturing labor force, and their offensive wage strikes were almost 30 percent more frequent among all their strikes than the rate for strikes in general with construction strikes excepted.[49] They led the way also in wage movements that did not result in strikes; in 1905, for example, masons conducted 507 such movements affecting 106,761 workers. These workers, along with printers, brewers, and others, had a "modern" idea of the wage and of advancing living standards. They were not for the most part new to their trade. Though many of them faced radical changes in business organization and substantial changes in working methods in this period, they could adjust through the wage. And, minority though they were, their numbers were not small.[50]

Examination of adjustment to work and the wage yields three groups of workers—an assortment that is not surprising but one that is decidedly hard to unify. At one end were the traditionalists in work habits and consumption expectations. At the other end craftsmen and metallurgical workers either found enjoyment in their work—remember the printers on the composing machines—or compensated by seeking higher wages, or, most commonly, both. This leaves the group in the middle, the reasonably skilled factory workers, many from small-town craft backgrounds. Most of them had not made a full transition to a progressive view of the wage and consumption. Some of them were content with their work—the middle group of the work-aggrieved was smaller than the middle group of consumption-conservatives. But there was a mass of workers, in textiles, mining, machine building, and shoe manufacture, who disliked their work

48 Walter Abelsdorff, *Beiträge zum Sozialstatistik der deutschen Buchdrucker* (Tübingen, 1900); August Busch, *Preisbewegungen und Kosten der Lebenshaltung in Frankfurt am Main* (Munich, 1914); Jeidel, *op. cit.*

49 Kaiserliches Statistisches Amt, *Streiks,* 1899–1914.

50 Habersbrunner, *op. cit.;* Zentral-Verband der Maurer Deutschlands, *Bericht des Verbandsvorstandes,* 1905–1906.

without finding full compensation in a new view of the wage. These workers were not yet capable of making the basic bargain that industrialization required, to admit new work methods, sometimes unpleasant ones, in return for advancing earnings.

LAZAR VOLIN

# THE RUSSIAN PEASANT: FROM EMANCIPATION TO KOLKHOZ

The very selection of the year 1861 as the starting point of this inquiry is symptomatic of the importance attached to the peasantry in the Russian social fabric. This is, I am sure, not due to a mere physiocratic bias or predilection. For 1861 is associated with a great milestone in the historic fate of the Russian peasant—the Emancipation Act of February 19. It decreed the abolition of what the great Russian historian Kliuchevsky characterized as the worst form of serfdom in Europe.[1] By the same token, 1861 became a great national landmark, ushering in a new era justly remembered in Russian history as that of the Great Reforms of the early reign of Alexander II. Following in the wake of a severe jolt administered to the Russian Autocracy by the humiliating defeat in the Crimean War of 1854–1855, these reforms revitalized national life after the sterile reac-

Reprinted by permission of the publishers from Cyril E. Black, ed., *The Transformation of Russian Society* (Cambridge, Mass.: Harvard University Press). Copyright 1960 by the President and Fellows of Harvard College.

1 V. O. Kliuchevsky, *Kurs russkoi istorii* (5 vols.; Moscow, 1910), I, 434. For a discussion of the Russian servile system, see also: G. T. Robinson, *Rural Russia under the Old Regime* (New York, 1932), chs. 3–4; Lazar Volin, "The Russian Peasant and Serfdom," *Agricultural History,* XVII (January 1943), 41–61, reprinted in Herman Ausubel, ed., *The Making of Modern Europe* (2 vols.; New York, 1951), II, 709–31. Of the voluminous Russian literature on the subject referred to in the above publications, there must be singled out the monumental *Velikaia reforma: Russkoe obshchestvo i krest'ianskii vopros v proshlom i nastoiashchem,* ed. A. K. Dzhivelegov and others (6 vols.; Moscow, 1911). The first four volumes are devoted to a description and analysis of various aspects of serfdom.

tionary regime of Nicholas I. Despite the abolition of serfdom, the dictum of Gustav Schmoller, that in Europe "from 1500 to 1850 the great social question of the day was the peasant question,"[2] continued to be applicable until much later in Russia. For in one form or another, it has never disappeared as a central political-economic issue at every critical juncture in modern Russian history, even after the peasantry ceased to be the predominant element of population.

Half a century after the emancipation, the peasant question or, as it was then called, the land or agrarian question was again in the foreground during the 1905 Revolution, and it emerged as an explosive issue a decade later during the revolution of 1917. It was central in the transition from War Communism to the NEP in 1921 under Lenin and, of course, in the collectivization crisis of the early 1930s under Stalin. After Stalin's death this question came back to plague the heirs of the late dictator.

This cursory review should make it clear that the peasant question in Russia was not settled by the emancipation in the 1860s as it was in Western Europe by the French Revolution and the subsequent agrarian reforms, and the industrial revolution in the nineteenth century. On the contrary, the historic contest between the Russian peasant and the landlord, shielded by the Tsarist state, continued until a complete victory was apparently won by the peasant in 1917. However, this was a Pyrrhic victory followed by a new conflict, this time between the peasant and the Communist state, bent on collectivization of agriculture and a rapid but lopsided industrialization. Throughout this period, while the institutional agrarian structure underwent significant changes, the peasant continued to be the Cinderella of the body politic, except for some transitory and sectional improvements.

The period between 1861 and the revolution of 1917 poses a crucial question: why, having begun with a promising agrarian reform, did it end with a peasant revolt resembling in many respects Pushkin's celebrated "Russian mutiny—terrible and senseless"? Certainly Alexander II recognized the dilemma—agrarian reform or eventual revolution—when he warned the serf-owning landlords in the beginning of his reign that it is better to liberate serfs from above than to wait until they liberated themselves. He saw the handwriting on the wall and hoped to forestall a possible peasant uprising, a rumbling of which was to be heard in frequent local mutinies of serfs, keeping alive that nightmare of the serf-owner—the *Pugachevshchina.*[3] When the government's intention to abolish serfdom became known about a hunded years ago, it was greeted with immense enthusiasm by the Russian intelligentsia of all shades of opinion: from the Slavophiles at the right, to liberals like Kavelin and (at that time) Katkov at the

2 *Volkswirtschaftslehre,* I, 520, quoted in J. H. Clapham, *The Economic Development of France and Germany, 1815–1914* (Cambridge, Eng., 1921), 1.

3 A term for a peasant revolt derived from the name of Emelian Pugachev, the leader of a formidable peasant rebellion in the 1770s during the reign of Catherine the Great.

center, to Herzen at the left of center, and even Chernyshevsky at the extreme left.

This enthusiasm, however, faded as the emancipation legislation, which was to affect so profoundly the life of the liberated peasantry, began to take shape.[4] Not only did radicals like Ogarev and Chernyshevsky damn the emancipation reform, but even Ivan Aksakov, the conservative Slavophile, was critical. For a strong impact was exerted on the new legislation by the landowning nobility, which was strongly entrenched at the imperial court and in the governing bureaucracy. The landowners were bent on making the liberation process economically as painless as possible to themselves when they realized its inevitability. The pressure of the landlord interests, though in some respects divergent (as between different geographic regions), resulted in many a compromise unfavorable to the liberated peasants.[5]

To be sure, the peasant ceased to be legally what Herzen called "baptized property." And, what is equally important in view of the attachment of the Russian peasants to their land, they were not liberated as landless proletarians. This was the fate of the peasants freed from bondage much earlier in the Baltic provinces (1818), and the idea was toyed with during the early preparatory stage of the emancipation reform but later abandoned.

The peasants did not obtain all the land they hoped for in accordance with the strongly implanted concept that land should belong to those who toil on it. Actually, the landowning nobility retained about 45 percent of the best land.[6] In the allotment of the remainder to the more than 20 million peasants, however there were considerable regional variations, dictated by the divergent interests of the landowning gentry in different areas.

A large section of the liberated peasantry in the more fertile regions, where land was valuable, was allotted even a smaller area than it had tilled for its own needs under serfdom. The holdings allotted were also often of poor quality and location, and lacking such important components as meadows (hayland) and woodland, necessitating the leasing of these types of land from the former

4 For a detailed treatment of the emancipation legislation, see: Robinson, ch. 5; George Pavlovsky, *Agricultural Russia on the Eve of the Revolution* (London, 1930); P. I. Lyashchenko, *History of the National Economy of Russia to the 1917 Revolution* (New York, 1949), ch. 21; *Velikaia reforma,* V, 4–5; A. A. Kornilov, *Krest'ianskaia reforma* (Moscow, 1905); chs. 3–5.

5 The divergence was principally between the landowners of the more fertile regions of the black-soil areas, where land itself was the most valuable element of the estate economy, and the much less fertile nonblack-soil area, where the landowners to a large extent derived their incomes not from farming of their own, but from quit-rents paid by the serfs, who gained their livelihood partly from agriculture and partly from nonagricultural pursuits.

6 Lyashchenko, 393. The reduction of the land area allotted to peasants after the emancipation amounted to 9.9 per cent in 15 nonblack-soil provinces and 26.2 per cent in 21 black-soil provinces, and 18.1 per cent for the combined 36 provinces. In some provinces the reduction exceeded 30 to 40 per cent (Lyashchenko, 384). It should be noted, however, that in addition to the more than 20 million private serfs there were also the so-called crown (state) peasants and those belonging to the imperial family, numbering altogether close to 20 million. These categories fared much better and suffered no reduction of their land area.

master. In these and other aspects of the land-allotment process was the genesis of the continued economic dependence of the liberated peasants on their former master which persisted long after the emancipation. Here was a source of irritation and conflict which poisoned the liberated peasant-landlord relations. . . .

The idea that all was not well with emancipated rural Russia began to gain ground in the public mind soon after the emancipation reform. As a matter of fact, as we saw above, serious criticism of the reform began with its very proclamation. A decade later, in 1872, an official commission of inquiry into rural conditions was set up, the Valuev Commission, before which much pessimistic testimony was given. Twenty years later, following the catastrophic famine in 1891, an even gloomier view that the Russian village was in the throes of a serious crisis because of increasing impoverishment gained wide acceptance. The paradox of a chronic undernourishment of the farm population in a country which had become one of the leading exporters of grain and other foodstuffs was stressed by numerous observers and witnesses before the official investigating commissions, such as that established under the chairmanship of the Minister of Finance, Count Witte. The increase in the number of peasant households without work horses and the generally poor condition of peasant livestock lacking an adequate feed-supply base, the increasing parceling of peasant holdings, the piling up of tax arrears—these were some of the symptoms of the growing deterioration of peasant agriculture.

If the peasant could still, with some difficulty, keep his head above water in years of good or average harvests, he was faced with disaster when crops failed, as they often did, especially in the large semiarid belt of Russia. Famine conditions, epidemics, increased mortality, decrease in the number of livestock (including work horses which, by striking at the sole source of farmpower, did more than anything else to undermine the very foundation of peasant farming)—this is the spectacle of the growing destitution of a famine-striken Russian village. The adverse effects of such conditions were felt long after the worst of the famine had passed. What Kipling wrote of the Indian peasant in the 1890s could be applied to his Russian counterpart as well: "His life is a long-drawn question between a crop and a crop."

The chronic rural distress should not obscure the fact that there always had been a small group which was economically better off than the great mass of the peasants. Leadership in the village and also a tendency to exploit the poorer peasants through usurious loans, and such, was often characteristic of this group. Such economic stratification in the village was noted, for instance, as early as the 1870s by the astute observer, A. N. Engel'gardt, in his celebrated *Letters from the Village* which, incidentally, can still be read with much interest and were recently republished by the Soviets.[7] But growing economic stratification in the village was particularly stressed by Marxist socialist writes, who appeared on the scene in the 1880s. At that time a split took place in the Russian socialist

7 A. N. Engel'gardt, *Iz derevni. 12 pisem 1872–1877* (Moscow, 1937).

movement between the new orthodox Marxist wing and the older populist (*narodnik*) or agrarian-minded current which based its socialist ideology on the peasant mir and not on the industrial proletariat. A vigorous controversy developed between the Marxists and the populists concerning the trend of economic development of Russia and, more specifically, the inevitability of its passing through a capitalist stage. The populists took a dim view of this. The Marxists, on the contrary, found supporting evidence for their traditional analysis of economic development (which postulates class stratification and polarization concomitant with the growth of capitalism) in the stratification process taking place in the Russian village. They claimed that the mir system with its egalitarian tendency of land tenure retarded but did not eliminate this process. However, in their preoccupation with economics, the Marxists neglected other influences in rural stratification, notably the demographic factor—that is, the composition and the size of the family. These, as Kaufman, Chaianov, and others showed, played an important role in the process of village stratification. Larger and stronger peasant holdings were usually associated with larger families, and vice versa.[8]. . .

And what about the peasant's attitude toward the crisis? What was his solution? It could be summed up in two words: ''more land.'' He saw the root of all his difficulties in a shortage of land and his only salvation in extension of the cultivated area. It was easier, of course, to continue the same type of farming in a larger area than to reorganize the system of farming on the old holdings, especially when capital and knowledge were lacking. Moreover, some holdings were too small for any practicable improvement of farming. There were also historical and psychological reasons for the peasants' attitude. There was the traditional view that only the tillers of the soil were entitled to land; hence the disappointment of the peasants when they did not obtain all the estate land after emancipation. What rankled most, however, was the loss of the land which they tilled as serfs on their own—the so-called *otrezki* (literally, cut-off land). Lenin sensed this feeling when he sought, as a means of enlisting the peasantry, the inclusion of a demand for restoration of *otrezki* in the platform of the Social Democratic Party.

While the peasants acquiesced in the new land arrangements more peacefully than the government expected, despite a number of local mutinies,[9] they

8 The larger the family, the greater as a rule the number of workers as well as of the mouths to be fed. This meant that more land could be and needed to be taken on from the mir or leased from the neighboring estate or fellow peasants. If a large peasant family, however, was short of work horses or farm equipment, some of its workhands could seek employment in the city and, with the money thus earned, purchase the needed draft animals and implements. See A. A. Kaufman, *Voprosy ekonomiki i statistiki krest'ianskogo khoziaistva* (Moscow, 1918), 19–20; A. A. Chaianov, *Organizatsiia krest'ianskogo khoziaistva* (Moscow, 1925), chs. 1–2.

9 Kornilov, 175. It was, however, by no means a submission without a protest, inasmuch as there were more than 1,100 cases of disorders and uprisings in different villages during the two years 1861–1863. V. Gorn, *Krest'ianskiia dvizheniia za poltora veka* (Moscow, 1909), 29.

never fully accepted them as a just solution. The peasants continued to dream, after emancipation, of a new partition of land to be ordered by the kind tsar, once he was able to overcome the resistance of the nobles and his ministers. Naturally, as the crisis deepened, they looked with increasingly covetous eyes on the broad acres of the "nobles' nests" which adjoined their narrow strips. How he could lay his hands on this land, of which he considered himself unjustly deprived, became the central preoccupation of the Russian peasant.

## CHAPTER 5

# MARRIAGE AND THE FAMILY

Nothing is harder to define, or to enforce, than a standard of morality. We associate the Victorian age with a strict and indeed prudish code of behavior, but that has little to do with the way in which most ordinary people actually conducted their private lives. How were childen raised and educated? What marital and sexual practices were countenanced at home? What role did religion continue to play in shaping moral values? These are some of the questions that the following selections attempt to answer.

*Jennie Kitteringham* grew up on a farm and knows whereof she writes concerning the rearing of children in a rural setting. Her essay is part reminiscence, part history, and altogether charming as well as informative. We learn about the strenuous mixture of work and play on a farm, and we are led to appreciate the difference between the perspectives of lower- and middle-class girls as they grew to maturity.

*Standish Meacham* distinguishes the subjective from the objective reality in evaluating why a working-class woman chose marriage as a way of life. She was usually eager to leave the confinements of the parental home, and she accepted her role as spouse and mother as a matter of course. If she thereby gained some status, she almost certainly became increasingly dependent on her husband, a pattern not soon to be altered by industrialization. Marriage might bring pleasures, but it also meant child-bearing, hard work, and daily routine.

*Theodore Zeldin* portrays the rituals of French family life. The penetrating values of property and social position affected every class. Yet romance and sex had their place as well. Zeldin uses popular nineteenth-century guidebooks to marriage in order to afford us an intimate glimpse into the private lives of French couples. We see that the church took an active part in attempting to mold sexual attitudes and practices. But we may wonder how successful such pious instructions actually proved to be in an increasingly secularized society.

While the evidence cited here is less than conclusive, it suggests that conceptions of morality evolve more slowly than economic and social change. Familial and religious traditions continued to exert an inhibiting influence on children as they grew and on young adults as they married. In these matters, what Friedrich Nietzsche called the transvaluation of values was to be, like industrialization itself, a long and distressing process—one that remains, and is likely to remain, incomplete.

*JENNIE KITTERINGHAM*

# *THE COUNTRY WORKING GIRL*

Country girls of the nineteenth century were by nature and necessity more hardy and practical than I was as a child. For instance the attitude my younger sister and I had to animals on the farm was that they were pets. We always had chickens which we used to rear from day-old chicks with the aim of them being the "Sunday joint." But it was fatal for us to get to know them—how could you eat something that you had reared and played with and liked? As soon as the weekend came round and there was the prospect of "Carole" or "Margaret" chicken being killed, Liz and I would start our pleading for her to be spared and a joint bought. For us there was that alternative; our predecessors would have had none. Killing was always done by my father, be it the chicken for dinner or newborn kittens.

A good example of the contrast in attitudes between today and then, is the killing of "the pig." Due to the lowness of wages, farmers sometimes allowed

Jennie Kitteringham, "The Country Working Girl," in *Village Life and Labour,* ed. Raphael Samuel (London: Routledge & Kegan Paul, 1975), pp. 75–76, 81–82, 127–33, by permission of the publisher.

their labourers to keep a pig for which they would supply some food, ground, etc. (this varied with the farmer). Possession of a pig, with its promise of future meat and bacon, was a great advantage for the labourer and his family; it was a walking investment for the harsh winter months, or, as F. G. Heath put it, a "live savings bank." It was fed all left-overs from meals, along with potato peelings, barley gleanings and acorns. In the North Oxfordshire village where Flora Thompson spent her childhood, and which she vividly evokes in *Lark Rise to Candleford,* all the family would be prepared to go without for the sake of the pig, and time would be spent collecting food for it. Leaves would be collected for its litter. As Flora put it:[1]

> The family pig was everybody's pride and everybody's business . . . The children, on their way home from school, would fill their arms with sow thistle, dandelion, and choice long grass, or roam along the hedgerows on wet evenings collecting snails in a pail for the pig's supper. These piggy crunched up with great relish . . .

There would be a "pig tub" at the back door, as Edwin Grey describes in his *Cottage Life in a Hertfordshire Village,*[2] into which all scraps would be thrown, and even the slops from the cooking and washing-up. (In some villages a local farmer would provide a communal tub to furnish swill for his own pigs, and the village pigless would contribute to it in return for a share of the pork when killed, or for payment—"We mayn't keep a pig, but instead of this master gives us 6*d.* a week for the wash," a Dorset labourer's wife told the Commissioner.)[3]

The killing of the pig was an important occasion, at once solemn and festive. Its death was a celebration—it was accepted that in order for them to live, the pig, no matter how much a friend, had to die. Its death was prepared with care. As Flora Thompson recalled:[4]

> When the pig was fattened—and the fatter the better—the date of execution had to be decided upon. It had to take place some time during the first two quarters of the moon; for, if the pig was killed when the moon was waning the bacon would shrink in cooking, and they wanted it to "plimp up."

This belief was also held in Dorset. I was told by Ruth Carey, who was born in 1882 the daughter of a tenant farmer, and later was a farmer's wife, spending most of her long and hard-working life in Dorset, that pig-killing had to be carried out whilst "the moon was growing," otherwise the meat would shrink. Her father would do the cutting of the meat and the females of the family would do the cooking and preserving but on no account was a female allowed to touch the

1 Flora Thompson, *Lark Rise to Candleford,* London, 1954, p. 10.

2 Edwin Grey, *Cottage Life in a Hertfordshire Village,* St Albans, 1935, pp. 50–1.

3 P.P. 1868–9 (4202–1) XIII, *2nd Report of the Commissioners on the Employment of Children, Young Persons and Women in Agriculture* (abbreviated *to AEC* II), Appendix pt II (g), p. 245.

4 Thompson, *op. cit.,* p. 11.

meat whilst she had a period as this would have given it a "peculiar taste," a taste which was easily discernible, as Ruth affirmed. Such attitudes indicate the gross importance of the quality and quantity of the meat to these workers and their families. . . .

For many country children in the nineteenth century, schooling was something that happened only in the winter time when the ground was too hard to work on—or when the market for the gloves, lace or plait that they had spent hours making, was low. Work came first. Where schooling was available, the hours were often such as to allow for children to do work before and after school: 10 A.M. until 12.30 P.M. and then 1 P.M. until 3 P.M., in an example given to the Newcastle Commission in 1861.[5] Though the three R's were taught to all, during recreation time it was considered that the girls should not take part in unsuitable athletic sports such as football, cricket, etc., but that they should ". . . find a little wholesome physical exercise . . . in cleaning out the school."[6] The parents often could not afford to send their children to school; wages were low, and every possible contribution to the family budget was needed. Where schooling tipped the balance from subsistence to starvation, school was easier to give up than food. An entry in the school log book from Braunton, in Devon, commented, "The poorer parents with long families think it hard if they cannot keep home their elder children two or three days in the week to earn a little to support the family generally," and at Ermington, also in Devon, another schoolmaster found it "hard to snatch a few pence from a parent's weekly income" by enforcing attendance.[7] Employers were often opposed to schooling for the labouring classes, and made it difficult for farm girls or boys to attend lessons, for instance, by making the working hours so rigid that they were not able to finish early enough to get to night school.

School log books from the latter half of the century, show how children were inextricably involved in the survival of their families and were called upon at particular seasons of the year to work and earn money at agricultural and rural forms of labour. There are mentions in these log books of children working at apple-picking, bird-watching, singling turnips, stone-picking and other jobs, as well as many references to unspecified field work. An entry in the log for Roxwell Church School, in Essex, from 11 August 1880, pinpoints the urgency of their seizing any chance to earn a few pence: "Pretty good school on Monday but many girls away in the afternoon for a report was spread that some gleaning was to be had, however proved to be incorrect."[8]

5 P.P. 1861 (2794–11) XXI–II, *Reports of the Assistant Commissioners appointed to Inquire into the state of Popular Education in England,* p. 86.

6 *Ibid.*, p. 99.

7 R. R. Sellman, *Devon Village Schools in the Nineteenth Century,* Newton Abbot, 1967, p. 121.

8 Essex Record Office, E/ML 171, log book, Roxwell Church of England School, 11 August 1881.

Summer holidays were important for the work done during them, and were often named accordingly: for instance in Kent the break was known as the Hopping Vacation or Hopping Holidays; elsewhere as the Harvest Holiday. The school log book from Yalding in Kent has an illuminating entry (6 October 1873): "Opened School today after the Hopping Holiday. Attendance rather small children not quite ready to come. Some are waiting to buy shoes."[9] Harvest times were used to accumulate money to pay off past bills (e.g., for the pig, or the doctor), or to buy shoes and other necessities for the coming winter and hard months; and everybody's work was needed. . . .

In all societies there is a predominant morality—a value system—which decrees the dos and don'ts of that particular society and by which its members are judged. This is not to say that all classes have the same value system—they don't—but each creates its own to suit its personal situation, ideals, etc. The Victorian and present-day societies are not exceptions to this rule.

The Victorian middle class used their own ideals as a yardstick to measure the failings of their inferiors. Theirs was the epitome of a "moral" existence; and anything different from it was thought to be immoral or a symptom of immoralities to come. The middle-class female was expected to be an ornament in the drawing-room, wholly withdrawn from physical toil and the world of men. Her children were given different roles according to their age and sex. Each room in the house had a definite and limited role assigned to it—the dining-room, the drawing-room, the study, the boys' bedroom, the girls' bedroom, the nursery and so on.

This segregation was a luxury that the working masses, with their crowded cottages, could not afford (and did not even consider as desirable). This did not stop them from being labelled as immoral. According to the *Saturday Review* of 3 April 1858 the "promiscuous herding of children in their immature years" was "not an infrequent prelude to a life of harlotry," "the cottage bedroom was the first stop to the Haymarket."[10] "They live like pigs," a witness told the Children's Employment Commission, ". . . great boys and girls, mothers and fathers, all sleeping in one room in many instances"; the alleged "boldness and shamefulness" of the girls, according to this authority, was not equalled by some of the "worst parts of London."[11] F. D. Longe, one of the commissioners, had a similar anxiety; he thought that the "want of decent sleeping room" and the "teaching of bad parents" had an even worse effect on the character of the girls than the bawdy influence of field work and the gangs.[12]

The immorality was in the eyes of the beholders. Living in close quarters doesn't make people immoral, any more than living in a country house or a vicarage kept their betters chaste. My counterparts were denounced by people

9 Kent Record Office, C/ES 408/2, log book, Yalding National School, 6 October 1873.

10 Cited in Duncan Crow, *The Victorian Woman,* London, 1971, p. 91.

11 P.P. Agricultural Gangs, Appendix (B), p. 167.

12 *Ibid.,* Appendix (A), p. 94.

too ignorant of the labouring classes—and too protected in the comfort of their drawing-rooms or studies, to see that there was another world, another culture than their own. Living so much on top of one another—as did the labourer's family—meant that adults and children were used to living together, and that the sight of a naked ankle did not stir them to immediate and lascivious desire.

The woman field worker was anathema to the middle class, the complete opposite to what they expected in their own women—helplessness. But wages paid to the farm labourer were too low for him to be the sole provider for his family; women and children had to sell their labour, too, in order to survive. Women were forced out of the isolation of the home into the society of the field: and thus out of domesticity into something more gregarious. In the eyes of clergymen and commissioners this was unwomanly, and their constant theme was that field labour did irreparable damage to the female character. Their work role was in conflict with the moral one prescribed for them. They were too independent, too free.

It was a dominant fear that heavy physical work would make girls unsuitable for their future roles of wife and mother; and that the "liberty" of the fields would disqualify them from employment as domestic servants. The fact that they might be injured or crippled at such work was not the issue. Women who worked in the fields were accused of neglecting their homes, their children, their husbands. "Loss of evening comfort to the husband" and "loss of female refinement" are just two examples of this abuse. Not only did field work ". . . almost unsex a women," making her rough, coarse, clumsy, masculine; but it generated "a further very pregnant social mischief by unfitting or indisposing her for a woman's proper duties at home."[13] Their independence of their menfolk was another fear which was made quite explicit.[14]

> That which seems most to lower the moral or decent tone of the peasant girls [wrote Dr Julian Hunter in 1864] is the sensation of independence of society which they acquire when they have remunerative labour in their hands either in the fields, or at home as strawplaiters, etc. All gregarious employment gives a slang character to the girls' appearance and habits, while dependence on the man for support is the spring of modest and pleasing deportment.

The work girl's clothing was also charged against her. If it was coarse and tough, to protect her from the mud and from the weather, it was said to be unwomanly—a degradation of her sex. But things were still worse if her clothing were flimsy and allowed her body to show through—an invitation to promiscuity in the summer harvest fields. To show an ankle was considered to be a sign of female moral depravity—thus the country girl who pulled up her skirt and tucked it between her legs when she was doing field work was depraved.

13 *AEC* I, pt I (A), p. 76.

14 P.P. 1865 (3484) xxvi, Appendix no. 6 to the *7th Report of the Medical Officer to the Privy Council,* p. 146.

Another alleged inducement to the sexual promiscuity of the country girl was the possibility of "seeing sights among the beasts."[15] The implication was that seeing animals copulating in the fields would induce them to emulate this pastime with members of the other sex. I remember seeing pigs, cats, dogs, cows, sheep and horses copulating, and I can't deny that I was curious to know what the animals were doing and why, but I don't remember waylaying the first unsuspecting lad that crossed my path; neither do I remember having such a functional analysis of the situation as Flora Thompson's heroine Laura who[16]

> at about 12 years old stumbled into a rickyard where a bull was in the act of justifying its existence, the sight [of which] did not warp her nature . . . The bull to her was but a bull performing a necessary function if there was to be butter on the bread and milk for breakfast. [brackets ours—eds.]

Many clergymen and writers of that time based their condemnation of the country girl on the amount of illegitimacy and cohabitation that occurred in the country. But once again they did not bother to look into the complete situation before making their value judgments. In many parts of England and Wales it was customary for a couple not to get wed until the woman had fallen pregnant—thus proving that she was capable of having children and providing the man with "sons." The *Morning Chronicle* of 18 January 1850 comments.[17]

> It really seems, in many places, to be taken as a matter of course that a young woman will be found with child before she is married. Many are married as soon as they become pregnant . . . Indeed, I have reason to believe that in an immense number of cases young people come to a distinct understanding with each other to cohabit illicitly, until the woman becomes pregnant, the man promising to "make an honest woman of her" as soon as that takes place.
>
> This they find more convenient than marrying at once, inasmuch, as the girl may be of service for herself, and the man elsewhere employed all the time. They meet occasionally, and are thus relieved at least of the responsibilities and the duties of housekeeping, living better on their separate earnings than they could do in a house of their own. This practice of cohabitation before marriage is almost universal. It is not only a characteristic of low rural life; it is also so with the miners and the fishermen.

When a girl found herself expecting an unplanned and "illegitimate" baby then, as today, there were limits as to what could be done. She could either accept the situation and have the child, or she might try to abort, by taking such drugs as savine or turpentine. This might not directly remedy the situation, but

15 *AEC* II, Appendix pt I (K), p. 197.

16 Thompson, *op. cit.*, pp. 35–6.

17 *Morning Chronicle,* 18 January 1850, Supplement, Labour and the Poor: Rural Districts, letter XIII.

it would have a debilitating effect on the unborn child, which when born would probably be in an even weaker condition than the mother's rundown state would have caused. There was not much choice after the child was born. If the girl was forced to work during the day—and bring up the child unsupported by the father—she had to find someone to mind it while she worked in the fields. She might leave it with her younger sister, mother, grandmother, the baby being taken to the fields to be fed at intervals. Or she would take the baby to a child-minder's house and leave it there whilst she was away at work, paying the child-minder out of her earnings. Many child-minders were inexperienced and this fact plus the often quite unhygienic and cramped conditions of the child-minder's "nursery" would do the young child's health no good. But the mother had to go and support herself and to work in the knowledge that some dreadful accident might happen to the child while she was away.

In the 1860s there was a general movement of opinion among the respectable towards the need to educate the children of the working classes; much interest was shown in the type of work that kept children out of school and it was for this reason that in the 1860s commissions were set up to investigate the condition and the employment of children in industry and agriculture in various regions of the country. The report on gangs by the Children's Employment Commissioners led to the passing of the Agricultural Gangs Act of 1867. This made it illegal for a child under the age of eight to work in agricultural gangs—amended by the Agricultural Children's Act of 1875 (taking effect from 1 January 1875) to read "no child under 10 years should be employed in agricultural gangs." These two Acts with the 1870 Education Act and its successors had the ultimate effect of removing girls from field labour, though it was difficult to enforce at first in the countryside because their work was an integral part of the village economy. It was not until mechanization had taken over the labour they performed, that compulsory education in the countryside became really effective. The people who had the power to enforce compulsory education locally also benefited from the results of women and girls' labour so it was not in their interest to be too diligent in this duty until they could find a cheap and efficient replacement.

By removing them from field labour and subjecting them to the influence of educational and religious institutions girls were placed under "respectable" influences. Many went on to be female servants, and were found situations through the educational and Sunday school machinery. Some went to the local farmers; some went to big houses in the district and then perhaps moved on to the town houses of the rich. Servants were status symbols. The social position of a household was measured by the number of its servants. The servants were a constant proclamation of their employers' social standing; and they were completely at their mercy, having to work long hours for very little money and with their free time strictly supervised by the "ladies" of the house. Escape from tutelage was difficult, except through marriage, because without a character reference from the mistress it was difficult to find another place. In such situations as these girls lived, they often fell prey to the appetites and lechery of the sexually repressed men of the household. It is not difficult for us to recall some story we have heard of how the under-housemaid was sent away in disgrace and the son of the house rebuked and sent back to university, etc. My great-grandfather, on my mother's side, was the product of such an occurrence: his mother, a kitchen maid, was sent home, while her seducer was packed off to America. Such servants were in a very precarious position alone in the big town, when it came to resisting the master or the mistress, because they knew they would need to have a character reference in order to get another job, and there was always another country girl willing to take up their place if, for whatever reason, they did not suit.

The inconsistency of Victorian middle-class attitudes towards female duties is illustrated by the notable absence of any commission inquiry into the working conditions and environment of their female servants. These servants carried out harsh and gruelling tasks, worked for long hours and were vulnerable to the whims and fancies of their employers; but such service was not thought degrading to the working-class female: far from it, it taught her to be feminine, a modest respectable girl.

*STANDISH MEACHAM*

# *WOMEN AT HOME*

Whether or not proximity afforded women the chance to establish themselves within some sort of matriarchal connection, their constant presence in the household, throughout the day, day after day, for years on end, unquestionably made them the central figures there: "She is the constant factor of the home. Others come and go, but she never disappears . . . Any week will find her at home in a long stretch of forty years."[1] Oral and written evidence sustains the assertion, confirming that in the eyes of the family members, it was she who

From Standish Meacham, *A Life Apart: The English Working Class, 1890–1914.* (London: Thames and Hudson, 1977), pp. 61–66, 78–79, 88–90, by permission of the publisher.

1 Alexander Paterson, *Across the Bridges,* p. 22.

"held things together." "She managed to find us all enough to eat." "Somehow mother managed." "She kept a lot from us, she didn't tell us anything . . . She bore it, most of it, herself." "As the family got larger, then of course mother moved about." (Father, in this case, was a navvy, living at home. But the assumption is clear: mother was expected to manage the moves.) When death, an accident, or a long spell of unemployment brought in train the inevitable financial crisis, mother coped, as she was expected to. Jack Jones's widowed mother put herself to work, and "by dint of hard scraping and economies that would terrify a church mouse, we did what we set out to do: we kept our little home over our heads." Will Crooks's father lost his arm in an accident: "I don't know what we should have done but for Mother. She used to toil with the needle far into the night and often all night long, slaving as hard as any poor sweated woman I have ever known." . . .[2]

The literature, whatever it may tell us about a working-class mother, undoubtedly confirms the central position within the household. It may also have played a role in persuading young women to forsake the independence and pleasures of life as an unmarried working girl—money at hand for cheap finery and a good time, responsibilities at bay—for a life of unremitting drudgery. For an exchange such as this, a woman would ask something in return. She could believe herself justified in expecting psychological cosseting, if physical comforts were to be denied her. An objective analysis, however, could not but reveal that, in most cases, she nevertheless got the worst of the bargain.

Of course, she did not see it that way—she was conscious of marriage not as a bargain, whatever its terms, but as a matter of course. What one sociologist has discovered to be true for modern working-class girls was true generally for their grandmothers: "She does not choose [whether or not to marry]. She does what appears to her to be natural. It is difficult to envisage what she might do otherwise."[3] Many marriages were, in part, the result of the discomforts of living at home, or of the not always pleasant experience of living in lodgings. Faced with a house overfilled with younger brothers and sisters, a woman of seventeen or eighteen would not look amiss at the chance to set up housekeeping with the young man who had been her steady companion over the past months. She "walked out" with him because there was no room to sit down: "If you lived with your father and mother, and many brothers and sisters, in one common feeding room, perhaps you would not be bold enough to present your fiancé."[4] And so you courted in the streets or in whatever seclusion the inhospitable urban landscape could provide. An Essex iron moulder, himself a self-professed failure, describes the ritual's first steps:

2 BBC Archives. LP 26422, X20298; T and V interviews, No. 237, p. 15; No. 8, p. 2; Jack Jones, *My Lively Life* (London, 1928), p. 16; George Haw, *The Life Story of Will Crooks,* p. 3.

3 Josephine Klein, *Samples from British Culture* (London, 1965), I, 39.

4 Robert R. Dolling, *Ten Years in a Portsmouth Slum* (London, 1896), p. 42.

> I just couldn't run a conversation on the silly little backchat that I've heard these other people do, you know. I was frightened off. The locals would go to White Colne, or something, Sunday evening and talk with a group of girls, just silly talk and . . . well, vulgar almost, not that I claim to be much different, but I just could not join that, or stand by shop doors and trip girls up as they come by, I just couldn't possibly.[5]

In this case, respectability was the inevitable consequence of shyness. More often it had to be preached by anxious mothers: "When I was going out with my husband, you know, courting, and I came back a bit late and she was behind the door. I needn't tell you what happened. She wasn't having me a little stop-out. That's what she said . . . Now I laugh but then I thought she was terrible."[6]

"Little stop-outs" got themselves pregnant. So long as they married before the baby came, in most cases they did their reputations no permanent damage. But they would be looked upon by some, at least, as being "no better than they should be." Pregnancy, along with convenience and convention, was simply another reason for marriage. Timing might depend on the availability of a house. Or simply the realization that nothing really stood in the way of a pleasanter, less overcrowded way of life. "Funny, ain't it, Helen," remarks the hero of Walter Greenwood's *Love on the Dole.* "Ah mean it's funny we ain't never thought of getting married afore . . . Fancy, though, us livin' in different houses when there's nowt t' stop us from gettin' a home of our own."[7] A wedding was seldom the great occasion that a funeral was. There was little fuss as a rule, and few presents. A Saturday wedding meant a celebration at a pub near the church, where friends not invited to the ceremony would drop in to wish the couple well. In most cases the groom would be back to work the following Monday, the bride as well if she was employed.

Straightforward economic common sense resulted in second marriages: "He wanted someone to look after his girls and mother wanted a few more bob—sort of financial agreement, I should imagine."[8] Some of these marriages were without benefit of clergy, often because one of the partners to an earlier union was guilty of desertion, not in itself grounds for divorce. Even supposing

5 T and V interviews, No. 12. p. 56. The speaker eventually found his future wife at the local W.E.A.

6 *Ibid.,* No. 117, p. 14.

7 Walter Greenwood, *Love on the Dole,* p. 125. A tabulation made by Rowntree of working-class marriages in York in 1898–1899 showed the largest percentage of women marrying at 21, with far fewer doing so in the years immediately before that age than in the years immediately after. Only 2.56 per cent of skilled women workers and 5.23 per cent of the unskilled, for example, married at 18. Rowntree discovered a marked difference in the ages at which skilled and unskilled males married: nearly one-third of the latter married before age 23, while only one-fifth of the former did so. B. Seebohm Rowntree, *Poverty,* pp. 400, 139.

8 T and V interviews, No. 417, pp. 35–36. In this instance, the speaker's stepfather slept apart from his wife, on her orders, "owing to his habits getting a little bit—I suppose—out of hand," p. 38. See also M. Loane, *The Queen's Poor* (London, 1906), p. 7.

the grounds sufficient, the cost, on the average bout £100, was an expense almost no one in the working class could bear.[9]

The nature of the tie between a working-class woman and her husband would depend, in great measure, upon the extent to which she remained bound to her own kin or to a network of nearby acquaintances. On unfamiliar ground in a neighbourhood new to her, and denied the sociability available to her husband at his place of work, she would rely on him for companionship and, in all likelihood, generally subordinate her life to his. If, on the other hand, she lived close by female relatives, if she could call in frequently at her mothers's house, her marriage would probably develop a double focus.

The shift from domestic to industrial production in the nineteenth century increased women's dependence on men, "not only in economic terms, but in the psychological subtleties of their relationships. Authoritarian patterns of behaviour, sanctioned by the factory, were carried into the home." More than ever, survival depended on the husband and father, "the one who 'earned life' for the whole unit."[10] A marriage in which, both partners led socially "segregated" lives was not, on that account, a marriage in which the husband was in any sense subordinate to his wife. Families could be both dominated by the father and centred about the mother; such appears to have been the case in the majority of working-class families at the turn of the century.[11] . . .

Economic uncertainty, the final arbiter of working-class existence, meant that a "successful" marriage depended first and foremost on simple survival. Poverty brought quarrels, desertions and death. To have made it beyond those pitfalls was cause enough for celebration:

> We've been together now for forty years,
> And it don't seem a day too much.
> There ain't a lady livin' in the land
> As I'd swap fer me dear old dutch.[12]

So sang the aged common-law husband in what was probably the most popular working-class tribute to marriage. He hymned the comradeship that was the

9 Charles Booth, *Life and Labour of the Poor in London,* Third Series, final volume, 41–42; Women's Cooperative Guild, *Working Women and Divorce* (London, 1911), p. 8. Women complained that although a husband could divorce his wife for one act of unfaithfulness, a wife was forced to put up with continued unfaithfulness if unaccompanied by cruelty and desertion. Even when a husband brought another woman into the house to live, wives had no grounds to proceed against him. The Women's Cooperative Guild recommended that grounds for divorce include cruelty and desertion by themselves, refusal to maintain, and serious incompatibility. "No other subject in the life of the Guild has aroused such immediate response and elicited such strength and earnestness of feeling," pp. 4, 14, 20.

10 Richard Titmus, *Essays on the "Welfare State"* (London, 1963, 2d ed.), p. 110.

11 Elizabeth Bott, *Family and Social Network,* p. 64.

12 Words by Albert Chevalier, music by Charles Ingle, 1893. Reprinted in *Music Hall Song Book,* Peter Gammond, ed., pp. 40–42.

reality of most married lives. The matter-of-fact air with which the working class went about courtship and marriage does not imply a lack of genuine and lasting fondness between husband and wife. Working-class men and women were as capable of affection as their middle-class counterparts. Their proximity to the facts of life, however—whether an empty food cupboard or an overfull bedroom—led them to expect little romance in life and left them even less time to look for it. The very modesty of their expectations could impart to them a simple, honest dignity: "I think all the pleasure that a woman got was living with this man . . . And I think they had to love one another and that was the pleasure that they got out of life . . . was loving one another and living with one another."[13]

The assessment tallies with conclusions Geoffrey Gorer reached in his study of English character: "What English men most value in their wives is the possession of appropriate feminine skills, whereas what English women most value in their husbands is an agreeable character."[14] The ability to endure crises together with common sense and without panic, an understanding of one's predetermined role and a willingness to assume it—these were the commonplace qualities which sustained a successful marriage as perceived by the working class.

An "agreeable" husband might be one who could, in addition, offer his wife the pleasure of sexual fulfillment. Yet if we can believe the admittedly scanty evidence, few women expected that satisfaction or considered it important to their marriage. More frequently, "agreeability" meant a husband's willingness to spare his wife as much as possible from the trials of a sex life which she conceived of as a duty but could not enjoy. Her attitude was determined in part by her ignorance. One might expect that the crowded conditions of working-class existence would have made sexuality an unavoidable fact of everyday life. Baths before the kitchen fire; beds and bedrooms shared not just by brothers and sisters, but by parents and children; adolescent gossip at the mill; evening walks unchaperoned into country lanes—surely all this might lead to sexual precociousness. The evidence is by no means clear cut. The anonymity of urban life might facilitate sexual adventuring for the curious young man; the connectedness within a working-class neighbourhood might as easily thwart it. Roberts writes of incest as a fact of working-class life; but he is quick to note that it was regarded as "the ultimate disgrace."[15] Hoggart concludes that although "sexual matters are nearer the surface, and sexual experience in the working classes is probably more easily and earlier acquired than in other social groups," the proximity of it all leads to its being locked up, or at least held at bay. There is, he points out, "a great shyness about some aspects of sex—about discussing it

13 T and V interviews, No. 162, p. 52.

14 Geoffrey Gorer, *Exploring English Character,* p. 125.

15 Robert Roberts, *The Classic Slum,* pp. 27, 74.

'sensibly,' about being seen naked, or even about undressing for the act of sex, or about sophistications in sexual behaviour.''[16]

Evidence from the late Victorian period bears Hoggart out. A girl of fifteen hits a boy in the groin for saying ''fuck,'' but will tell her father of the incident only when the house has been cleared of her brothers and sisters. A mother keeps her boys outside on Friday nights until the girls have had their bath. Parents are loathe to discuss sexual matters with their children: ''Everything was kept hidden from us. We couldn't talk like the . . . mothers and daughters today . . . Everything was hushed up. You didn't know life as we . . . know it now.''[17] Reticence induced a remarkable degree of ignorance in young, unmarried working-class women. Nor did marriage itself necessarily enlighten them. . . .

Meat was a gauge by which the working-class families measured their prosperity. Its consumption increased markedly in the period between 1875 and 1914. Prosperous working-class households could expect to dine on meat as often as four or five times a week. The son of a Bradford boilermaker, whose mother worked part-time as a fancy laundress, recalled weekly menus of Sunday roast joint and Yorkshire pudding, liver and onions, meat and potato pies, and stews with left-over scraps from the joint. ''We always had good meals.''[18] In Ben Turner's house there was usually some sort of meat for the noontime meal, ''always providing the funds ran to it.''[19] Left-over meat became part of what were called ''resurrection meals''; ''scouse,'' a stew of meat scraps and vegetables, appeared as a staple in working-class diets. When scraps were scarce, barley was added, and the mixture dubbed ''blind'' scouse.[20] The price of meat depended, naturally, on its quality. ''Pieces'' were sold for anything from 6d to 3d a pound, though in the latter case, the meat was bound to consist mostly of sinew and gristle. Entrails of various sorts—hearts, lights, tripe—were favoured by those women who knew how to stew them up in a tasty fashion. Pork rinds, stewing bones, and faggots, made of pig entrails, could be combined with rice or potatoes into a satisfying meal: ''I've often made a good supper for my man and myself for three halfpence. When faggots are cold you can get one for three farthings. I boil a pennyworth of rice till it is quite soft, and then cut the faggot through it and boil up together. The faggot makes the rice so savoury that anyone could eat it.''[21] The fact that quantities are measured, not by their bulk, but by their cost, documents the attention housewives were constantly forced to pay to their budgets.

16 Richard Hoggart, *The Uses of Literacy,* p. 83.

17 T and V interviews, No. 162, p. 44; No. 51, p. 7; No. 39, p. 16.

18 T and V interviews, No. 187, p. 15.

19 Ben Turner, *About Myself* (London, 1930), p. 46.

20 T and V interviews, No. 43, p. 9.

21 Anna Martin, *The Married Working Woman,* pp. 14–15; see also T and V interviews, No. 320, p. 12.

Tinned and imported frozen meats, substantially cheaper than the fresh domestic, did not find universal favour among working-class wives, despite their price. Beef in tins did not appear to resemble meat at all: "I have a vivid recollection of the unappetizing look of the contents—a large lump of coarse-grained meat inclined to separate into coarse fibres, a large lump of unpleasant-looking fat on one side of it—and an irregular hollow partly filled with watery fluid."[22] "Chilled" meats from abroad were assumed, on very little basis, to be of a generally inferior quality. Roberts discloses that no respectable artisan's wife before 1914 would deal with a butcher who sold only imported, frozen beef and mutton.[23]

The fact that meat became a mark of respectability was a measure of its cost. Families that upon occasion enjoyed meat in some form or other, nevertheless lived on bread. Potatoes were a staple as well, and in the north, porridge. Those lucky enough to rent an allotment supplemented their diet with vegetables. But week in, week out, bread furnished the working class with the bulk of its nourishment. In some houses baking was a part of the weekly ritual; housewives prided themselves on their ability to turn out a variety of loaves—white and brown, tea cakes, ginger snaps, and the like. More relied upon local bakeries, where two two-pound loaves—a quartern—could be purchased for from 4d to 6d. Bread was what has now come to be called "convenience food." It was cheap, it came ready cooked; one could eat it any time and anywhere. . . .

No ritual assumed a greater importance in the eyes of respectable working-class women than the weekly house cleaning. With few tools to make their work easier, but with a determination to prove themselves equal to the challenge, they set about their tasks with fanatical determination. Overcrowding further increased their difficulties. When each room contained more than its share of furniture, as was the case in most respectable homes, the dirt and grime found many more surfaces upon which to settle. When five or six people lived in only three or four rooms, they had that many fewer hooks, cupboards, and drawers in which to keep their possessions tidy. Houses poorly and thoughtlessly constructed were houses with more cracks into which both the dust and the soap suds of the years might alternately sink; they were houses with scullery floors of stone, damp and difficult to keep free from mould or mildew. Some women surrendered to it all, preferring "to have a weekly tilt at the demon dirt and leave the field to him for the next six days."[24] Others, undaunted, waged constant war: on the stove, with blackleading, "which sends particles of lead into the cleaner's lungs, fills her nails and pores with a filthy mixture of grease, lead, soot, and coal dust"; on the furniture:

> A job I detested was dusting the . . . sewing machine that we had, and I had to get into all those little curves and nooks and crannies with the frames of the sewing

22 J. C. Drummond, Anne Wilbraham, *The Englishman's Food* (London, 1939), p. 382.

23 Robert Roberts, *The Classic Slum,* p. 88.

24 Walter Greenwood, *Love on the Dole,* p. 11.

machine. And the chairs . . . [Mother] was very particular about getting into all the nicks and getting all the dust out.

On the front steps:

You sort of had to wash your step, then wet . . . the sandstone, like you do a pumice stone style, sand it along right on the edge and then you had to get your fingers and go nice and smooth . . . [I] used to love scouring those steps. It's a work of art, you know.[25]

To some women, a line of freshly laundered clothes was also a work of art. To achieve it might take them as much as one full day. In houses without heated copper boilers, water was boiled first on the stove and then transferred in buckets to the copper. Even with a proper boiler, the laundress was usually saddled with the task of filling it by hand. In went the clothes, having soaked, perhaps, overnight, in went the soap and the soda. Out again, and into the dolly- or peggy-tub, a wooden contrivance with mallet which was used to thump the clothes clean. Then, finally, to the line which, on rainy days, would be strung in the kitchen.

Underclothes were changed twice a week in more affluent households, once a week elsewhere. Generally the weekly change coincided with the weekly bath. Once again the copper was filled, children bathed first, then parents.[26] Coppers without plugs had to be emptied by hand, into the scullery sink or outside into the drain.

Given the difficulties and discomforts involved in keeping their houses and families clean, the wonder is that more working-class women did not give in and admit defeat. Instead, one encounters the determination of a very poor Canning Town mother, her husband an invalid, who collected, washed, and sold rags to earn the penny or two necessary to wash her children's clothes:

She'd get a couple of coppers for [the rags], well then she'd get over the soap and soda and . . . rub all our clothes for us and have 'em dried and ironed, and she put them on next morning. If they . . . came home from school at night and she thought they was a bit grubby, well that's what she used to do. Put us to bed—wash us and put us to bed and then she'd go out and get [the soap and soda] . . . nobody can say we was ever left dirty.[27]

Why the compulsion? In the case of this one woman, perhaps, a determination to turn her children out respectably despite the odds. The craving for respectability, while it may have driven a wife to the copper with an armload of dirty

25 M. L. Eyles, *The Woman in the Little House,* p. 45; T and V interviews, No. 187, p. 10; No. 168, p. 35.

26 The older members of the household, particularly the males, might, instead, avail themselves of public baths.

27 T and V interviews, No. 126, p. 12.

clothes, or to her steps with the sandstone, did not compel her to look upon the scouring of her steps as "a work of art." There is something in those remarks of the step-scrubber—"you had to get your fingers and go nice and smooth"—that reflects a state of mind described by Alexander Paterson in his 1911 survey of working-class south London: "Dust and dirt accumulate despite restrictions, and with them comes a stickiness that creeps from the fingers up the arm, and puts washing on almost the same plane as smoking, as a soothing practice associated with home and with repose."[28] There is a reassuring rhythm in a task repeated again and again with the certainty that it is being done as well as it can be done. Routine, which might weigh upon one housewife as painful monotony, might to another bring welcome certainty.

28 Alexander Paterson, *Across the Bridges,* p. 8.

THEODORE ZELDIN

# MARRIAGE AND MORALS

The family, as organised in France in these years, had an effect on people's lives as profound as any political regime or any economic force. It was a powerful institution which resisted change with remarkable vitality—the counterpart, in private life, of the administrative centralisation of the *ancien régime* which, for all the attacks on it, survived into the mid twentieth century. It deserves attention as much as the changing governments and the industrial revolutions, but it seldom receives it because there are very great difficulties—many of them insuperable—in discovering the facts about it. Its activities were inevitably hardly ever recorded and research on it is still fragmentary. . . .

How should a man choose a wife, what should he expect of her and what could he expect their relations to be? The answers throughout the period were varied. So long as obedience was the principal virtue inculcated into children, so long as girls were brought up to be models of innocence, to be ignorant of the world, skilled in domestic arts, and destined for marriage, then the choice was

From Theodore Zeldin, *France 1848–1945, Volume One: Ambition, Love, and Politics* (Oxford: Clarendon Press, 1973), pp. 285–87, 291, 295–99, by permission of the publisher.

made by the parents, using their own criteria. Parents seem to have been influenced by the position they held within their class. The marriage of their children was a public valuation placed on the parents' position, and it was also a method of improving that position. The great problem was to avoid a *mésalliance,* which was why love was the great enemy, the rebel against parental authority which could bring disaster on all their plans. The aristocracy laid greatest stress on the antiquity and nobility of the families they married, though if they were strong themselves in the matter of antiquity, they were willing to marry for money—provided the sums to be acquired were very large—and many did. In any case, it was generally accepted that property arrangements had to be satisfactory, to maintain both the couple immediately and their children after them. The bourgeoisie accepted these values. Marriage was for them the great means of social ascension. The larger the dowry they could obtain for their son, the better the situation he could buy and the more optimistic his prospects. In the lower commercial bourgeoisie, the combination of two fortunes was often used to start up or expand businesses. The peasantry had the same practise on a more modest scale, with the accumulation of land into larger units as the aim. Only the poorest industrial workers were the pariahs of this society. Quite often in the nineteenth century they did not marry at all, because they could not afford the expense of the ceremony. Rootless in the city, there was not the same family pressure. But when they rose to the artisan class and accumulated some property, they followed the same pattern. . . .

The history of the emotional relations between married couples is even more difficult to trace. The flowering of the romantic ideal did not of course necessarily mean an increase in domestic intimacy. On the contrary, the idealisation of women placed even greater distances between them and men. The cult of their purity made them inaccessible: pleasures in sexual intercourse could not in such circumstances be sought with them, who were dedicated to motherhood. Romanticism probably made the prostitute even more necessary. . . .

The notion that women could obtain pleasure from sexual intercourse was no invention of the twentieth century and Marie Stopes has wrongly been credited with inventing the female right to orgasm. The works of the seventeenth-century Dr. Nicolas Venette, frequently reprinted in the nineteenth, painted a picture of women as being naturally more lascivious than men, and offered advice on how to meet their sexual demands. A doctor who produced a revised edition of Venette's book on conjugal love in 1907 urged married men to treat their wives sexually in the same way as they treated their mistresses.[1] Among the numerous guides to sex and marriage published in the nineteenth century, there were some moralistic ones, but quite a few stressed the importance of satisfying women emotionally. One particularly successful one, by a retired army medical officer, which went through 173 editions between 1848 and

1 Dr. Nicolas Venette, *Tableau de l'amour conjugale* (new edition by Dr. Caufeynon (pseudonym for Dr. Jean Fauconney) (1907)).

1888, was quite specific about women enjoying intercourse as much as men. It advised men that whereas some women go into a delirium of pleasure at the least contact, others require frequently repeated caresses to reach orgasm. For extreme cases of inhibition he prescribed flagellation, but his main advice was to win women by tenderness and kindness. He said that doctors were agreed that a married man between twenty and thirty should only exercise his conjugal rights two to four times a week, but always with an interval of a day; twice a week till forty, once till fifty, once a fortnight till sixty, but never beyond that age. Over-activity—"five or six times a day as many young men do"—produced regrets later. Women were capable of indulging more often than men, but they should restrict themselves because it could lead to diseases and to cancer. "The solitary masturbation practised by many women dissatisfied with their husbands" should be avoided for the same reason.[2]

Another doctor, who published *A Little Bible for Young Spouses* (1885), though writing with more discretion, stressed the need for husbands to give their wives sexual pleasure and to aim for simultaneous orgasm.[3] But all this advice had to work against firmly engrained prejudices in both sexes. There is a case recorded of a wife demanding a divorce because of the excessive zeal and "unnatural caresses" of her husband: he pleaded that he was only trying to please her and increase her affection for him. . . .

The lady who asked for a divorce because her husband's love-making alarmed her was very likely the victim of the conflict produced by the hostility of many conservatives to the enjoyment or discussion of sex. The doctrine preached by the Catholic clergy was that the purpose of marriage was definitely not pleasure, but the constitution of families and the procreation of children. In 1920, Abbé Grimaud, in a work which was to go through at least 33 editions and which was crowned by the French Academy, summarised their attitude well when he said that "God foresaw in his wisdom that couples would not accept the heavy obligations of paternity unless they were pushed by the charms of pleasure." But sexual pleasure should not be an aim in itself. The clergy generally spoke of the husband as having sexual urges and the wife as submitting to them. Taking their own practise as an ideal, they urged the repression of sexual desire as the ultimate aim: Joseph and the Virgin Mary, who loved each other but never copulated, represented ultimate virtue. Few people could be expected to reach these heights, but, after procreation, continence by mutual consent in marriage was recommended as desirable, even though it would mean abstention from all touching, looks or words of affection, which might reinflame desire. The clergy were genuinely concerned with the dignity of women, but sometimes conceived it in a way which restricted women's intellectual aspirations. Thus Abbé Grimaud, in discussing what kind of wife a man should choose, vigorously advises men to steer as completely clear of intellectuals and

2 A. Debay, *Hygiène et physiologie du mariage* (n.d., 54th edition).

3 Dr. Charles Montalban, *La Petite Bible des jeunes époux* (1885), 36, 56.

professional women (unless they were willing to give up their jobs) as of prostitutes. A woman must be primarily a mother devoted to bringing up her children as Christians. For all his belief in the equality of souls, he likewise urges men to marry only girls of their own class. If a man feels that he is about to fall in love (he likens it to being attacked by a microbe) his first thought should be to go to his parents and ask them to ascertain whether the girl was suitable. Then, when all the demands of reason were satisfied, he could allow his passion to capture him. Passion would of course pass rapidly and could not be the basis of marriage. That is why it was so deplorable that employers were putting "young men and girls to work at the same tables. Go into a bank, for example, and in a flash, if you are just a bit of a psychologist, you will appreciate how much a young man, even though he would like to remain honourable, is menaced by the possibility of contracting an unhappy marriage. Next to boys—often very distinguished ones, who have studied, and come from a certain level of society—one sees typists, among whom are some of excellent education, but also many others less *sérieuses.* One can judge what the majority of these girls are like from the clothes they wear. One suspects that in this mixed company it will not be the good quiet girls, modest like nuns and reserved like mothers of families, who will attract the men's glances. They will be called boring and unattractive. The others on the contrary will not fail to please the young men rapidly, because they do not hesitate to surround them with the most provocative attention."[4]

The Church's view of marriage laid stress on gravity, devotion to duty, the bringing up of children, resignation, acceptance of one's lot, and consolation from prayer and piety. It was vigorously opposed to contraception and, through the confession, some clergy even pressed women to resist their husband's embraces if they practised *coitus interruptus,* which was the commonest contraceptive method employed in this period. It sought to maintain morality by preaching self-control. It offered a great deal of emotional consolation, but it was God and prayer, not the husband, who were the consolers. The only true and full love women could have, one author pointed out, was love of God. Bishop Dupanloup in the 1860s stressed that marriage brought dignity to the mother but it also gave authority to the father. In 1920 when General de Castelnau issued his Declaration of the Rights of the Family at the Estates General of the French Family (an anti-contraceptive organisation), he defined the family as being "founded on marriage, hierarchically constituted under the authority of the father, having as its goal the transmission, support, development and perpetuation of human life." The stress was on the family unit against the rights individuals claimed against it.[5] Sexual education was seen mainly as an exhortation to piety, chastity and repression. The Church opposed sexual education in schools and insisted that it should be left to the parents.[6] One author held up as a model on how the

4 Abbé Charles Grimaud, *Futurs Époux* (1920), 287–90, 301–15.

5 H. Bordeaux, [*Le Mariage* (1921),] 208–10.

6 *L'Église et l'éducation sexuelle.* Proceedings of the seventh national congress of the Association du Mariage Chrétien (1929).

facts should be told the history of a pious father who, when his son reached the age of eighteen, summoned him to his study and told him: "My son, I have some great truths to tell you. Let us kneel and say an Ave Maria." Asking whether his son had understood the prayer he explained the divine mystery of the Incarnation, and from that moved on to show the less sublime origins of miserable humanity; then he pointed out our duties, the dangers that would be encountered and the precautions to be taken. The boy listened, hardly asking any questions, and understood the ideas which would transform him. "I felt," he said, "that I became a man." The conversation ended with a prayer as it had begun.[7] Marriage was thus seen as a duty, second best to the complete dedication of the self made by the nun or the monk.

7 Grimaud, 37–8.

CHAPTER 6

# THE EFFECTS OF URBANIZATION

If the most difficult days of early industrialization had been overcome by the mid nineteenth century, at least in the West, it was by no means certain that Europe could thereafter expect a bright and glorious tomorrow. In terms of economic development, there was a striking surge of growth from 1850 to the early 1870s. This was followed by two decades of fitful depression, and then by a remarkable upturn once again in the years prior to the First World War. A social pattern is more difficult to discern. One might perhaps posit a gradual improvement of living conditions, but that would ignore the wretched housing and lugubrious streets still existing in the big cities. Or one could imagine a general simmering down of lower-class dissatisfaction, but this would overlook such violent episodes as the Paris Commune in 1871, the appearance of militant trade unionism, and the rising wave of industrial strikes at century's end. The only safe conclusion is that social protest was beginning to erupt in new forms.

*Jenni Calder* takes us into the working-class slums of Great Britain, where we had best watch our step. We quickly perceive that poverty and despair hang in the air, mixing with the stench of garbage and refuse in the streets. All who are physically able must work incessantly—provided they can find jobs. Adequate housing is rare, and sanitary toilets even more so. It is sobering to remember that just a few generations ago many of our own families grew up under these conditions. And we cannot fail to be reminded of the slums in American cities today.

*Guenther Roth* explores the reasons why members of the German working class began to organize. Obviously their motive in many cases was to seek an escape from poverty through collective action. But there was something more in the comradeship of trade unions and political parties, which Roth defines as "sociability and self-respect." Maybe this is another way of saying, as Karl Marx once did, that the workers were starting to share a class consciousness.

*Charles Tilly* summarizes the leading conclusions drawn from a team study of collective violence in western Europe, especially France, following the onset of industrialization and urbanization. He asserts that violent means are a "normal" function of the political process of modern society, but he advances the surprising hypothesis that a greater concentration of population initially militated against the tendency to group violence. His view of the longer-run potentialities is more cautious, however, and it is also less comforting for those whose preoccupation is the maintenance of law and order.

In no way can we accurately measure the level of tension in a society. Appearance is often deceptive. Strikes and local insurrections may be only adjustments to a given situation rather than preludes to a paroxysm of widespread violence. Acts of destruction or incidents of criminality may be a justifiable corrective to social injustice rather than the wanton aggression of misfits. We have learned to be cautious in making categorical judgments. The surface does not always betray the profound sources of social unrest, and we know in retrospect that the relative equilibrium that had ostensibly been attained by 1914 was not to endure.

—*JENNI CALDER*

# *CITY SLUMS*

Slums were a widespread feature of Victorian existence. In most parts of the country it was impossible to avoid the presence of poverty and squalid living conditions. It was not just age and deterioration that created the slum, but overcrowding, inadequate drainage, lack of access to water. In slum conditions it was impossible to keep dirt and disease at bay. A slum was an environment in which

From Jenni Calder, *The Victorian Home* (London: B. T. Batsford Ltd., 1977), pp. 64–66, 73–75, by permission of the publisher.

a human being was lucky to survive: the phrase "home life" could not begin to conjure up any of the suggestions of comfort or harmony that it contained for the better off.

There were damp mud floors, unmended roofs, lack of sanitation in every part of the country, but the most obvious concentrations of slums were in the cities, and many of them were relatively new, dating as they often did from the period of rapid expansion immediately before Victoria's reign. There were the slums that had ripened out of decaying old housing in the centre of Manchester, in Glasgow, in London's East End, but there were also the new slums, like the terraces put up for cotton operatives in Preston, with an open sewer flowing between them at the back. Each house had an earth closet in the backyard which emptied into the sewage ditch, and twice a year the landlord sold the contents. Dust heaps in the streets were a common feature of the urban landscape, and they were a saleable commodity. In some places night-soil carts made the rounds daily and collected the accumulated excrement of the previous 24 hours: an unwholesome job, but a profitable one. Life must have been dominated by smell. The impossibility of separating human waste from water supply meant that infection and disease could spread like lightning. There were frequent epidemics, and it was a long time before their causes were understood.

In *Mary Barton* Elizabeth Gaskell described the life of the Manchester poor, and amongst her many striking pictures—and they came from direct experience—there is this one, of a slum street and a cellar home.

> It was unpaved; and down the middle a gutter forced its way, every now and then forming pools in the holes with which the street abounded . . . As they passed, women from their doors tossed household slops of *every* description into the gutter; they ran into the next pool, which overflowed and stagnated. Heaps of ashes were the stepping-stones, on which the passer-by, who cared in the least for cleanliness, took care not to put his foot. Our friends were not dainty, but even they picked their way till they got to some steps leading down into a small area, where a person standing would have his head about one foot below the level of the street, and might at the same time, without the least motion of his body, touch the window of the cellar and the damp muddy wall right opposite. You went down one step even from the foul area into the cellar in which a family of human beings lived. It was very dark inside. The windowpanes were many of them broken and stuffed with rags, which was reason enough for the dusky light that pervaded the place even at mid-day. After the account I have given of the state of the street, no one can be surprised that on going into the cellar inhabited by Davenport the smell was so foetid as almost to knock the two men down. Quickly recovering themselves, as those inured to such things do, they began to penetrate the thick darkness of the place, and to see three or four little children rolling on the damp, nay wet, brick floor, through which the stagnant, filthy moisture of the street oozed up; the fire-place was empty and black; the wife sat on her husband's chair, and cried in the dank loneliness.[1]

Between 40,000 and 50,000 families lived in similar Manchester cellars, many of

1 Elizabeth Gaskell, *Mary Barton* 1848, Chapter 6.

them Irish, the most exploited labour of the period. The husband of the family described above is sick and unemployed. Soon he will be dead. There is no money and no means of relief apart from that provided by the neighbours, two of whom are visiting the cellar in this passage. The homes of the employed when times are good make a striking contrast, Mary Barton's own, for instance, where that heartwarming tea was enjoyed. Mary's home is frugal, but it is neat and clean and supplied with fire and food. In bad times though, when wages could be reduced and men laid off, or when the operatives were on strike, life deteriorated rapidly. A subsistence wage could provide necessities, less than that meant suffering. Lack of food and lack of warmth brought inevitable demoralization, and a demoralized human being, starving and cold, cared less and less about the domestic virtues of order and cleanliness.

The Manchester cellars and the "rookeries" of London, which Dickens and Gissing and social commentators of the last quarter of the century describe so unforgettably, were amongst the most notorious of Victorian slums. But millions of families all over the country lived on a borderline between poverty and squalor, and it took so little to send the poor into the depths of destitution. There was bound to be a point beneath which it seemed hopeless even to try to maintain a plausible existence. Ill-health, an accident at work, a strike, an epidemic, sacking, all could deprive a family of the major breadwinner, and although the wife, and after 1833 children over the age of nine, might also be wage earners, they could not earn as much as a man. A woman, perhaps at the mill for a 12-hour stint or longer (before the Ten Hours Bill of 1847), still had domestic chores and very likely younger children to care for before and after work. Those children who were old enough were often expected to work all their waking hours. Life for the working class was, indeed, filled up with work—for those who were in employment. For many, especially for the young and the women, there was scarcely any other feature of life for six days of the week. There was no way of disguising the realities of its demands. Work was the only weapon against disease, filth and squalor, all of which could destroy human beings with frightening rapidity, but very often the work itself involved the risk of dirt and disease, of deformed or maimed limbs, or contaminated lungs. For most of the working class the environment of home was preferable to the environment of work, but nevertheless there was not the time or space or opportunity for many positive qualities. . . .

Much of the improvement was general, and not particularly aimed at the labouring classes. Sanitation, for example. By the 1850s many cities were making some attempt to control the problem of human waste. Covered drains were built to replace open sewers (though many of these continued to empty into the rivers: the Thames remained a sludge of disease-carrying filth) and more care was taken to provide an uncontaminated water supply. But disease was still rife. Cholera, typhus, smallpox, diphtheria and lung diseases were the major killers, and the slowness in bringing them under control was partly due to a reluctance to believe that a contaminated water supply was the means of contagion. The miasmic theory of disease, which held that infection was carried by bad air, predominated in the nineteenth century, even when the connection between cholera, for instance, and contaminated water, was patently demonstrated. In 1849 William Fair first suggested a correlation between water, elevation and the spread of cholera, and by 1866 all doubts concerning the murderous role of contaminated water had been removed. But bad air was a concept the Victorians were reluctant to part with. There was, though, in the 1840s, an increasing concern about public health and a growing commitment to action, and Edwin Chadwick, determined sanitation reformer, had a great deal to do with this. In 1848 there was a Public Health Act which set up a General Board of Health and Local Boards of Health, which was a first step towards cleaning up the towns. But even this was six years after the publication of Chadwick's report on *The Sanitary Conditions of the Labouring Classes* which had established in detail the intimate connection between disease and bad sanitation.

Work on improving sewage systems and water supply was slow and variable. The middle classes, who were of course most likely to be benefiting from such facilities as did exist, did not take kindly to the idea of paying rates to provide improvements that would most radically affect the lives of others. The fundamental facts of sewage were so much in evidence in early Victorian life that perhaps to a certain extent they were accepted as part of the landscape. That there might be ways of disposing of excrement efficiently, and removing the smells and the disease and the filth underfoot, came slowly to some. And sanitary improvements alone could not transform the lives of those whose need was greatest.

Concern for the housing of the poor had grown initially out of the need to provide housing in the rapidly growing industrial areas. Most of what was put up, in mill villages, in towns, anywhere it was necessary to house large numbers of factory workers within reach of the factory gates, was jerry-built, cramped, destined to lapse in some cases almost instantly into slum conditions. Primitive sanitary arrangements were often responsible. With the infamous back-to-back terraces the sharing of privies and water supply often meant that these essential amenities were some considerable distance from the home. Water was precious if every drop had to be carried, and not likely to be used lavishly in the interests of keeping clean. The temptation not to make use of the privy, which was probably stinking and filthy, was great. In Sunderland there was an average of one privy to 76 people, in parts of Manchester over 7000 shared 33. On the landlords' part there was a reluctance to spend money, reflecting a general assumption that the factory operative was barely more than an animal, that his needs were not those of a civilized human being, and that for the purposes of work he could be treated with less care than a (considerably more valuable) machine. It was hardly surprising that workers sometimes took their revenge on these machines.

—*GUENTHER ROTH*

# *ORGANIZED LABOR*

The attractions of solidarity and collective action can be illustrated in three different contexts: at the time of joining the movement, while doing lower-level party work, and during extreme political crises. A few examples, covering the whole period under investigation, may be mentioned. Anton Weiguny described in his memoirs the first attempts to organize journeymen tailors and garment workers (*Schneidergehilfen*) of small business in upper Austria in the 1870's. The thrill of involvement in "serious" collective action for one's own economic group was so strong it enabled a radical break with past clique behavior and rivalry among different vocational groups of journeymen. The young workers suddenly became quite serious at the prospect of responsible group action. Weiguny's colleagues, each in his turn, sacrificed an hour's wage in order to read aloud during work hours, a practice previously observed by the tobacco workers.[1]

When Buttinger was a 15-year-old boy, forced by his proletarian family's poverty to work on a farm, he experienced "the most sublime feeling" of his young life as 400 workers poured into his village to demonstrate against the mistreatment of a Social Democratic health insurance official: "Their appearance . . . awakened a sense of forces that would lift a man above the personal selfishness that, in the village, had shaped his outlook on life."[2]

The "workers' poet" Karl Bröger (1886–1944) at first resisted demands to pay union dues, preferring to be forced off a job. Finally, he yielded to pressures. The conversion, with the experience of solidarity and the renunciation of individualism, came when he listened to the speech of a functionary who threatened a strike if a fired worker was not rehired:

> He who yelled loudest and applauded most was [Bröger]. He was glowing with zeal and conviction. He nodded again and again and searched for the reflection of his own

From Guenther Roth, *The Social Democrats in Imperial Germany: A Study in Working-Class Isolation and National Integration* (Totowa, N.J.: The Bedminster Press, 1963), pp. 203–9, by permission of the author.

1 Cf. Anton Weiguny, *Erinnerungen eines Alten aus den Anfängen der oberösterreichischen Arbeiterbewegung*, 17, quoted in Richard Wagner, *Geschichte der Kleiderarbeiter in Österreich im 19. Jahrhundert und im ersten Viertel des 20. Jahrhunderts* (Vienna: Gewerkschaft der Kleiderarbeiter Österreichs, 1930), 122.

2 Buttinger, *op. cit.*, 403 f. By permission of the publisher.

agitation in the faces of the others. Everywhere he found it. . . . He suddenly grasped the value and power of community and was anxious to support this newly found recognition. He began to talk about trade union problems, read what was worthwhile in this field, although he found it strange at first, and passionately accepted the socialist doctrine of salvation.

He had known that there were the rich and the poor and that there were more, infinitely more poor people. But he had been satisfied with this knowledge and derived from it the incentive to become rich himself. He had not been concerned with the goals of his own life sphere. Indeed, he had rejected his world, he had painfully tried again and again to transcend it spiritually. When he looked back, in the light of his socialist wisdom, on his youthful struggles, they appeared to him like the hopeless fighting of a soldier who, cut off from his troops, desperately carried on his own war. He believed the new order of life would come for all the poor, not just for one alone. It will come for everyone or it will not come at all. His difficult attempts during all those years were bound to end in defeat, for he had desired betterment only for himself; he had dreamed of millions of Marks to give him the good life in harmony with his tastes and capabilities. He had no thoughts for other people or only those of a rich man handing out alms. There is no right to personal happiness, there is only the duty to further the general welfare.[3]

Sons of Social Democrats were likely to join the labor movement, but not merely because of their fathers' example. A case in point is William Bromme.[4] He joined after the fall of the antisocialist legislation because of the appeal of "serious" collective pursuits.

At first Bromme did for the party only what his father demanded. He carried socialist pamphlets and newspapers and shouted slogans during an election campaign. For a while he sympathized, for reasons not given, with the Advanced Liberals. He also spent much time with a nonpolitical group of friends who had formed a regular "table group" (*Stammtisch*) in 1889, unimaginatively called *Frohsinn,* as many of the hundreds of German glee clubs were named. When he first attended socialist meetings at the age of 16, he was much impressed. Even the cheerfulness after the meetings appeared to him different from the boisterousness of his glee club friends. At first, his positive reaction may have been primarily due to the appeal of seriousness and adulthood. But he gradually came to understand, as his father had before him, that the combination of the workers was the only means to improve their conditions. As isolated individuals they could neither change their immediate nor their wider social environment. The labor movement offered a solution. As the father became a victim of his political activity, the direct and indirect achievements of the labor movement began to benefit his son. When the son was dismissed for political reasons and indicted for political blackmail in 1898, the organizations which the father had helped to build supported the son. Under the impact of the labor movement's

3 Karl Bröger, *Der Held im Schatten* (Jena: Diederichs, 1930), 135 f. This autobiographical novel covers the period from the nineties until 1914.

4 Cf. William T. Bromme, *Lebensgeschichte eines modernen Fabrikarbeiters,* Paul Göhre, ed. (Jena: Diederichs, 1905). The following refers especially to 128–32, 233–39, 326 and 334.

growth, the state accepted some responsibility for securing improved working and living conditions. Bromme's mother died of tuberculosis; his tubercular condition was treated under the provisions of the sickness insurance. However, Bromme was incapable of further physical work at the age of 33—the year that he finished his autobiography.

When Bromme writes that his political attitude and innermost conviction made him continue to work for the party, despite his ill health and his wife's opposition, he bares only one part of the meaning of the labor movement for him. His memoirs clearly reveal his personal need for sociability and self-respect. Party work was the most meaningful activity of his life. To give it up would have made him just a party member or voter, no longer belonging to the ingroup of the local party organization.

This raises the problem of the meaning of the labor movement for the more active members, the lower-ranking functionaries in particular. A relevant example here is Adelheid Popp, who became one of the most prominent women of the Austrian labor movement. Her case shows that material deprivations alone were not usually enough to make a worker turn to the labor movement. Adelheid Popp paints a picture of her youth exposing fully the physical and psychical mutilation inflicted on many men and women of the first lower-class generation recruited for large-scale industrialization.[5] However, extreme suffering made her no more favorable to socialism than it made the thousands of other women at work in Viennese factories during the eighties. She believed the anti-Semitic propaganda and the characterization of Social Democrats as anarchists. But when she was without a job for several weeks her Catholic faith was shaken. Trials of Social Democrats aroused her compassion and interested her in the labor movement. After meeting her first Social Democrat in the eighties, she expected the revolution within a short time. Gradually her grasp of socialist ideas improved, and the party speakers and newspapers formulated for her those ideas she was unable to develop on her own:

> I heard clearly and convincingly expressed that which I had instinctively felt but had never been able to think out. . . . The more consciously I became a socialist, the more free and strong I felt to meet all opponents.[6]

Reading pulp magazine fiction had kept her for several years in an imaginary world. Socialism, on the other hand, was concrete in a double sense: it was

5 Adelheid Popp, *Autobiography of a Working Woman* (London: Unwin, 1912). Popp's family came from Bohemia. As industralization progressed in Austria, many non-German citizens of the Double Monarchy migrated to Vienna, the industrial center of the country. Thus, there was a development similar to, though not as pronounced as, the development in the United States where the lowest social group was to a large extent made up of the most recent wave of immigrants. "Undesirable" workers could be deported from Vienna to their native villages. For her political activities Popp was threatened with deportation to Bohemia although she could not speak Czech.

6 *Op. cit.*, 99 and 34.

a theory explaining her material living conditions and promising a millennium, and a political movement to which she could belong. The labor movement provided her with meaningful work and an articulate class consciousness. Absorbed in everyday party work, she completely identified with the movement. This is what it meant to her to become a full-time functionary:

> I was now endlessly happy. I had a sphere of work which satisfied all my longings but which I had considered quite unattainable for myself. It was to me the Promised Land.[7]

The intense identification with the labor movement and the great sense of personal satisfaction were shared by both moderate and radical functionaries. Both groups were equally interested in efficient organization, but the radicals, such as Buttinger, were also concerned with the Marxist indoctrination of the workers, particularly those who were already followers. The more radical functionaries could afford such concern because they did not carry the responsibilities, sustained by the top leaders, for the survival of the movement and for dealing with the government and the public; they could operate nearly exclusively within the classbound and isolated realm of the Social Democratic subculture. Many moderate functionaries, too, immersed themselves completely in this realm. Typical of them was Bromme. He was very useful as a member of a party which aimed primarily at increasing the number of its parliamentary seats and at expanding its organization.[8] The considerable material sacrifices he made for the party were partly borne by his wife and children, who could not share the emotional gratifications which compensated him. He tried to avoid provocations, but was not deterred from party work by the ever present possibility of dismissal for political reasons, criminal prosecution on *ad hoc* pretexts or the danger to his health through overexertion. This is no mean record, but he was not the kind of man likely to impress the more radical functionaries. His absorption in administrative work, membership drives and electoral campaigning, to the more or less tacit exclusion of theoretical interests, placed him clearly in the ranks of the moderates, among whom the editor of his autobiography, Pastor Göhre, was prominent.[9]

7 *Op. cit.,* 120.

8 Cf. Bromme, *op. cit.,* 240 f.

9 In his composite portrait of a middle-aged, female proletarian party worker, Buttinger described one consequence of uncritical immersion into the Social Democratic subculture, namely, the unrelatedness of routine activities to their object: To her "anything written in a book or pamphlet issued by the party was the Gospel truth, sight unseen. Her job was not to read the party literature but to circulate it. It did not occur to her to doubt the contents. To do so would have seemed silly and unjust as if the 'leaders and theoreticians' at the top had questioned the accuracy of her accounting for party buttons and publications. Frau Meier's faith in the party did not rest on its doctrines but on its life." *Op. cit.,* 64. By permission of the publisher.

Just as the reasons for joining the labor movement and the activities to which an individual devoted himself shed light on the movement's meaning to each person, so the personal meaning became visible in those moments that threatened the very life of the movement. The events of 1933 proved that the beliefs of the Social Democratic and Communist functionaries and rank and file were not functioning to produce mass resistance against the destruction of the labor movement in Germany. Both movements collapsed when they were outlawed and confronted with totalitarian methods of suppression. But this is no argument against the assumption that the labor movement was the life center of masses of workers.

*CHARLES TILLY*

# *COLLECTIVE VIOLENCE*

As comforting as it is for civilized people to think of barbarians as violent and of violence as barbarian, Western civilization and various forms of collective violence have always been close partners. We do not need a stifled universal instinct of aggression to account for outbreaks of violent conflicts in our past, or in our present. Nor need we go to the opposite extreme and search for pathological moments and sick men in order to explain collective acts of protest and destruction. Historically, collective violence has flowed regularly out of the central political processes of Western countries. Men seeking to seize, hold, or realign the levers of power have continually engaged in collective violence as part of their struggles. The oppressed have struck in the name of justice, the privileged in the name of order, those in between in the name of fear. Great shifts in the arrangements of power have ordinarily produced—and have often depended on—exceptional movements of collective violence.

Yet the basic forms of collective violence vary according to who is involved and what is at issue. They have changed profoundly in Western countries over

Charles Tilly, "Collective Violence in European Perspective," in *Violence in America: Historical and Comparative Perspectives,* ed. Hugh Davis Graham and Ted Robert Gurr (New York: Frederick A. Praeger Publishers, 1969), pp. 4–5, 10–13, 31–37.

the last few centuries, and those countries have built big cities and modern industries. For these reasons, the character of collective violence at a given time is one of the best signs we have of what is going on in a country's political life. The nature of violence and the nature of the society are intimately related.

Collective violence is normal. That does not mean it is intrinsically desirable, or inevitable. For century after century, the inhabitants of southern Italy endured malaria as a normal fact of life; today, American city dwellers endure smog and nerve-rending traffic as normal facts of life; few people hail malaria, smog, or traffic jams. Europeans of other centuries often destroyed children they could not provide for. Now infanticide has become rare. Few of us mourn its passing. But the fact that infanticide persisted so long in the face of persuasive teachings and fearsome penalties tells us something about the poverty and population pressure under which people once lived in Western countries. It also may help us understand some apparently barbaric practices of people outside the West today. In a similar way, both the persistence of the phenomenon of collective violence and the changes in its form within European countries over the last few centuries have something to teach us about their political life, and even about contemporary forms of protest. . . .

## *POLITICS AND VIOLENCE*

My own explorations of Western Europe, especially France, over the last few centuries suggest a more political interpretation of collective violence. Far from being mere side effects of urbanization, industrialization, and other large structural changes, violent protests seem to grow most directly from the struggle for established places in the structure of power. Even presumably nonpolitical forms of collective violence like the antitax revolt are normally directed against the authorities, accompanied by a critique of the authorities' failure to meet their responsibilities, and informed by a sense of justice denied to the participants in the protest. Furthermore, instead of constituting a sharp break from "normal" political life, violent protests tend to accompany, complement, and extend organized, peaceful attempts by the same people to accomplish their objectives.

Over the long run, the processes most regularly producing collective violence are those by which groups acquire or lose membership in the political community. The form and locus of collective violence therefore vary greatly depending on whether the major ongoing political change is a group's acquisition of the prerequisites of membership, its loss of those prerequisites, or a shift in the organization of the entire political system.

The impact of large structural changes such as urbanization, industrialization, and population growth, it seems to me, comes through their creation or destruction of groups contending for power and through their shaping of the available means of coercion. In the short run, the growth of large cities and rapid migration from rural to urban areas in Western Europe probably acted as a damper on violent protest, rather than a spur to it. That is so for two reasons:

(1) The process withdrew discontented men from communities in which they already had the means for collective action and placed them in communities where they had neither the collective identity nor the means necessary to strike together.
(2) It took considerable time and effort both for the individual migrant to assimilate to the large city, and thus to join the political strivings of his fellows, and for new forms of organization for collective action to grow up in the cities.

If so, the European experience resembles the American experience. In the United States, despite enduring myths to the contrary, poor, uprooted newcomers to big cities generally take a long time to get involved in anything—crime, delinquency, politics, associations, protest, rioting—requiring contacts and experiences outside a small world of friends and relatives. These things are at least as true of European cities.

In the long run, however, urbanization deeply shaped the conditions under which new groups fought for political membership, and urbanization's secondary effects in the countryside stirred a variety of protests. The move to the city helped transform the character of collective violence in at least three ways:

(1) It grouped men in larger homogeneous blocs (especially via the factory and the working-class neighborhood) than ever before.
(2) It facilitated the formation of special-interest associations (notably the union and the party) incorporating many people and capable of informing, mobilizing, and deploying them relatively fast and efficiently.
(3) It massed the people posing the greatest threat to the authorities near the urban seats of power, and thus encouraged the authorities to adopt new strategies and tactics for controlling dissidence.

For the people who remained in the country, the rise of the cities meant increasingly insistent demands for crops and taxes to support the urban establishment, increasingly visible impact on individual farmers of tariff and pricing policies set in the cities, and increasingly efficient means of exacting obedience from the countryman. All of these, in their time, incited violent protests through Europe.

Of course, definitive evidence on such large and tangled questions is terribly hard to come by. Until very recent times few historians have taken the study of collective violence as such very seriously. As Antonio Gramsci, the Italian socialist philosopher-historian, put it:

> This is the custom of our time: instead of studying the origins of a collective event, and the reasons for its spread . . . they isolate the protagonist and limit themselves to doing a biography and pathology, too often concerning themselves with unascertained motives, or interpreting them in the wrong way; for a social elite the features of subordinate groups always display something barbaric and pathological.

Since World War II, however, a considerable number of French and English historians, and a much smaller number of Americans, have begun to study and write history "from below"—actually trying to trace the experiences and actions of large numbers of ordinary men from their own point of view. This approach has had a special impact on the study of protests and rebellions. As a result, we are beginning to get a richer, rearranged picture of the political life of plain people in France and England (and, to a lesser extent, other European countries) over the last few centuries.

The new variety of evidence makes it possible to identify some major shifts in the predominant forms of collective violence in those countries over the modern period. Without too much difficulty we can place the forms of collective violence which have prevailed during that long period in three broad categories: primitive, reactionary, and modern. The primitive varieties once predominated, until centralized states began dragging Europeans into political life on a larger than local scale. As Thorstein Veblen put it in his sardonic *Imperial Germany and the Industrial Revolution,*

> . . . so soon as the king's dominions increased to such a size as to take him personally out of range of an effectual surveillance by neighborly sentiment . . . the crown would be able to use the loyalty of one neighborhood in enforcing exactions from another, and the royal power would then presently find no other obstacle to its continued growth than the limit placed upon it by the state of the industrial arts.

In the process, the king's retinue produced the apparatus of the state, which then acquired momentum of its own. That transformation accelerated through much of Western Europe after 1600. Since then, the primitive forms of collective violence have dwindled very slowly, but very steadily. Now they occur only rarely, only at the margins of organized politics.

The reactionary forms, by contrast, burgeoned as the national state began to grow. That was far from coincidence; they most often developed as part of the resistance of various communal groups to incorporation into the national state and the national economy. But the state won the contest; in most countries of Western Europe the reactionary forms of collective violence peaked and then faded away in their turn during the nineteenth century. They gave way to modern forms of collective violence, characterized by larger scale, more complex organization, and bids for changes in the operation or control of the state apparatus, rather than resistance to its demands. [Also] during very recent years we have seen what might be signs of another large shift in the form and locus of collective violence, for in the last century the modern forms have pushed all others aside. . . .

The twentieth-century figures from France include almost no primitive violence. By the beginning of the century the primitive forms had been fading slowly through most of Western Europe for three centuries or more. In some countries, however, the transition from predominantly reactionary to predominantly modern forms of collective violence occurred with striking rapidity. In England, the reactionary forms were already well on their way to oblivion by the time of the last agrarian rising, in 1830, although they had prevailed thirty years before. In Germany, demonstrations and strikes seem to have established themselves as the usual settings for collective violence during the two decades after the Revolution of 1848.

The situation was a bit more complicated in Italy, because of the deep division between north and south. The transition to modern forms of collective violence appears to have been close to completion in the north at unification. By the time of Milan's infamous *fatti di Maggio* of 1898, in which at least two policemen and eighty demonstrators died, the newer organizational forms unquestionably dominated the scene. In the south, mixed forms of the food riot and tax rebellion still occurred at the end of the century. Within ten years, however, even in rural areas the agricultural strike and the organized partisan meeting or demonstration had become the most regular sources of violence on the larger scale.

Spain, as usual, is the significant exception: while the country as a whole displays the long-run drift from primitive to reactionary to modern forms of collective violence, it also displays a marvelous array of regressions, mixtures, and hesitations. Surely, the country's erratic industrialization, uncertain, fluctuating unification, and exceptional military involvement in politics lie behind its differentiation from the rest of Western Europe in this respect. Spain, as Gerald Brenan says,

> . . . is the land of the *patria chica.* Every village, every town is the center of an intense social and political life. As in classical times, a man's allegiance is first of all to his native place, or to his family or social group in it, and only secondly to his country and government. In what one may call its normal condition Spain is a collection of small, mutually hostile, or indifferent republics held together in a loose federation. . . . Instead of slow building-up of forces such as one sees in other European nations, there has been an alternation between the petty quarrels of tribal life and great upsurges of energy that come, economically speaking, from nowhere.

Thus Spain becomes the exception that tests the rule. For the rule says the shift from predominantly reactionary to predominantly modern forms of collective violence accompanies the more-or-less durable victory of the national state and the national economy over the particularisms of the past. In Spain, that victory was not durable, and the forms of violence wavered.

The precise timing and extent of the shift from reactionary to modern forms of collective violence in these countries remains to be established. For France, it is fairly clear that the shift was barely started by 1840, but close to complete by 1860. Furthermore, France experienced great, and nearly simultaneous, outbreaks of both forms of collective violence in the years from 1846 through 1851. The well-known events we customarily lump together as the Revolution of 1848 and the less-known but enormous insurrection of 1851 stand out both for their magnitude and for their mixture of reactionary and modern disturbances, but they came in the company of such notable outbreaks as the widespread food riots of 1846–47, the Forty-Five Centime Revolt of 1848–49, and the unsuccessful coup of 1849.

If this account of the transition from reactionary to modern collective violence in Western Europe is correct, it has some intriguing features. First, the timing of the transition corresponds roughly to the timing of industrialization and urbanization—England early, Italy late, and so on. Furthermore, the most rapid phase of the transition seems to occur together with a great acceleration of industrial and urban growth, early in the process: England at the beginning of the century, France of the 1850s, Germany of the 1850s and 1870s, Italy of the 1890s.

Second, there is some connection between the timing of the transition and the overall level of collective violence in a country. Over the last one hundred fifty years, if we think in terms of the frequency and scale of disturbances rather than the turnover of regimes, we can probably place Spain ahead of France, France ahead of Italy, Italy ahead of Germany, and Germany ahead of England. France is in the wrong position . . . but [nevertheless] there is some tendency for the latecomers (or noncomers) to experience greater violence. If we took into account challenges to national integration posed by such peoples as the Catalans, and differences in the apparatus of repression, the connection would very likely appear even closer.

The information we have on hand, then, suggests that the processes of urbanization and industrialization themselves transform the character of collective violence. But how? We have a conventional notion concerning the life cycle of protest during the course of industrialization and urbanization: an early stage consisting of chaotic responses to the displacements and disruptions caused by the initial development of urban industry, a middle stage consisting of the growth of a militant and often violent working class, a late stage consisting of the peaceful integration of that working class into economic and political life. This scheme has many faults, as we have seen. Certainly we must correct and expand it to take account both of other groups than industrial workers and of the connections between industrialization and urbanization . . . .

The experience of France challenges the plausible presumption that rapid urbanization produces disruptions of social life that in turn generate protest. There is, if anything, a negative correlation over time and space between the pace of urban growth and the intensity of collective violence. The extreme example is the contrast between the 1840s, with slow urban growth plus enormous violence, and the decade after 1851, with very fast growth and extensive peace. Cities like St. Etienne of Roubaix that received and formed large numbers of new industrial workers tended to remain quiet while centers of the old traditional crafts, like Lyon and Rouen, raged with rebellion. When we can identify the participants in political disturbances, they tend to grossly underrepresent newcomers to the city and draw especially from the "little people" most firmly integrated into the local political life of the city's working-class neighborhoods. The geography of the disturbances itself suggests as much. It was not the urban neighborhoods of extreme deprivation, crime, or vice, George Rudé reports, "not the newly settled towns or quarters that proved the most fertile breeding-ground for social and political protest, but the old areas of settlement with established customs, such as Westminster, the City of London, Old Paris, Rouen, or Lyon." The information available points to a slow, collective process of organization and political education—what we may loosely call a development of class consciousness—within the city rather than a process of disruption leading directly to personal malaise and protest.

As a consequence of this process, the great new cities eventually became the principle settings of collective violence in France. Furthermore, collective violence moved to the city faster than the population did. Even at the beginning of the nineteenth century, the towns and cities of France produced a disproportionate share of the nation's collective violence. Yet tax rebellions, food riots, and movements against conscription did occur with fair regularity in France's small towns and villages. After these forms of disturbance disappeared, the countryside remained virtually silent for decades. When rural collective violence renewed, it was in the highly organized form of farmers' strikes and marches on Government buildings. This sequence of events was, to some extent, a result of urbanization.

Early in the nineteenth century, the expansion of cities incited frequent rural protests—obviously in the case of the food riot, more subtly in the case of other forms of collective violence. We have some reason to believe that groups of people who were still solidly established within rural communities, but were losing their livelihoods through the concentration of property and the urbanization of industry, regularly spearheaded such protests. The most important group was probably the workers in cottage industry. Their numbers declined catastrophically as various industries—especially textiles—moved to the city during the first half of the century. Large numbers of them hung on in the countryside, doing what weaving, spinning, or forging they could, seeking out livings as handymen, day laborers, and farmhands, and railing against their fate. Within their communities they were able to act collectively against power looms, farm machines, tax collectors, and presumed profiteers.

Slowly before midcentury, rapidly thereafter, the increasing desperation of the French countryside and the expanding opportunities for work in the new industrial cities drew such men away from their rural communities in town. That move cut them off from the personal, day-to-day contacts that had given them the incentive and the means for collective action against their enemies. It rearranged their immediate interests, placed them in vast, unfamiliar communities, and gave them relatively weak and unreliable relations with those who shared common interest with them.

The initial fragmentation of the work force into small groups of diverse origins, the slow development of mutual awareness and confidence, the lack of organizational experience among the new workers, and the obstacles thrown up by employers and governments all combined to make the development of the means and the will for collective action a faltering, time-consuming process. Collective violence did not begin in earnest until the new industrial workers began forming or joining associations—trade unions, mutual-aid societies, political clubs, conspiratorial groups—devoted to the collective pursuit of their interests. In this sense, the short-run effect of the urbanization of the French labor force was actually to damp collective violence. Its long-run effect, however, was to promote new forms of collective action that frequently led to violent conflicts, and thus to change the form of collective violence itself.

This happened in part through the grouping together of large numbers of men sharing a common fate in factories, urban working-class neighborhoods, and construction gangs. Something like the class-conscious proletariat of which Marx wrote began to form in the industrial cities. This new scale of congregation combined with new, pressing grievances, improving communication, the diffusion of new organizational models from Government and industry, and grudging concessions by the authorities to the right of association. The combination facilitated the formation of special-interest associations. At first workers experimented with cramped, antique, exclusive associations resembling (or even continuing) the old guilds; gradually they formed mutual-aid societies, labor exchanges, unions, and national and international federations.

The new associations further extended the scale and flexibility of communication among workers; they made it possible to inform, mobilize, and deploy large numbers of men fast and efficiently in strikes, demonstrations, and other common action. These potentially rebellious populations and their demanding associations proliferated in the big cities, in the shadows of regional and national capitals. They therefore posed a greater (or at least more visible) threat to the authorities than had their smalltown predecessors. The authorities responded to the threat by organizing police forces, crowd-control tactics, and commissions of inquiry. The associations, in their turn, achieved greater sophistication and control in their show of strength. The process took time—perhaps a generation for any particular group of workers. In that longer run the urbanization of the labor force produced a whole new style of collective violence.

The experience of the industrial workers has one more important lesson for us. In both reactionary and modern forms of collective violence, men commonly express their feeling that they have been unjustly denied their rights. Reactionary disturbances, however, center on rights once enjoyed but now threatened, while modern disturbances center on rights not yet enjoyed but now within reach. The reactionary forms are especially the work of groups of men who are losing their collective positions within the system of power, while the modern forms attract groups of men who are striving to acquire or enhance such positions. The reactionary forms, finally, challenge the basic claims of a national state and a national economy, while the modern forms rest on the assumption that the state and the economy have a durable existence—if not necessarily under present management. In modern disturbances, men contend over the control and organization of the State and the economy.

What links these features together historically? The coordinate construction of the nation-state and the national economy simultaneously weakened local systems of power, with the rights and positions which depended on them, and established new, much larger arenas in which to contend for power. In Western European countries, as locally based groups of men definitively lost their struggle against the claims of the central power, reactionary disturbances dwindled and modern disturbances swelled. The rapid transition from one to the other occurred where and when the central power was able to improve rapidly or expand its enforcement of its claims. Accelerating urbanization and industrialization facilitated such an expansion by providing superior means of communication and control to the agents of the central power, by drawing men more fully into national markets, and by spreading awareness of, and involvement in, national politics. In the process, special-purpose associations like parties and labor unions grew more and more important as the vehicles in the struggle for power, whether violent or nonviolent. Thus urbanization and industrialization affected the character and the incidence of collective violence profoundly, but indirectly.

# PART 3

# BRAVE NEW EUROPE: 1914 TO THE PRESENT

The history of Europe in the twentieth century can logically be divided into two successive parts. In the first half of the century Europeans were rocked by two disastrous international wars and plagued by chronic political instability. In the period since then, however, they have gradually settled down to an era of unprecedented tranquility and prosperity. True, the cold war has separated the European peoples into two armed camps. Yet the separation has in many ways been salutary insofar as it has provided breathing and growing space for social developments long retarded. Specifically, this has become the age of the welfare state, whether in a western or eastern version, and more common people have been better cared for through public agencies than in any time past. As Bertolt Brecht once wrote, *"Erst kommt das Fressen, und dann kommt die Moral"* (roughly, "First comes chow and then morality"). Despite the national and ideological antagonisms of contemporary Europe, in other words, there has everywhere been a concerted attempt to raise the general standard of living. To a remarkable degree that effort has been successful, and in the final quarter of this century all Europeans are enjoying an extraordinary bonanza. Class differences persist, of course, and the wealth is unevenly distributed, as it always has been. But on balance Europeans are probably more alike now in dress and habit and outlook than ever before. Slow though it may be, what we are witnessing in our day is the social homogenization of an entire civilization.

If that observation is correct, it may mean that social history has a momentum of its own, apart from political events and military conflicts. For instance, it is striking that everywhere in Europe urbanization has continued, feminism has advanced, and youth have become more prominent. In this section we have singled out these three examples of a social metamorphosis that appears irresistible and irreversible. These tendencies are just as characteristic of our age as, say, slavery was in the city-states of ancient Greece. They have become essential and enduring aspects of European culture.

Perhaps we should not be too quick, however, to wave politics aside. What would have occurred if Nazi Germany had been victorious in the Second World War? Our imagination boggles at such a counterfactual thought, but it is safe to speculate that European society would have been quite different beneath a Nazi tyranny than it has become under its present variety of capitalist and communist regimes. When we remain within the known historical data, considering that Germany lost both world wars, we can see that the pattern of social change has been far from uniform. That should hardly surprise us, since divergence has always been the European rule. From a social standpoint, the growth of Bolshevik Russia after 1917 and the subsequent spread of communism into eastern Europe have merely created a new kind of division between East and West to replace the old. Generalizations about the entirety of European society therefore remain handicapped because of elemental political circumstances that we must take into account. Homogenization or not, careful distinctions must still be drawn.

The pattern of economic growth has, of course, also been of primordial importance. In the first half of this century Europe experienced the most extreme fluctuations between inflation and depression. The only common feature was an economic instability that tended to produce, in one form or another, political radicalization. The institutions of parliamentary democracy were consequently shaken or swept away. Nazi Germany was only the most conspicuous incarnation of this turbulence, which was economic in its immediate origin. Since mid-century, as we noted, the picture has changed markedly for the better and Europe has entered a relatively calm period of extraordinary prosperity. If the durability of that phenomenon is still in doubt, especially as the menace of a prolonged energy crisis looms over it, the lines of political development now seem firmly etched and the future of European society looks promising. We need not lose ourselves in a cloud of false optimism to believe that the prospects of Everyman in Europe are brighter now than at any time in the past.

## CHAPTER 7

# MECHANIZATION AND COLLECTIVIZATION

The sturdiest of Europeans have been the peasants. They have endured through it all. Yet the daily round of their existence has obviously changed since the days of slavery and serfdom; today they are more likely to be found sitting on a tractor than bending in the field. Change and progress, certainly. From the standpoint of efficiency there has undoubtedly been a remarkable advance in rural labor since the eighteenth century. But what of the quality of country life? Intangibles cannot be measured in average yield per acre, nor in the number of motorcycles owned by peasants. It is unnecessary to romanticize times past in order to grasp that the peasant has entered the modern era with some reluctance and a certain nostalgia.

*Henri Mendras* analyzes the impact of machinery on the traditional livelihood of the peasant. Farm life has become in some ways easier but also far more complex than in centuries past. Scientific techniques are being introduced to agriculture. Consequently, old habits no longer suffice and must be replaced by expert knowledge. Farming is another business enterprise in a commercial society. The results are much tension and some confusion about what it now means to be a peasant in Europe. Maybe the term itself is no longer appropriate?

*Edward C. Banfield* records how changes in agricultural methods are reflected in the customs and social patterns of the rural population of a small community in southern Italy. The outside world has manifestly intruded there. The dress, the food, and the pleasures of a village have all been altered. If people seem more prosperous at first glance, Banfield detects among them a sadness and a sense of confinement. He uses psychological testing to confirm his conjecture that peasants of today are depressed by their station in life and that they share a pervasive melancholy with their fellow villagers.

*Merle Fainsod's* classic account of the sovietization of Russia treats the difficulties that the Stalinist and post-Stalinist regimes inherited from tsardom. The establishment of thorough political control has not yet guaranteed adequate agricultural production, nor has it overcome the reluctance of Russian peasants to be absorbed into the regimentation of collective farming. Fainsod argues that agricultural interests have, to a great extent, been sacrificed to those of industrialization, and that the Soviet government has displayed toward the peasantry an attitude of dependence and hostility. He traces first the successive stages of official policy and peasant reaction before the Second World War, the impact of Nazi occupation and postwar upset, and finally the enforced merger of collective farms under Khrushchev in the 1950s. An unfavorable result has been a marked tension between different generations and various strata of the rural population. Still, an enduring basis for Russia's agricultural development has apparently been laid and, as far as one can see, the lot of the peasants has been irretrievably determined.

The peasant population of Europe is today embattled. As industrialization has proceeded, the peasantry's numerical and political importance has visibly declined. Yet the farm is an essential economic and social element that must remain, since the urban population is forever dependent on rural labor to provide its food. It is evident that the decline of the agricultural sector would strike down the entire economy of Europe. The implications are already apparent: the increasing subsidization of agriculture by industry and the unrelenting application of technology to farm production. A civilization that has treated rural workers so shabbily for so many centuries now finds that they are indispensable members of modern society.

HENRI MENDRAS

# THE VANISHING PEASANT

In traditional agriculture, there is no division of labor, no separation between production and consumption, no distinction between economic and family life. The family and the enterprise coincide: the head of the family is at the same time head of the enterprise. Indeed, he is the one because he is the other. This is a purely intellectual distinction rather than a realistic analysis of his situation; in most of his activities the peasant is one and the other, and he lives his professional and his family life as an indivisible entity. The members of his family are also his fellow workers. The father usually directs the management of the farm, or is at least an advisor who enjoys the respect and support of the family. His wife busies herself with her own activities and shares much of the men's work. The children are apprentices and assistants wherever needed. Tasks are assigned by custom according to sex and age,[1] not by the organization of production according to the skill of the workers.

The position of the sons is particularly revealing. Their father teaches them their trade both in his capacity of father and in that of master of apprentices, with the result that the child never knows if a reprimand, a piece of advice, or a set of instructions belongs to everyday or professional life. The authority of the father is based on his position in the family as much as on his professional competence. The young peasant cannot derive from his apprenticeship any clear idea of what the farmer's trade is, or of the techniques of which it is constituted; it is part of a way of life he has learned from his elders, and of the position he was assigned at birth. For him, *savoir faire* (ability) and *savoir vivre* (good breeding) are the same thing: in his life as a child and an adolescent the technique of plowing is tied to the family field where it is learned, and integrated into a way of life just as are all the other "techniques" of professional and social life—language or the rules of polite behavior, for example. Every effort to isolate his activity as a farmer from the rest of the peasant's life violates a reality whose fundamental characteristic is syncretism, a reality that must be analyzed and understood rather than minimized.

Not only is it impossible to dissociate the role of father from that of farmer; the latter is itself of a complexity with hardly any equivalent in other occupations.



1 Varagnac, 1942.

In his polyproductive enterprise, the farmer assumes all the functions that elsewhere would be divided among several specialized workers and organized into a hierarchy of command.

For the peasant of the past, it was enough to know how to handle his hoe, his scythe, and his sickle and to drive his plowcart or swingplow. Manual dexterity and physical endurance were the essential qualities. For the farmer of today, who is still a manual laborer in more than half his tasks, these qualities remain essential. However, machines are multiplying, improving, specializing, and creating new tasks for man, and the machines must be prepared, repaired, adjusted, and operated. They increase the efficiency of the work and ease the hardships of the worker, but at the same time they complicate the profession by demanding new skills and mechanical knowledge. Aptitudes useful in the operation of a tractor, a harvester-thresher, a binder, and other equipment are becoming at least as important as strength and dexterity in the handling of tools. In short, the farmer is still the man with the hoe and must be at the same time a mechanic and tractor operator.

Only one skill is losing its importance: the art of breeding, training, and managing draft animals, oxen or horses. On the other hand, the breeding of animals for profit is becoming more and more scientific. It has always been necessary for the breeder to look after his herd and know it with a thoroughness that depends on the peculiar sympathy he develops through long experience. Today, in addition, he must be able to prepare a balanced diet and should know enough to call a veterinarian if he feels that his lack of experience makes a scientific diagnosis advisable.

Knowing how to handle implements and machines is enough to make a farmhand, but not a peasant, who must also know soil, plants, and animals. Pedology, phytology, and zoology are perhaps big words to designate the variety of agronomical knowledge that is necessary. The peasant had only the rudiments of this knowledge, the results of his father's experience and of his own work. It is what used to be called a ''feeling for'' the land and the animals, something that has always been necessary but is becoming more scientific and rational as techniques develop. The period of apprenticeship shows a gradual tendency to transform this traditional attainment and give it scientific basis, thanks to certain aspects of physics, chemistry, anatomy, and other sciences. Soils, plants, and animals are too diverse for the farmer to be satisfied with a few manipulative procedures that have lost all meaning. The more carefully selected plants and animals are less hardy and more sensitive to parasites and sickness. To know which fertilizer to use and the right way to treat each case at each moment is no longer a question of habit or instinct but one of knowledge. While he is often obliged to resort to the expert's advice, the farmer must normally be his own expert. The rudiments of science are also useful for consultation with the veterinarian or the agricultural advisor.

If the family is large or the property extensive enough to require that one or two salaried workers be employed, the "employer" must know how to give orders, assign each one his task, maintain the rhythm of the work, see that the time schedule is respected, and supervise the work so that it is done well. In a word, he must be a good foreman. And the fact that he is the father and the husband makes his job no easier. He can certainly expect his son to be more conscientious than a hired hand, but by the same token the son will have a more independent spirit and character. Their very intimacy gives an emotional dimension to their work relationship. The clearly defined relationships of the salaried condition are simpler than those that exist between father and son, unpaid journeyman and eternal apprentice.

. . . the organization of work is a discipline that the peasant can impose only on himself; it is not easy to impose it on his assistants. Certainly the work dictates the time schedule and the rhythm, but its urgency and the manner of doing it can be determined in varying ways, and the "employer," a hard worker himself, has only his personal, family, or employer's authority to make his wife, son, or employee fall into line.

Producer and foreman, the peasant is also seller and buyer. The fair and the market hold a prominent place in the social life of the traditional village. Since these activities are social as much as economic, it can be said, paradoxically, that the more autarchic the agricultural economy the more important are the fair and the market. They are occasions for meeting one's neighbors and relatives and finding out how things are going. The bargaining itself used to be a strictly ritualized social game, permitting the parties to prove their cleverness and cunning. For certain investments, notably cattle, knowing how to buy and sell at a good price was at least as important as knowing how to produce well, and some breeders were horse traders rather than farmers.

Today the fair is gradually being replaced by the merchant who stops at the farm to buy, and by cooperatives, to which the farmer turns over all of his produce. Face to face with the merchant, the farmer can always bargain, being free to sell or not to sell. But this freedom is less real today than it used to be. Once the peasant could return home with his cow or his sheep if he could not get a good price, and speculate on market fluctuations; he had no urgent need for cash because there was not much daily use for money in an autarchic economy. Now, on the contrary, he constantly "has his hand in his pocket." To buy necessities for his family and his farm, the farmer must sell whether the price is good or bad. On the farm, confronted by the merchant who makes him an offer, he is not really free to refuse. Without precise knowledge of the ins and outs of the market and unable to set several buyers into competition with each other, he finds himself at a disadvantage and must accept the conditions offered to him.

At the cooperative too, no discussion is possible. Rather, a new form of commercial regulation is in force, since the management of the cooperative is at least nominally in the hands of all the members. It is indeed true that most of the cooperatives entrust management to the skilled hands of a director. However, the farmer who belongs to a cooperative remains in theory a seller and a buyer, as was his father at the fairgrounds; furthermore, since the cooperative does the work of the middleman and the horse trader of the past, it replaces them in the economy.

Cooperatives of all sorts are multiplying, and more and more farmers are being called upon to accept responsibility for their direction. But to participate in the management of an important cooperative, even if only for the purpose of keeping informed, demands knowledge and time that average farmers do not have at present.[2] In any cooperative the management of the enterprise extends far beyond the framework of the traditional farm. As far as the economist is concerned, the farm is a "firm" and the farmer an entrepreneur. Liberal economics has built its models on this simplistic image, as false today as it ever was.

We have shown that in traditional self-sufficient polycultivation, since the peasant had few choices to make, the economic and technical management of the property was reduced to a few objectives: to avoid debts, to save enough to settle the children, to enlarge the estate if the occasion presented itself. The principles were those of domestic and family economy rather than of economic management of an enterprise. The only possible investment, the purchase of land, was made without any calculation for amortizing debts or increasing income. It was simply a transfer of capital from one form of hoarding (cash or livestock) to another, more highly valued by society.

Today, on the contrary, the peasant is gradually becoming an economic agent who chooses to engage in a particular speculation according to the technical means at his disposal and the returns he can anticipate. He invests in land, buildings, machines, livestock, fertilizer, and seeds, usually with the aid of credit in anticipation of profits from his investments. Economic reasoning, in the sense in which the term is used by economists and accountants, is entering farm management, often by devious and surreptitious paths. . . . The farmer can no longer be content to manage his farm "as a good father"; he must do so as a shrewd enterpreneur. To aid him in this effort, management counselors and centers for rural economics are springing up everywhere, while techniques of farm bookkeeping are constantly improving and spreading.

The growing complexity of machines and techniques of cultivation, the increased importance of marketing, over which the farmer must retain control, the penetration of an economic rationale into the management of the enterprise: these are evidence that the farmer's occupation is becoming more complex and diverse each day; and there is no division of labor to help relieve him of some of his tasks. He remains the jack-of-all-trades who must be competent in everything, as clever at handling the scythe and regulating a harvester-thresher as at reading a balance sheet from the cooperative or a booklet on zootechny.

2 No study has been done on this subject in France, but there are many by American, Dutch, and Scandinavian scholars.

There is a visible contradiction between the growing complexity of the profession and the demands of traditional polycultivation.

. . . the real solution will involve much more specialized farms. In the meantime the farmer, torn between traditional needs and the economic and technical imperatives of progress, is deeply affected by this crisis in the survival of a form of agriculture that preserves its ancient structures at the same time that it is penetrating the realm of business management and adopting scientific techniques.

This tension is all the more painful because the farmer does not analyze or isolate each of his roles as we have just done, but rather lives them closely united, as they are in his daily experience. Hence it is impossible for him to distinguish the logic and the exigencies of each role and the expectations it arouses. The natural result is confusion in analyzing each situation, a jumble of motives and desires.

*EDWARD C. BANFIELD*

# *A PEASANT VILLAGE IN SOUTHERN ITALY*

Consumption patterns are changing very rapidly in Montegrano. These changes reflect others that are deep-lying and fundamental.

Twenty years ago every peasant woman wore a blouse and skirt. Nowadays only old women dress in this way. Peasant women who are not of the older generation wear print dresses that come secondhand from America. Formerly almost all women wore funeral black; deaths occurred frequently and the period of mourning was ten years. Now, because of antibiotics, deaths are few. Meanwhile, people have come to feel that one or two years is long enough to wear mourning.

Some peasant girls have permanent waves. A groom may give one to his bride as a wedding present. Twenty years ago peasants generally went barefoot. Now they all wear shoes. A man used to wear a jacket and pants and nothing else; now almost every man has some underwear and many even have stockings and a handkerchief. Formerly only a few prosperous peasants had holiday suits, and the pants and jackets of these seldom matched. Today most peasants have a suit for holiday wear, and a few are almost indistinguishable from the upper class as they stroll in the *piazza* on *festa* days.

Ten years ago peasants tanned their own leather and made their own shoes. Now they all buy their shoes at the store. Shirts used to be made at home. Now they are made by the tailors. Seamstresses and tailors work from pattern catalogues that show the styles in Rome, Paris, and New York.

A generation ago peasant women made little preparation for their babies. Now they see the midwife well in advance and have a supply of clean sheets and dressings ready for the parturition, and a *corredino* of diapers, undershirts, and the like for the new baby. Grandmothers are no longer listened to at childbirth; the midwife is in charge. Some peasant mothers even bathe their babies.

Even the most prosperous peasants bought nothing but salt and sardines at the store a few years ago. Montegrano's wheat is not hard enough to make a good spaghetti, but even so spaghetti was made at home. Nowadays people buy *pasta* from the store or go without it. The peasant who has money to spend at the store buys the same foods, including canned ones, that are bought by the upper class.

Several years ago there was no bar and no movie in Montegrano. Now there are two bars and two movies. Some peasants feel deprived if they do not see a movie twice a month. A few go occasionally to a bar for a cup of *espresso* coffee.

These changes are not the product of greater prosperity. Most peasants are probably poorer than they were a generation ago: they have less to eat and less in savings. Soil erosion has left Montegrano's land base smaller than it was then, and the gradual depletion of the fertility of the soil that remains has led to a less intensive agriculture. The population to be supported by the reduced resources, however, is slightly larger than it was a generation ago.

One cause of these changes has been improvement of highways by public works projects. Isolated as it still is, Montegrano is more accessible to the cities than formerly. Salesmen who would not have thought of journeying there a few years back stop more or less regularly now.

Another cause of change (and also an effect of it) is reduction of cultural distance between the peasant and the outside world. A generation ago peasants seem to have taken it for granted that they were a different breed than other folk. Some of them—Prato, for example—still do. But many see no difference between themselves and others except that the others are better off. Those who take this view are unwilling to wear a peasant costume or to be set apart in other ways.

Paolo Vitello, a laborer who works at a forge, may be taken as an example of the new-style consumer. He spent some time in the cities of the north during his military service and has not forgotten what he saw there.[1] Although his income is twenty percent less than Prato's, he somehow manages to spend a great deal more.[2] His house has electric lights, bottled gas, and a toilet—all luxuries which Prato thinks are forever beyond him. He buys a bit of meat, fish, cheese, and sugar now and then—something Prato almost never does—and when he feels flush he buys his wife a handkerchief, his youngest child a toy or a cookie, or himself a beer, a cigarette, or a sixteen-cent lottery ticket. Prato, it is safe to say, has never in his life bought a luxury. On holidays Vitello takes his ease in the public square, dressed in a black suit like a gentleman. Prato has no holiday suit. Vitello's wife suffers from chronic headaches; she goes frequently to the doctor and buys vitamins and other drugs. Prato's wife is also chronically ill, but her medical expenses for the year consisted of the price of two aspirin tablets. Vitello hopes to persuade a relative in Naples who is a tailor there to take one of his boys as an apprentice. Although Prato is deeply dissatisfied, the possibility that his children might leave Montegrano and become something other than peasants seems so remote to him as not to be worth consideration.

Now that buying things from the store has become one of the possible ways of showing love for one's family, not to do so seems to a new-style consumer like coldness or indifference. One evening, Pasquale Dura, an intermittently employed farm laborer with seven children, came home with a radio for which he had promised to pay eight dollars a month. At first his wife was furious and demanded that he take it back at once. Then he explained that, although he could go to the public square for amusement, she and the children had to be always at home; it would be good, he said, for them to have one thing that would give them pleasure—one thing to relieve *la misèria.* In fact, he went on, it was not fair to the children that they should grow up with nothing at all. Who knows? Perhaps they might learn something from the radio. When she heard the explanation, his wife was touched. The Duras kept the radio and it at once became the active agent of further change. "I was in mourning," Signora Dura explained later, "but when we decided to keep the radio, of course I took the

1 Prato was not in military service and he has only once seen a big city. No doubt Vitello's military experience accounts in part for his more sophisticated standards of consumption. But it would be a mistake to suppose that war-time travel accounts in general for the changes that are underway in Montegrano. Some villagers saw more of the world than did Vitello and were utterly unaffected by what they saw. Moreover, some very important changes were underway before the war: peasants had begun to practice birth control, for example, at least a decade before the war. Perhaps the decisive difference between Vitello and Prato is not in travel experience but in the fact that Vitello (although the objective circumstances of his early life, including schooling, were not much different from Prato's) has always thought of himself as an artisan and a townsman rather than as a peasant. There are, however, new-style consumers who cannot make the slightest claim to being anything but peasants.

2 The Vitello family's expenses for the year [show that] Vitello went deeply into debt. It was obvious that the next year he would have to earn more or spend less.

mourning off. After all, you don't have a radio going in the house and wear mourning at the same time.''

When the peasant speaks of *la misèria,* he refers first to his hard physical labor, to his patched rags, and to the bread that is often all he has to eat. Cruel as it is, however, his poverty does not entirely account for his chronic melancholy. Many peasants are idle a good part of the time because there is no work for them to do. Those who have a little land trudge up and down the mountainside driving a pig to pasture or gathering firewood, but this is not exhausting labor. Much of the peasant's incessant going and coming is nothing but a way of passing time. ''Our house is so small and crowded that we couldn't stand each other if we were cooped up in it all the time,'' an old woman explained when asked why she and her crippled husband struggled through the summer heat to a barren garden patch at the foot of the mountain. Winter temperatures are seldom below freezing, and although many people are extremely uncomfortable for lack of clothing, no one freezes or suffers serious injury. Many are ill from dietary deficiencies, but no one starves to death and few are painfully hungry more than now and then.

In part the peasant's melancholy is caused by worry. Having no savings, he must always dread what is likely to happen. What for others are misfortunes are for him calamities. When their hog strangled on its tether, a laborer and his wife were desolate. The woman tore her hair and beat her head against a wall while the husband sat mute and stricken in a corner. The loss of the hog meant they would have no meat that winter, no grease to spread on bread, nothing to sell for cash to pay taxes, and no possibility of acquiring a pig the next spring. Such blows may fall at any time. Fields may be washed away in a flood. Hail may beat down the wheat. Illness may strike. To be a peasant is to stand helpless before these possibilities.

But neither his present hunger nor his anticipation of worse to come fully accounts for the peasant's deep dissatisfaction. There are primitive societies in which the level of biological well-being is even lower, but in which people are not chronically unhappy. What makes the difference between a low level of living and *la misèria* comes from culture. Unlike the primitive, the peasant feels himself part of a larger society which he is ''in'' but not altogether ''of.'' He lives in a culture in which it is very important to be admired, and he sees that by its standards he cannot be admired in the least; by these standards he and everything about him are contemptible or ridiculous. Knowing this, he is filled with loathing for his lot and with anger for the fates which assigned him to it.

''Getting ahead'' and ''making a good figure'' are two of the central themes of the peasant's existence. But he sees that no matter how hard he works he can never get ahead. Other people can use their labor to advantage, but not he. If he has a bit of land, he may conceal the waste of his time from others and perhaps even from himself by some monumental labor—terracing a hillside with soil carried on his back from the valley, for example. He knows, however, that in the end he will be no better off than before.

The knowledge that no matter how hard he struggles he will remain behind (*indietro* ) is galling. Prato, for example, can never save enough to get his daughter properly married. In his eyes it is the impossibility of improving his position which distinguishes the peasant from others. "The peasant," he said, "always keeps his place; others have the possibility of improving themselves." In only two of 320 stories told by 16 Montegrano peasants who were given Thematic Apperception Tests[3] did a family prosper by thrift or enterprise, and even in these cases the success was not great enough to raise it out of the peasant class. In the TAT stories, dramatic success came only as a gift of fortune: a rich gentleman gave a poor boy a violin, a rich gentlewoman adopted an abandoned child, and so on.

By the standards of the larger society, the peasant's work, food, and clothing all symbolize his degradation. It is on this account, as much as for biological reasons, that he finds them unsatisfying and even hateful. Southern Italians attach great importance to being mannerly (*civile*); the peasant feels that he is the very opposite: association with earth and animals, he thinks, has made him dirty and animal-like. "We poor peasants," one said, "work from morning until night always touching the earth and always covered with mud." Prato's jacket keeps him reasonably warm, but it marks him as one to whom no respect is due. When he was asked his impressions of a big city, he spoke of the way people dressed. "In the city," he said, "everyone dresses the same and you cannot tell whether a man is a peasant or not."

Peasants often complain that they have no recreation, and they speak as if this were as much of a hardship as hard work or hunger. Taken at its face value, this complaint is ridiculous. Except at the busy times of planting and harvesting, there is nothing to prevent the peasants from playing as much as they like. What is to stop them from dancing and singing? Or from playing cards? Or telling stories? What the peasant lacks is not opportunity for recreation, but opportunity for those particular kinds of recreation—having coffee in the bar in the public square, for example—which are *civile* and which would therefore identify them as persons entitled to respect and admiration.

*La misèria,* it seems safe to conclude, arises as much or more from social as from biological deprivations. This being the case, there is no reason to expect

3 The Thematic Apperception Test is a method widely used by the psychologist to reveal the dominant emotions, sentiments, and conflicts of a personality. The subject is shown a series of 20 pictures and asked to make up stories about them on the spur of the moment. The pictures are of varying degrees of ambiguity (one is actually a blank card). The subject interprets them in ways which consciously and unconsciously shed light on his sentiments, values, wants, and preoccupations. Psychologists can infer from clues in the stories some important aspects of the storyteller's personality. Here, however, the TAT has been used mainly for what it may tell about ethos rather than personality. The pictures used were prepared by Dr. Henry A. Murray of the Harvard Psychological Clinic.

that a moderate increase in income (if by some miracle that could be brought about) would make the atmosphere of the village less heavy with melancholy. On the contrary, unless there were accompanying changes in social structure and culture, increasing incomes would probably bring with them increasing discontent.[4]

4 An instructive contrast may be drawn between Montegrano and the Spanish village vividly described by J. A. Pitt-Rivers in *The People of the Sierra,* Weidenfeld and Nicolson, London, 1954. The Andalusian village seems to be about as poor as Montegrano, but its mood is not melancholy. This difference is perhaps both cause and effect of other differences: the Andalusian peasant identifies strongly with his village, his kinship and friendship ties are numerous and significant, and he does not feel humiliated by his social status. Boasting and vanity are striking features of Andalusian (but not of Montegrano) culture; perhaps these are compensatory devices by which the Spaniard protects his ego from total destruction.

—*MERLE FAINSOD*

# *CONTROLS AND TENSIONS IN SOVIET AGRICULTURE*

The peasantry, perhaps more than any other element in transitional societies, tends to be distrustful of change. The world of the peasant is bounded by a profound attachment to the land. When he is landless or has only dwarf holdings, his revolutionary aspirations take the form of a hunger for land. When he is established on his own property, he obstinately resists being swept into the anonymity of the collective. Of all the major revolutionary transformations of the Soviet period, none was more difficult to effect than the collectivization of agriculture. Once achieved, the persistent efforts of the peasantry to evade its discipline presented the regime with problems of control and adjustment which have still to be satisfactorily resolved.

In its inception the Communist attitude toward the peasantry represented a curious combination of dependence and hostility. The dependence came from the necessity of appealing to the peasants' land-hunger in order to win and consolidate power in an overwhelmingly agrarian country. The hostility and distrust carried over as an ineluctable legacy from Marx, deriving from the conviction that the petty-bourgeois aspirations of the peasantry made it a natural enemy of any form of collectivism. In Lenin's words, "Small-scale production gives birth to capitalism and the bourgeoisie constantly, daily, hourly, with elemental force, and in vast proportions.

The strange amalgam of hostility and dependence is reflected in Soviet agricultural policy. When the regime feels powerful enough to disregard peasant sentiment, opposition is brushed aside, and the Communist leadership ruthlessly imposes its will on the peasants. When it operates under the necessity of wooing peasant support or holding out greater incentives to stimulate output, concessions to the peasantry are forthcoming. Although the pendulum of policy has swung back and forth with the regime's changing assessment of its own position and needs, its ideological commitment is firmly to collectivism. In the words of the 1961 Party program, "The economic flowering of the collective-farm system creates the conditions for gradually bringing closer together collective-farm ownership and public ownership and in the long run for their merging in a single communist ownership."

## *THE DEVELOPMENT OF SOVIET AGRICULTURAL POLICY*

The course of development of Soviet agricultural policy illustrates this tendency. The peasant revolution of 1917–18, which involved the expropriation of the landlords' estates and their division among independent peasant households, was fully sanctioned by early Soviet legislation. But this was primarily a tactical expedient. As Lenin observed in 1919, "In October 1917 we seized power *together with the peasantry as a whole.* This was a bourgeois revolution, inasmuch as the class war in the rural districts had not yet developed . . . the real proletarian revolution in the rural districts began only in the summer of 1918." In carrying on this struggle, the major enemy was identified as the kulak, or rich peasant, while the major support on which the Bolsheviks relied was the so-called Committees of Poor Peasants. The middle peasants were treated as a vacillating force whom the Bolsheviks could not afford to alienate. Lenin frequently urged his followers to refrain from coercion in dealing with them.

In practice, the pressures of the Civil War drove Soviet authorities to seize grain wherever they could lay hands on it. Little distinction was made among different social strata of the peasantry in carrying out the requisition policy. The response of the peasants to this type of confiscation was what might be expected. Peasants reduced their plantings to meet only their own consumption needs, did their utmost to conceal their reserves from the requisitioning authorities, and occasionally responded to seizures by violent attacks on the food collectors. The catastrophic decline in production caused severe food shortages in the cities as well as in many rural areas. Grumbling mounted as food became increasingly scarce, and the Bolsheviks stood in danger of completely alienating the countryside. The Kronstadt revolt in March 1921 and the peasant rising in Tambov and other provinces in the winter of 1920–21 marked the height of the crisis. Even though the Bolsheviks ruthlessly punished the participants in these disorders, they also concluded that a change of policy was imperative.

The New Economic Policy, which was introduced in 1921 and lasted until 1927–28, marked a reversion to the policy of concessions to the peasantry. A tax in kind replaced compulsory requisitioning, and peasants were free to dispose of their surpluses after satisfying their fixed obligation to the state. Although the title to land remained in state hands, the tenure of the peasant in the land was guaranteed by law. Peasants were permitted considerable freedom in leasing additional land and employing hired labor, practices which had been prohibited under War Communism. The peasant was given an incentive to produce, and a considerable revival in agricultural output soon followed. Peasant home consumption increased substantially, and a general improvement in the living standard of the countryside was visible . . .

[thereafter] . . . The policy of concessions to the peasantry was terminated, and a new era of open warfare loomed.

The first victims were the kulaks, the more prosperous peasants on whom the regime had to depend heavily during the NEP to provide surpluses for urban consumption. The efforts of the kulaks to withhold grain from the government because of their dissatisfaction with the low prices offered by the state were met with what Stalin described as "emergency measures . . . methods of public coercion." In plain language, force was employed to seize the kulaks' stores. As the kulaks fought back, the regime intensified its offensive. In 1929 it launched the policy of eliminating the kulaks as a class. Under the banner of this slogan, approximately a million peasant families were deprived of their farms and property and sent into exile or forced labor.

In order to replace and expand the grain surpluses which the kulaks had produced and to avoid the difficulties which had attended compulsory requisitioning under War Communism, the regime turned confidently to collectivization and mechanization. Soviet agriculture was to be reorganized around two types of large-scale production units, the *sovkhoz,* or state farm, and the *kolkhoz,* or collective farm. Initially, great hopes were placed in the sovkhozes to provide a quick substitute for the kulak output. The sovkhozes were visualized as great grain factories which would be completely mechanized with tractors and combines, which would be operated by skilled agricultural technicians and workers, and which would serve the peasants as socialist models of large-scale farming and advanced technique. Beginning in 1928 a number of huge new state farms were organized on free land in the southeastern, eastern, and southern regions of the USSR. Difficulties quickly developed. The land allotted to the grain sovkhozes was usually semiarid, full of weeds, and sparsely settled. Crop failures were common because of drought. The soil required intensive cultivation and weeding, but seasonal labor to perform these operations was difficult to obtain and was not particularly efficient. Combines and tractors were not effectively utilized. Skilled operators and repair facilities were lacking. Combines became clogged with weeds and were put out of commission. Tractors broke down and could not be mended. Because of the vast expanse of the sovkhozes, supervision was difficult in the best of circumstances, and inexperienced managers had great difficulty in providing the necessary skillful leadership. The grandiose expectations which were centered on the sovkhozes met bitter disappointment. At the Seventeenth Party Congress in 1934 Stalin openly acknowledged the "discrepancy" between "the enormous sums the state has invested in the state farms with the actual results they have achieved to date." The decision was made to subdivide the large farms into smaller, more manageable units, and a halt was called on their expansion. For the rest of Stalin's reign, the state farms receded in importance, and it remained for Khrushchev to provide a new impetus for their expansion.

The original plan for the establishment of kolkhozes contemplated a relatively slow tempo of development. By 1932 the crop area included in collective farms was expected to embrace about 36 million acres, compared with 298 million acres to remain in individual holdings. This relatively modest objective was apparently dictated by the shortage of mechanical power. Until tractors and combines could be provided in large numbers, there appeared to be little advantage in rushing ahead with wholesale collectivization. Meanwhile, the available tractors, combines, and other farm machinery were pooled in the MTS or machine-tractor stations, which were designed to serve the needs of a group of neighboring collective farms and to make possible maximum utilization of equipment.

## *THE DRIVE FOR COLLECTIVIZATION*

Toward the end of 1929 the policy of gradual collectivization was suddenly reversed. In a series of speeches and decrees, Stalin gave the signal for a rapid acceleration of the collectivization program. It was no longer necessary, he claimed, to wait until tractors and combines were produced in large quantities. "A tremendous expansion of the crop area" could be achieved simply by merging individual holdings and by tilling waste land, field boundaries, and virgin soil. The land of the kulaks would be absorbed into the new collective farms, and this additional "sweetening" would serve as an extra inducement to make the poor and middle peasants join. . . .

The collectivization crisis of the early thirties exacted a terrible price. The liquidation of the kulaks involved the uprooting and exile of millions of peasants and robbed the countryside of its most efficient and enterprising element. The slaughter of livestock and draft animals inflicted a wound on the Soviet economy from which it took nearly a decade to recover. The disorganization of work in the new collective farms contributed to the disastrous harvests of 1931 and 1932. Despite the drastic decline in crop yields, the authorities were ruthless in enforcing their demands on the countryside, and near-famine conditions prevailed in many rural areas. Motivated by an overriding compulsion to feed the rapidly growing industrial centers and to provide supplies for export, the regime "contracted" with the kolkhozes to obtain grain and other items in amounts determined exclusively by the regime's needs and quite unrelated to the problem of keeping the members of the kolkhozes alive. An unknown number of peasants, variously estimated at from one to several million, died of starvation in these hungry years. The "contracts," by which obligatory deliveries to the state were enforced, were in effect a revival of the compulsory requisitions of War Communism. Although the substitution of a relatively small number of collective farms for millions of peasant households greatly facilitated the state's food collection activities, the large-scale expropriations of the early thirties offered the collective farmers little impetus to produce. The regime again found itself faced with the problem of fashioning incentives to stimulate output. . . .

Though the attitude of the peasants toward the collective farms remained largely negative, from the point of view of the regime collectivization marked a triumphant step forward. As an accompaniment of collectivization and mechanization, a substantial migration of rural labor to the new industrial centers was achieved without impairing the output of the countryside. Even more important, collectivization, after overcoming its initial difficulties, provided a greatly improved system for ensuring the urban food supply. The collective farms were an infinitely more efficient food-gathering device than the millions of small farms which they replaced. Instead of trying to collect taxes in kind from twenty-five million peasant households, each with its developed techniques of evasion, the regime could now largely limit its procurement activities to a quarter of a million collective-farm units. From the administrative point of view, this represented a vast improvement and simplification. Moreover, evasion was rendered difficult by the intimate participation of machine-tractor stations in the harvesting of crops of many collective farms. The MTS themselves functioned as procurement agencies, since they collected fees in kind for their services, while they also operated as an unparalleled local intelligence service to check on the performance records of the collective farms they served. The dimensions of state procurement steadily mounted.

As the Soviet authorities consolidated their ascendancy in the countryside, they intensified their demands on the collective farmers. In 1939 a new campaign was launched to tighten control of the collective farms. Investigation revealed that more than two and a half million hectares of land had been unlawfully diverted from the collective farms to private garden plots and that many so-called collective farmers had only a nominal attachment to their kolkhozes and spent most of their time on their own gardens. The joint Party and governmental resolution of May 27, 1939, "On Measures toward Safeguarding the Collectivized Land from Being Squandered," was designed to put an end to these abuses. A survey to check the size of all garden plots was ordered, so that land stolen from the collective farms could be reclaimed. Severe penalties were provided for those farmers found in unlawful possession of such land. A minimum number of workdays was prescribed for each member of the kolkhoz regardless of sex. The USSR was divided into three zones, and the minimum for each was fixed respectively at 100, 80, and 60 labor days. Nonfulfillment of these minima was to be punished by explusion from the kolkhoz and loss of garden plots. A joint Party and governmental resolution of April 13, 1942, subsequently raised the minima to 150, 120, and 100 labor days and provided a specific allocation of labor days which had to be worked during different seasons of the year.

Meanwhile, efforts were also made to stiffen work discipline and to provide additional inducements for increased productivity. On August 1, 1940, Soviet agricultural authorities were ordered "to put an end to the intolerable practice that in some kolkhozy, MTS, and sovkhozy, kolkhozniki and the workers of the MTS and sovkhozy, instead of starting work at 5–6 o'clock, report for harvesting work at 8–9 o'clock and stop work in the field before sundown." A government degree of December 31, 1940, first introduced in the Ukraine and later extended to other areas, provided a premium system to encourage output in excess of planned goals. Under this system, kolkhoz brigades exceeding their plan were to be rewarded with a certain proportion of the surplus they produced. This was to be made available either in kind or in the form of a cash equivalent.

At the same time, the regime made further demands of the peasantry. In 1940 the basis for computing crop deliveries to the government was shifted from the actual acreage planted to the amount of tillable land in possession of the kolkhozes. This change in the method of assessing compulsory deliveries was accompanied by a substantial boost in the amounts which the collective farms were required to yield to the state. While this measure was probably influenced by the pressure to accumulate reserves against the contingency of war, its effect on the collective farmers was onerous and sharpened their resentment of the burdens which the state imposed on them.

## *WORLD WAR II AND POSTWAR DEVELOPMENTS*

The impact of World War II on Soviet agricultural production was critical. In the first years of the war the Nazis occupied a large part of the richest and most productive land in the Soviet Union. The regime attempted to compensate for this loss by substantially increasing the production of foodstuffs in Siberia and Central Asia, but despite these efforts and the encouragement of urban workers to cultivate vegetable plots, food shortages were frequently desperate. Though the basic needs of the armed forces and essential industry were met by drawing on reserves and Lend-Lease aid, malnutrition accounted for many civilian casualties, and in besieged localities such as Leningrad there were few families whom starvation passed by.

Despite the disorganization of war, the kolkhoz remained the basic form around which Soviet agriculture was organized. In areas occupied by the Nazis, many kolkhozniks hopefully looked forward to the dissolution of the collective-farm system. These expectations were disappointed when the Nazis determined to retain the great majority of the kolkhozes because of their convenience as food-gathering devices. Disappointment was succeeded by complete disillusionment as the Nazi requisitions became increasingly burdensome and many villages began to experience the full brunt of Nazi atrocities. The patriotic sentiment aroused by Nazi brutality led many of the kolkhozniks in occupied areas to identify their fate with the survival of Soviet power. While the Soviet authorities continued to be regarded as oppressors, they were, as some of the kolkhozniks are reported to have remarked, "at least ours." In nonoccupied areas, similar patriotic impulses narrowed the gap between collective farmers and the regime. As the armed forces drained the kolkhozes of manpower, the women, old men, and children who replaced them worked all the harder because they were bound to the front by the knowledge that the fate of husbands, brothers, and sons depended on them. The reservoir of patriotism on which the regime was able to draw buttressed the wartime effectiveness of the kolkhoz as a procurement mechanism.

Another effect of the war, however, was to weaken the fabric of kolkhoz controls. In areas abandoned by the Nazis, the kolkhozes usually had been stripped of their cattle and draft animals, and only the most primitive farm implements remained. Collective farmers utilized the general confusion and disorder to enlarge their garden plots at the expense of the kolkhoz. In the reoccupied areas, farms usually had to be reorganized from the ground up, and the shortage of supervisory personnel, draft animals, and mechanical power heightened tendencies toward individual self-help. In nonoccupied as well as reoccupied areas, collective farmers were under a powerful incentive to pour maximum effort into their own garden plots rather than into the communal enterprises of the kolkhoz. With food scarce, prices skyrocketed on the free market. Any surpluses from the garden plots could be readily bartered at advantageous rates for the possessions of the hungry population of the towns. Collective farmers who were in a position to do so used the war emergency to accumulate stores of goods as well as substantial hoards of currency. Within the framework of the collective-farm system, a lively revival of individual enterprise found spontaneous expression. While the war still raged, little was done to curb these tendencies. Indeed, rumors were rife in the villages (and were apparently tolerated by the regime) that the end of the war would see a fundamental revision of the kolkhoz system and a new charter of freedom for the peasantry.

These sanguine expectations met a sharp rebuff. The history of Soviet agricultural policy in the post-World War II period is essentially a record of tightening control over all kolkhoz activities. . . .

The postwar drive to re-establish effective control over the kolkhozes was . . . accompanied by a campaign to replace the *zveno* (literally, link) or small team by the much larger brigade as the basic unit of agricultural production. During the early and middle thirties, the brigade had been the officially approved form of organizing kolkhoz labor. Toward the end of the thirties, there was an increasing tendency to break down the brigades into *zvenya* or teams of a dozen or so workers who concentrated on working a small plot from the sowing through the harvest. Originally, the zveno was used in connection with technical crops such as sugar beets and cotton where a great deal of hand labor was required, but in the late thirties it spread rapidly to grain farming. At the Eighteenth Congress of the Party in 1939, Andreyev, the agricultural spokesman of the Politburo, strongly endorsed the zveno system. He argued that "the collective farmers working in large brigades are not held personally responsible for the quantity and quality of their work . . . the more the work on the collective farm is individualized, that is, performed by teams of separate collective farmers, and the greater the material encouragement of their labor, the more efficient it will be as regards crop yields and stock raising." During the war and immediate postwar years, the zveno system was widely heralded as the most efficient method of organizing kolkhoz labor. The loss of tractor power during the war and the consequent necessity of relying on hand labor contributed to strengthening the position of the zveno system.

Suddenly, in one of these sweeping reversals in which Soviet history is embarrassingly rich, the zveno system was repudiated. On February 19, 1950, an unsigned article in *Pravda,* entitled "Against Distortions in Collective Farm Labor Organization," explicitly condemned Andreyev for his advocacy of the zveno system, criticized the use of the zveno in grain farming as obstructing the effective use of tractors, combines, and other machinery, reasserted the importance of the brigade as the basic form of organizing kolkhoz labor, and indicated that the zveno system would be retained only temporarily for the cultivation of sugar beets, vegetables, and certain other intensive crops "inasmuch as production of these crops is not yet adequately mechanized." The appearance of this authoritative pronouncement was followed on February 25 by the publication of a letter in *Pravda* by Andreyev in which he confessed his errors and promised "to rectify them in deeds."

This unusual spectacle of the use of a Politburo member as a whipping boy to signal a change in policy pointed to the importance of the issues at stake in this seemingly minor conflict over methods of organizing kolkhoz labor. Behind the attack on the zveno system, as Lazar Volin has indicated, was the apprehension "that the small zveno unit might eventually supplant not only the brigade but also the kolkhoz itself." As the *Pravda* article put it, "Substitution of teams for brigades would signify the splitting of a single large-scale collective unit into small cells, scattering the energies and reserves of the collective farm, and a return from advanced technology and collective forms of labor to individual, manual labor. It would mean shaking the very foundations of large-scale collective socialist agriculture." The fear of the disintegrative potentialities of the zveno system was reinforced by the difficult control problem which it presented. The zveno system required a much greater number of politically reliable leaders than the brigades, and such leadership was in short supply in rural areas. From the point of view of the regime, the kolkhoz could be more effectively controlled through a few trusted brigadiers who were amenable to Party influence than through a large number of zveno leaders whose interests were identified with the rank-and-file collective farmers.

The replacement of the zveno by the brigade was closely linked with the kolkhoz merger movement which was launched almost simultaneously. On March 8, 1950, Krushchev, who had succeeded Andreyev as the Politburo's agricultural spokesman, used the columns of *Pravda* to signal the opening of the new campaign. In calling for the amalgamation of contiguous small kolkhozes into larger units, Krushchev listed a number of benefits which the regime hoped to attain. The mergers, he claimed, would facilitate mechanization and the adoption of the most advanced agricultural practices. They would yield increased production and higher income for collective farmers, greater farm surpluses, and, presumably, larger deliveries to the state. They would also make possible a substantial reduction in administrative expenditures and the selection of outstanding managers and agricultural specialists to direct the new kolkhozes.

One of the paramount objectives of the merger campaign—left unstated by Krushchev—was the regime's desire to tighten its control over the collective-farm structure. The merger of small collective farms resulted in a substantial increase in the number of kolkhozes with primary Party organizations and an intensification of Party influence. The reduction in the number of collective-farm chairmen meant that those who were retained were likely to be the most politically reliable, as well as technically proficient. The regime appeared headed toward the consolidation of a managerial corps in the kolkhozes which would be increasingly isolated from the rank-and-file farmers and which would function as an effective state instrument to extract maximum output from them. . . .

## *THE VIRGIN-LANDS PROGRAM*

In the first year after Stalin's death, the new Soviet agricultural program centered on livestock products, potatoes, and vegetables as critical deficiency sectors. Relatively little attention was devoted to grain, since it was assumed that the problem was well in hand. This turned out to be an incorrect assumption.

The sharp drop in the 1953 grain harvest as compared with the preceding year dramatized the failure of grain production to keep up with the demands of the growing urban population. The grain problem now came into the forefront, and in a speech to the Central Committee on February 23, 1954, Khrushchev unfolded a new grandiose program to open up and cultivate so-called virgin lands in Kazakhstan, Siberia, the northern Caucasus, the Volga, and the eastern regions. The program as originally announced called for 32 million new acres; by 1960 it had been expanded to more than 101 million acres, equal to more than one third of all the grain area in Russia in 1953 and considerably in excess of the total wheat area cultivated in the United States. The new lands were seeded mostly with spring wheat and cultivated largely by tractor power. The organizational form chosen to achieve this vast expansion of acreage was the state farm rather than the collective farm.

More than 150,000 workers and technicians—predominantly young people—were initially mobilized to settle on the new lands. Special financial inducements were held out to encourage migration, but these were also reinforced by appeals to sacrifice and by pressure through Party and Komsomol channels to accept virgin-land assignments. The campaign was conducted with great fanfare and excitement. Tens of thousands of students from all corners of the Soviet Union were shipped to the virgin lands to help in the harvests, and the heroic exploits of the new pioneers were widely celebrated and extolled. But a great many of those who volunteered or who were mobilized for service in the virgin lands did not remain there. "In 1960 and 1961," according to *Pravda,* "103,650 tractor drivers and combine operators were trained [in Kazakhstan] and 53,744 equipment operators arrived from other parts of the country to take up permanent jobs. During that same period, more than 180,000 equipment operators left the state and collective farms." Harsh living conditions and lack of accommodations and amenities led them to abandon their posts on the new frontier. The regime faced the challenge of creating sufficiently attractive conditions in the virgin lands to hold its labor force as the initial wave of enthusiasm and self-sacrifice dimmed. . . .

Thus far, the gamble on the new lands appears to have paid off, despite the bad record in Kazakhstan over the 1959–1961 period. The large additional acreage brought into cultivation has not only operated to lift the average level of total output, but has also served to diversify the risks of Soviet agriculture. To be sure, there remains a real danger that careless plowing up of the dry steppes and a succession of dry years may create dust-bowl conditions and lead to a series of disastrous crop failures. But Krushchev himself has been inclined to minimize the danger. "Some comrades might ask," he reminded the Twentieth Party Congress, "whether we are doing right in developing virgin lands in areas subject to drought." He answered in the affirmative:

> If in five years we have only two good, one average, and two poor crops, it is possible with the relatively small outlays needed for grain cultivation in these conditions to farm at a big profit and produce grain at low cost.

> The results of our work in virgin-land development make it possible to draw the indisputable conclusion that the line of the Party is correct. This policy assures a substantial increase in grain production within the shortest possible time and with the least outlay of labor and resources.

He should perhaps have added that both human and capital investments in the new land program will have to mount substantially if the fertility of the soil is to be preserved and its future productivity safeguarded. . . .

## *THE FUTURE OF SOVIET AGRICULTURE*

Despite the many shortcomings in the organization of Soviet agriculture and the difficulties which have been encountered in meeting production and procurement goals, it would be a mistake to assume that Soviet agricultural output is destined to stagnate. The scientific and technical potentialities for increasing yields exist, and over time they will probably be exploited to the full.

In many respects, agriculture represents the least developed sector of the Soviet economy. As Khrushchev pointed out in his Central Committee report of March 5, 1962, even on the state farms where mechanization is most advanced, "not more than one fourth of the cows are milked mechanically . . . a large part of the corn for grain is harvested by hand . . . the harvesting of sugar beets and potatoes is not mechanized, and . . . there is extremely little equipment for loading and unloading work." The output of agricultural equipment, mineral fertilizers, and herbicides still falls far short of current needs.

The future growth of Soviet agriculture is likely to depend less on any tinkering with organizational controls than it is on the willingness of the Soviet leadership to improve its incentive system and to make large additional capital investments in agriculture. If resources can be mobilized to increase the stock of agricultural machinery, fertilizer, pesticides, and improved seed varieties, to extend irrigation facilities, to train skilled agricultural personnel, to raise the income of agricultural workers, and to provide them with the equivalent of urban amenities, it can safely be predicted that agricultural output will rise substantially. Until such measures are taken, Soviet agriculture will remain a problem area.

# CHAPTER 8

# WOMEN IN AN URBAN SOCIETY

The twentieth century has witnessed remarkable technological improvements and also dreadfully destructive wars. Both have been largely the work of men, and the exploits of industrial and military "heroes" are the main subject of most history textbooks. Yet the more silent half of the population has been all the while emerging to establish the right of women to speak, to vote, and to participate in a changing European society. This gradual but inexorable emancipation has taken a variety of forms, of which the following readings give a fair indication.

*Robert Graves* and *Alan Hodge* examine urban life in Britain during the two interwar decades. They describe one of the first instances of a mass-consumer society, in which taste and fashion have been significantly altered from times past. Everywhere we look—at buildings, shops, houses, or streets—the character of public life has changed. No sight is more symptomatic than the appearance of women. The way they dress, what they buy, and how they decorate their homes have all been instrumental in defining the modern age.

*Patricia Branca* admits that evidence for a study of working-class women is scant, but she argues that they cannot be understood simply as imitators of their social betters. More women have entered the industrial-labor force in this century than ever before. Courtship patterns have changed accordingly, and the age of marriage has steadily dropped. New freedom has brought new problems, among them an apparent increase in premarital sex, illegitimate births, and abortions. At the same time, the institution of marriage has been slow to evolve, and traits of male dominance have remained obvious among the laboring class. Just as in earlier times, material deprivation renders homemaking and child rearing less than an unmitigated joy. Motherhood and modernity do not always mix.

*Claudia Koonz* tells a particular story about the fate of women in Nazi Germany. Before the Nazi seizure of power in 1933, German women had attained at least a formal equality under the Weimar Republic: they joined the labor force in large numbers, they exercised their newly acquired right of suffrage, they began to enter university and political life. But there were powerful undercurrents of opposition to such advances, and Nazism was one conspicuous example. Pro-Nazi women were placed in the paradoxical position of seeking equality through a party that basically had no interest in feminism. Not surprisingly, then, the Nazi period proved to be a clear retrogression for German women, who found themselves glorified but oppressed.

*Edgar Morin* ends this chapter on a less depressing note. His account of marriage and family life in contemporary French towns should strike us as more typical of our time. Current European society, like its American counterpart, has unquestionably opened new possibilities to females since the Second World War. We are all acquainted with the young women that Morin depicts, and we now have reason to believe that their emancipation will be more than a myth.

It is all too convenient to regard a strident feminism with cynicism or contempt. Some women themselves are so inclined, and historically they have not always been their own best boosters. But an alteration of sexist attitudes has demonstrably been occurring in the twentieth century, and a transformation in popular conceptions of the proper social role for women has become both a characteristic symptom and a criterion of modernity. Woman's emancipation is certain to be among the most enduring achievements of our time.

—ROBERT GRAVES AND ALAN HODGE

# CHANGING STYLES

By 1923 building materials had cheapened and the government subsidies granted to urban and rural District Councils were tempting enough to set the housing boom gradually in motion. This boom, which kept a great many trades occupied and benefited the workers themselves by giving them comfortable homes to live in, took another five years to get well under way; but it was a great steadying factor in national life. Builders of houses had to conform to certain specifications of size, airiness and convenience before they could earn the subsidy, and the sites had to be approved by the district surveyor; the result was a great improvement in the general health of the nation, a remarkable decrease in infant mortality, and the elevation of slum-dwellers to lower-middle-class rank by virtue of such amenities as gas, electricity, bathroom, and water-closet. The Conservative papers joked at first about the uses to which these unfamiliar baths would be put, but on the whole the filthy habits of the slums were left behind with the foul air and bugs and the communal earth-closet. Ruffianism in crowded trains and buses, at places of public entertainment, and in public houses, grew most exceptional and if ever it occurred was likely to be put down at once by some strong-armed champion of popular opinion—usually an ex-serviceman. For the habits of discipline and cleanliness learned in the Army and Navy had contributed largely to this improvement in public behavior. Another main cause was a new-found pride of the younger women, who wished everything to conform in cleanliness and respectability to their new domestic standards. . . .

The most remarkable outward change of the Twenties was in the looks of women in the towns. The prematurely aged wife was coming to be the exception rather than the rule. Children were fewer and healthier and gave less trouble; labor-saving devices were introduced, especially for washing, cleaning, and cooking—the introduction of stainless plate and cutlery saved an appreciable amount of time daily and this was only one of a hundred such innovations. Provisioning also had become very much easier. The advertising of branded goods was simplifying shopping problems. Housewives came to count on certain brands of goods, which advertisers never allowed them to forget. The manufacturers' motto was: "Swear not by the moon, the inconstant moon, but swear by constant advertising." They made things very easy for the housewives by selling their foods in the nearest possible stage to table-readiness: the complicated processes of making custard, caramel, blanc-mange, jelly, and other puddings and sweets, were reduced to a single short operation by the use of prepared powders. Porridge had once been the almost universal middle-class breakfast food. It now no longer took twenty minutes to cook, Quick Quaker Oats reducing the time to two; but even so, cereals in the American style, eaten with milk, began to challenge porridge and bacon and eggs in prosperous homes, and the bread and margarine eaten by the poor. At first the only choice was Force and Grape-Nuts; but soon there was a bewildering variety of different "flakes"; and grains of rice, wheat and barley "puffed" by being fired at high velocity from a sort of airgun. Bottled and tinned goods grew more and more various and plentiful. When the war ended the only choice was soup, salmon, corned beef, California fruits, and potted meat; but by the Thirties almost every kind of domestic and foreign fruit, meat, game, fish, vegetable could be bought, even in country groceries. Foodstuffs that needed no tin-opener were also gradually standardized: eggs, milk, and butter were graded and guaranteed and greengrocers began selling branded oranges and bananas. Housewives could send or ring up for goods without inspecting them, more and more shops called daily or weekly for orders and delivered free of charge, as light commercial vans displaced the horse and cart. The fish-van brought fresh fish to the door even in inland towns and villages. The cleanest and neatest shops secured the best custom; flies and wasps disappeared from grocers' counters, finding no open pots of treacle or boxes of sugar to attract them, and the butchers began keeping their carcasses in refrigerators out of sight, not suspended bleeding from hooks in the full glare of the sun. By the Thirties cellophane, a cheap wood-pulp product, was coming into general use for keeping dry groceries and cigarettes fresh and clean, and soon also covered baskets of strawberries, lumps of dates, and even kippers and other cured fish.

Woolworth's stores were the great cheap providers of household utensils and materials. There had been a few "6½d. Bazaars" before the war, but the Woolworth system was altogether new. It worked by small profits and quick returns in a huge variety of classified and displayed cut-price goods; some, such as excellent glass and hardware, were even sold below cost price to attract custom. The *Daily Herald* reported in 1924 that the T.U.C. was reviewing complaints about working conditions in Woolworth's—"the well-known bazaar-owners"—and that this was the more serious because the stores were patronized chiefly by the working class. But the firm never had any difficulty in engaging unskilled sales-girls at a low wage; for the "the local Woolworth's" was increasingly the focus of popular life in most small towns. And the name of Woolworth was a blessed one to the general public; wherever a new branch was opened, the prices of ironmongers, drapers, and household furnishers in the neighborhood would drop twopence in the shilling. The middle class at first affected to despise Woolworth's goods, but they soon caught the working-class habit and would exclaim brightly among themselves: "My dear—guess where I got this amazing object—threepence at Maison Woolworth! I don't know *how* they do it."

Woolworth's, the Building Societies, and the Installment System made it financially possible for people of small means to take over new houses. The installment or "never-never" system was being applied to all major household purchases, such as furniture, sewing-machines, vacuum-cleaners, gas-ovens, wireless sets. A *Punch* illustration showed a young mother, watching her husband writing out the monthly check to pay off the maternity-home debt: "Darling, only one more installment and Baby will be *ours*. . . ."

The great change in women's clothes in the Twenties was mainly due to the development of the artificial silk industry. Rayon (as it was first officially called in 1927) was light, warm and cheap, and took bright colors well. By its use, the weight of clothes that a woman carried was reduced from pounds to ounces and the amount of material for a complete costume from nineteen yards to seven. Underclothes, blouses, dresses, stockings, scarves—all were soon rayon.

Since rayon was not very durable, new clothes were bought more frequently; which shortened the time-lag in fashions between their sale to the well-to-do and their adoption by the poor. It was now at last possible to mistake working girls for titled ladies, if one judged by dress; and since educated speech was a valuable asset in business, and the B.B.C. taught it free, as time went on one could not always judge even by the voice. The American habit of buying cheap mass-produced goods for short use was a novel one to the British: it was gradually extended from clothes to shoes, handbags, and household goods. If the old-fashioned shop assistants still mumbled "I can guarantee this—it will last a lifetime," the modern come-back was "Then for goodness' sake show me something else!"

The general outline of women's dress did not change much in these years, though there was constant variation of trimmings and draperies attached to blouses and skirts; sometimes blouses had square necks instead of pointed ones, and there were fashions in waistcoats and "different" jackets. Each season brought in a "new color," meaning a new name for a hitherto unfashionable shade. The Twenties showed great bravado in names—"Yes, modom, we stock it in all the new shades: Mud, Nigger, Rust, Gunmetal, Old Boots, Dust, and Self."

By 1925 the skirt, after a temporary drop in 1922–3 to just above the ankles, had receded to just below the knees even for women of sixty and seventy, and in 1926 the knee-caps were often free and there was a glint of knickers. Yet bathing-dresses remained modest, with high necks and long sleeves, and after bathing one either wore a wrap or got dressed again. To play tennis without stockings was considered immodest; and as late as 1923 the Underground refused advertisement-space to a French film showing girls wearing backless evening-dresses. In the following year the employers of Birmingham waitresses started a "morality crusade," forbidding their staff to wear short skirts at all.

Short hair did not come into fashion among the well-to-do until 1923, when it was reported that "many men are wearing their hair long and permed at Deauville while women are almost all "shingled," as the Americans call the new, very ugly bobbed and shaved haircut." Newspapers mistook this for a passing fashion only and came out with comments such as "Bobbed Hair and Bobbed Love," "Shingle's Blow to Marriage." But the "bob," "shingle," and "bingle" were succeeded in 1926 by the boyish "Eton crop." Heavy make-up was not yet practiced. In 1922 the first Elizabeth Arden advertisements appeared, but they were only for powder and eye-lash dye.

PATRICIA BRANCA

# WORKING-CLASS WOMEN

Ironically, given the great popularity among social historians for study of the working class, we know very little about the working-class family beyond what the vital statistics tell us. The role of the woman in the working-class family remains a particular mystery until illuminated by sociological research dealing with the last two decades. Even more than her middle-class counterpart she remains, once married, locked inside her home. Lack of material from magazines and manuals compounds the problem of grasping her role and outlook, for literature was rarely directed to working-class women with their lack of funds and general reluctance or inability to read. Perhaps, indeed, she needed less guidance from outside experts anyway. For we are beginning to understand that working-class women made their own family adaptations and may be judged remarkably successful in dealing with change.

The role of the working-class woman in the family certainly underwent significant alteration in the nineteenth century as a result of the forces of modern living. By the end of the century the working-class family seemed to be adopting many aspects of middle-class culture and behaviour patterns, most particularly as it too began to limit family size after 1870–90. However, the working-class family's forging of a modern life style involved far more complexities and

From Patricia Branca, *Women in Europe since 1750* (London: Croom Helm Ltd., 1978), pp. 131–35, 137–40, 143, 150–51, by permission of the publisher.

subtleties than mere imitaton of the middle-class model. Even shared behaviour could result from different causes, and much behaviour was not shared at all, for the role of the working-class woman was and remains substantially different from that of her middle-class sisters. Birth control, a possible case of imitation in that it followed middle-class adoption chronologically and was indeed the subject of intense middle-class propaganda (as reformers saw benefits to the well-being of the poor if there were fewer mouths to feed), was part of a distinctive adaptation to the new forces of urban and industrial life. The physical health of the working-class woman was obviously to benefit from fewer pregnancies, but this does not seem to have been as important in the decision to cut births as it was in the middle-class family since there was little or no effort to improve the woman's pre-natal and child delivery care until much later than the advent of family planning. In fact it seems possible that women in working-class families were not really emotionally prepared for birth control. For many women the decline in children was viewed as a deterioration in their importance in the family. Recent polls indicate that the working class still views numerous children as a sign of family success far more commonly than does the middle class. This is not to downgrade the importance of birth control in the class; by 1900 the rate of decline was as rapid as that of the middle class although, starting later, the working class continued to have larger families. However, the process here was not simply middle-class culture taken with a slight time lag. In the working class, economics was the primary factor in the decision to limit births. The economics of a large family became a definite burden by the late nineteenth century with the extension and strict enforcement of laws limiting child labour and requiring school attendance.

To appreciate the adjustment of the working-class woman we must begin with marriage itself. Greater variety of jobs and steadier employment meant that most working-class girls spent some part of their lives, about ten years on the average, actively earning a living. What impact this work experience had on their marriage is not entirely clear. It enhanced the opportunity for marriage by providing social contacts and some savings that could help start a household, and this opportunity represented a vital goal in the culture of working-class women, mothers and daughters alike. At the same time, working-class girls were getting married earlier in the nineteenth century than in pre-modern times and one to three years earlier than middle-class girls in industrial society itself. In England the mean age at marriage for young women dropped from 27 in pre-modern times, reflecting peasant patterns, to about 24 in the mid-nineteenth century to twenty in the twentieth century. Marriage ages declined more slowly in France as agriculture remained far more dominant, yet there was a drop from between twenty-eight and thirty in the seventeenth and eighteenth centuries to between twenty-five and twenty-seven in the nineteenth century as the working class gained ground.

Along with some economic independence through separate earnings, the new skills and values gained at work might make a girl a more attractive marriage partner. Her work experience might aid her in her lifetime job as household manager. She gained experience handling money, for example, sooner than her middle-class counterpart, and this could give her an advantage in dealing with financial matters in marriage. Those who had worked as servants might acquire housekeeping and childrearing skills.

With increasing urbanisation the basis for many working-class marriages continued to evolve; love relationships steadily replaced purely economic unions as social contacts and economic self-sufficiency increased. Working-class courtship patterns also modernised, becoming shorter and more informal as parental consent became less essential. More important, working-class girls found themselves freer from parental chaperonage than middle-class girls. There was far more mixing of the sexes in these early years. Nightly visits to the pub after work, Saturday night dances or attendance at the music halls, and Sunday afternoon excursions through the park enabled many working-class girls to meet men. No doubt some became victimised in these strange surroundings without family around to provide traditional guidance and protection. The high rates of illegitimacy are only one indicator of the potential problems the young girl encountered during her work years.

For the first half of the nineteenth century premarital sex among the working class remained an accepted aspect of the culture, as it had been developing in the late eighteenth century. We must stress, as against some common impressions, that this culture had rural origins and predated factory experience; a German worker, noting high rates of illegitimacy, said that they hardly rivalled those she had left behind in the countryside. For some, illegitimacy formed part of a pattern of promiscuity that could drive girls to ruin. Factory girls in Rheims in the 1830s often served as prostitutes in their scant spare time, calling this their "fifth quarter of the day."[1] Increasingly, however, premarital sex led to marriage; indeed pregnancy became an accepted way to convince the man of the values of matrimony. And some men wanted to be sure a future wife was fertile, like German automobile workers in the 1890s who said they "didn't want to buy a pig in a poke."[2] A working-class novel described a common pattern in England: a girl courted a co-worker for almost two years, the boy being in "no hurry to marry until he could not honourably delay."[3]

After about 1870, in fact, outright illegitimacy began to stabilise, even fall slightly, as working-class culture took more definite form. It is possible that prebridal pregnancies declined as well; certainly they were now usually followed by marriage, as responsibility was expected by girls and accepted by boys. Some

1 Rene Villerme, *Tableau de l'état moral et physique des ouvriers employés dans les manufactures, de laine, et de soie* (1840).

2 Fritz Schuman, *Auslese und Anpassung der Arbeiterschaft in der Automobil industrie* (1911).

3 Robert Tressell, *The Ragged Trousered Philanthropists* (1914), p. 49. This novel presents an unusual insight into working-class life in England in the late nineteenth century.

believe this change was due to increased use of birth control techniques by the working class,[4] which cut illegitimacy without necessarily changing premarital behaviour or outlook. Others have argued, more persuasively, that there was a changing culture in the working class which frowned upon sexual promiscuity. There may in fact have been some imitation of the middle-class value of the virgin bride. But this was not a middle-class culture overall. Illegitimacy rates, for example, continued to be well above both pre-modern and middle-class levels, which shows that premarital sex was still common. We know also that many working-class women, married or unmarried, had to resort to abortion to achieve what birth control there was; 25 per cent of all working-class wives in one Berlin survey in 1900 had had at least one abortion, often before marriage.[5] Some women thus preserved premarital "purity" only by resort to illicit dangerous practices. At the same time we must give the stabilisation of working-class families its due. Some parental control and a good sense of self-interest caused most working-class girls to avoid sexual promiscuity and premature pregnancy, as the differential between the age of puberty and the age of marriage was long, at least eight to ten years. And personal choice was commonly involved when premarital sex was accepted. It was not just a titillating part of courtship but an accepted means of converting courtship into marriage.

With marriage the working-class woman's experience remained dissimilar to that of the middle class in a number of important respects. The relationship between husband and wife was different, in some ways more traditional than the new middle-class relationship. In the working-class marriage the husband remained the major decision-maker in principle, the wife submissive to his will. There was to be a strict segregation of roles. Undoubtedly the lines were less clear in practice and there was much variation according to individual personalities. Nevertheless there was no pretence within the working class to the new concomitant relationship of the middle-class husband and wife. The concept of sharing in marriage remained rudimentary. We need only a few key examples. The social spheres of the husband and the wife were distinct; the working man's world was a man's world.[6] The husband now went off to work away from the home, but in contrast to middle-class patterns his limited leisure was also spent away from home, with his male companions. Pub visits and soccer games were the male preserve. The wife was expected to socialise with her own set of friends, apart from her husband, except perhaps for a family walk on Sunday afternoon. . . .

4 For a discussion of birth control and the working classes see Shorter, *Modern Family;* and Daniel Scott Smith, "Family Limitation, Sexual Control, and Domestic Feminism in Victorian America," in Mary Hartman and Lois Banner, *Clio's Consciousness Raised* (1974), pp. 119–36.

5 This information was found in Edward Shorter's, "Female Emancipation, Birth Control, and Fertility in European History," in the *American Historical Review* 78 (1973).

6 F. Zweig, *The Worker in an Affluent Society* (1961) discusses the parent-child relationship at some length.

It is not surprising that the task of managing the home was far more difficult for the working-class woman than it was in the middle-class. Material differences were stark, and there were cultural differences too. One wonders why the working-class woman's role in the family never brought her the same prestige (especially in view of her economic support) as the middle-class woman achieved. After all the working-class wife was also home-centred, urged not to work outside. She too served as consumer agent, in the new specialisation of labour that added to the woman's new economic functions. Yet she never found praise because in many ways she was doomed to fail. For the working-class woman, outside forces were such that she was rarely able to maintain any sense of control even in the late nineteenth century. Women and their husbands alike found it difficult to believe that the housekeeping was being done properly. Crowded housing and meagre diets made rational management of domestic chores impossible. The problem was compounded by the fact that there was little precedent in traditional rural society for the domestic skills needed in the new urban centres and we have seen experience hardly improved the situation, particularly as the steadily declining age of marriage plunged more and more ill-prepared adolescents into the responsibility of running a household.

The many complaints about the decline of the art of housekeeping in nineteenth-century England were more easily levelled at the working-class than at the middle-class woman. Whatever hard times came, depression or inflation, she was, indirectly at least, held responsible. A husband, noting that provisions had deteriorated as prices rose after 1900, summed up many a household battle: "I never interfere about anything, because I think it's your part to attend to the house, but it seems to me you don't manage things properly."[7] Such judgements could only lead the housewife to doubt her own worth. With the combination of emotional and material stress, the working-class wife could rarely develop a new sense of self, and without a positive self-image it was difficult for her to challenge old ways, but was bound to fail in her attempt to maintain traditional values in an increasingly modern environment. Thus she created her own vicious circle. We know, for example, that there was growing indignation over infant mortality in nineteenth-century England. By the end of the century working-class women were beginning to make an emotional investment in the child. But even after 1904 half the women in one factory town were judged resigned to a child's death, so long as they could provide a proper funeral. And even the women newly anguished over a child's death, which most would experience at least once, took scant measures to ensure against it. Suspicion of strangers as well as poverty kept women away from doctors even for childbirth. Health problems were the concern of the local herbalist or quack, who was known in the neighbourhood, or in the final analysis of God or fate; there was little positive action to be taken. Whether we are prepared to accept statistics in such emotional matters or not, it strikes us that both groups stood to lose. The

7 Tressell, *The Ragged Trousered Philanthropists,* p. 58.

traditionalists avoided sorrow but failed to gain the emotional support of real attachment to the majority of children who did live, in the urban environment. The cautious innovators failed to go far enough to protect themselves from grief by demanding the medical care which was at last available.

The situation on the Continent was less traumatic than that in England. More working-class families lived outside big cities, the husband commuting to work by rail. France had far fewer massive agglomerations and the French working class cut its birth rate earliest, providing another relief for the wife. But German as well as French housewives were judged to manage better than the English, keeping closer to customary ways. They were less trapped between tradition and novelty, less likely for example to mourn a child's death with new intensity. They were also held to a less rigorous material standard. Differences in eating habits make it easier for the Frenchwoman than for her English counterpart. Meat early became an essential in the working man's diet in England, to be served at least once a day; as this was the most expensive item in the working-class woman's budget this break from the traditional diets pressed household resources. Women were also unskilled in preparing meat meals, which caused waste and, perhaps, the notoriously poor level of English cooking; there were complaints that working-class women either bought pre-cooked meat and served it cold, at needless expense, or squandered it by cooking it too rapidly.[8] Of necessity they had to buy the poorest quality of meat as well. French diets were not as radically changed as the English. The growing emphasis on meat was found only in areas of heavy industry such as mining and metallurgy, and many French workers took a main meal at restaurants. Still, French working-class wives were scarcely able to plan ahead any better than their English sisters, and housekeeping difficulties were common in the class generally. . . .

Added to dreary unrelieved household duties was the burden of motherhood. Again the hand of tradition remained strong here and little new prestige accrued to the working-class woman as mother. Workers were slow to cut their birth rate, long seeing children as economic assets and ignorant of the methods that might best be employed. New male workers often had no knowledge of condoms and some delighted in expressing their masculinity by siring large families. Women's views were ambiguous. Frequent pregnancies were customary and expected, but as children stopped being economic contributors, barred from work by factory laws and school requirements, they added to the problems of budget management. Some women lamented when most of their children lived, expecting the traditional 50 per cent mortality rate to ease their lot. A German wife with six children berated her husband, shouting "Why don't they die?" Yet there were no new methods adopted, no eager receptiveness to innovation, to provide relief through birth control, which reached large

8 [Peter N.] Stearns, "Working-Class Women [in Britain 1890–1914," in Vicinus, *Suffer and Be Still*], p. 104.

segments of the class only after 1890. Even afterwards the average family had two children more than the middle-class model. Furthermore, working-class control methods more commonly involved abortions, condoms or sexual abstinence; there is no sign of sexual pleasure or imaginativeness in marriage, as initiative had clearly passed to the middle class.[9] Another potential outlet for expression and enjoyment remained unchanged.

Even after birth control began to limit family size, repeated pregnancies and the anxiety of providing material sustenance for the family proved an all-consuming task for the working woman; there was precious little time for new emotional support or new emotional enjoyment of the mothering process. While middle-class mothers strove to provide their children with toys and close personal attention and entertainment, the working-class woman took in washing or sewing or even went out to char in order to put food on the table and shoes on her husband and children.

Mothering thus remained fairly traditional. In both England and France, working-class women had their babies at home with the attendance of a midwife of mediocre quality. A few women went to the new hospitals but doctors were rarely consulted in pregnancy or afterwards. Patent medicine and traditional folk remedies were heavily relied upon. Feeding methods also remained traditional. Breast-feeding lasted for up to two years, primarily to save on food but also as a means of birth control.

With crowded accommodation which allowed no privacy for the woman, children always underfoot, and household chores and work from the outside, the working-class woman could not allow her children to be free before her. There was consequently more reliance on traditional disciplinary techniques, including physical beatings. The picture was not totally unchanged from the pre-industrial past. Women paid new attention to toilet training, a virtual necessity in cramped urban apartments, and children were not swaddled. Working-class children responded by at least fond memories of their mother, against the image of a seldom-seen, authoritarian father. . . .

The working-class woman remained highly vulnerable to change, for her approach stressed the most gradual adaptations of tradition. Even birth control brought confusion and may have been encouraged primarily by the husband (whose co-operation was vital in all the methods used save abortion) on economic grounds. Family limitations came along with the rapid decline of domestic manufacturing and left many women confused about what role they had. A response was to continue to have more children than the middle-class, to fulfil the woman's more traditional expectations, and to encourage the children to stay within class boundaries so that, in her own later age, conventional kinship networks would be preserved. Only after World War II was there a sign of a new loosening of the culture of working-class wives, beyond grudging and limited adaptation to the necessities of a rapidly-changing society. And even now we must ask how much the world of the working-class woman has enlarged.

9 Shorter, *Modern Family;* Alfred C. Kinsey, *Sexual Behaviour in the Human Female* (1965).

—CLAUDIA KOONZ

# THE IDEAL NAZI MOTHER

The ideal Nazi man was a fighter; the ideal Nazi woman, a mother. Women were not to aspire to great achievements in the competitive, masculine worlds of politics, government, industry, and the military. Rather, women's lives ought to revolve around their true calling, motherhood. Apparently this doctrine appealed to both men and women in postdepression Germany. In the last free elections before the Nazi seizure of power, about one third of both male and female voters supported the Nazis. Just after the 1933 elections, Adolf Hitler boasted to an American woman, "Women have always been among my staunchest supporters. They feel that my victory is their victory. They know I serve their cause."

Feminists wondered how German women could vote to disenfranchise themselves. How, they asked, could women oppose the new emancipation granted to them in the Weimar Republic? Nazi politicians pointed out that anyone who voted Nazi voted to disenfranchise himself *or* herself and to undo the liberal reforms inaugurated after World War I. Yet this response is at best only a half-truth. The male voter for National Socialism may have been voting to end elections—but he could still envisage himself as a trooper in the Sturm Abteilung (SA), party official, or civil servant. And he could identify with the blatantly masculine élan of the party. Nazi men did not vote to remove themselves from all aspects of political life. Nazi women did. We cannot explain women's support for Hitler by assuming they were ignorant of National Socialist attitudes toward women, nor can we attribute the popularity of the Nazis among women to vague psychological propensities such as female passivity. To understand why women voted for and sometimes joined the Nazi party we will have to consider their criticisms of the emancipation of women in the Weimar Republic and to evaluate the changes they anticipated in the Third Reich. On the "woman question," as on so many other issues, early party supporters frequently expressed disillusionment with the realities of post-1933 society.

Although Nazi leaders consistently emphasized the primacy of motherhood for all women, their definition of that role expanded and contracted according to the needs of the Nazi party and state. In a first phase, before 1933, women in the Nazi movement struggled shoulder to shoulder with their male comrades in

From Claudia Koonz, "Mothers in the Fatherland: Women in Nazi Germany," in *Becoming Visible: Women in European History,* ed. Renate Bridenthal and Claudia Koonz (Boston: Houghton Mifflin Company, 1977), pp. 447–48, 448–53, 455–57, 470–471, by permission of the publishers.

whatever capacity the situation demanded. After the seizure of power, Hitler ordered employed women to relinquish their jobs and dedicate their full energies to rearing large families. By 1937, this policy was reversed as Hitler prepared for war: mothers, he decreed, must now also work in factories, offices, and fields. During all three phases, Nazi leaders saw women as ancillary, yet crucial to their cause. Leafletting amidst a hostile crowd, altering national consumption patterns, or building bombers could all be reconciled with motherhood. One policy, however, remained consistent. At no time could Nazi women expect to exert the slightest influence over the policies that affected their lives. Except within their own organizations, women could not hope to attain positions of leadership or control. From the foundation of the party through the defeat of the Nazi state, the needs of women—like the needs of all citizens—remained subservient to the demands of the Nazi elite. Girls learned to "Be brave! Be pure! Be German!" while boys in the Hitler Youth marched to the slogan, "Be brave! Be strong! Die smiling!" Traditional sex-role stereotypes were preserved to the detriment of men and women alike. . . .

In the early 1920s women comprised about 20 percent of the Nazi party membership. Although they played virtually no role in policy making, they did contribute money and moral support to the movement. Years later Hitler thanked the women of the party who had preserved party unity during his imprisonment. However, at the time neither Hitler nor the other Nazi men had paid much attention to their women colleagues. Not even at election times did they campaign for the female vote; and no woman ever held any party office. Because they were deemed so unimportant, women were unintentionally given the opportunity to organize their own relatively independent associations, edit their own newsletters, pamphlets, and broadsides, proselytize among other women, and discuss their views on the "woman question." While no Nazi orthodoxy on the "woman question" emerged, it is possible to discern some trends in the writings of women who joined or supported the Nazi movement prior to 1933.

Like their male counterparts, Nazi women expressed contempt for democracy, liberalism, individualism, and decadence. But in addition they deplored the emancipation of women. The Weimar Constitution of 1919 stipulated that "men and women shall have basically the same rights and duties." This meant that women were eligible to vote, hold public office, and pursue whatever career they wished. In fact, one-third of the labor force was female; between 70 and 90 percent of all eligible women voted in Weimar elections; between 6 and 9 percent of the parliamentary delegates elected were women; and about 20 percent of all university students were women.

These signs of emancipation, which so greatly impressed foreign observers, did not reflect the realities faced by most German women. Nazi critics complained that though the Weimar reforms may well have meant personal emancipation for a few well-educated, privileged women, the average women merely felt more exploited. Paula Siber, an early adherent of National Socialism, noted that while the women's movement produced a few women judges and parliamentarians, it "forced hundreds of thousands of German women out into the streets of the big cities and produced thousands of wage slaves to the capitalist economic order." Nazi women argued that it was unjust to force women into a man's world in which they were unwanted and for which they were unprepared. Instead of reforming that male world, they urged women to return to the security of their traditional spheres of activity. In these roles women could exercise control over their lives and command respect from society. Besides the personal rewards of such a life, traditional women could have the additional satisfaction of knowing they contributed to the national cause by raising a loyal, decent future generation.

Women who supported the Nazis hoped to stem the tide of decadence they believed was engulfing their society. Unable to explain what appeared to be the demise of all morality and order, these women often blamed foreign influence and women's emancipation. A new English "girl type," a "movies-sport-jazz-flirt," behaved so scandalously that women in general came to be regarded as mere sex objects. Liberty, claimed one Nazi supporter, had been a French import in the first place and naturally produced only libertinism and prostitution. Another author blamed the increasing "materialism, naturalism, and Americanism" on the emancipated women who abandoned their homes and joined women's organizations. These "emancipationists," claimed Nazi women, had declared a "sex war" that promised to become as damaging to national solidarity as the socialists' class war. Nazi women, like Nazi men, came from predominantly lower-middle-class backgrounds. Whereas working-class women had long been accustomed to working outside their homes and upper-middle-class women often received educations that equipped them for careers or charitable social work, lower-middle-class women were unprepared to benefit from the changes initiated by Weimar Germany. Many had worked as sales clerks or servants prior to marriage, but these were not jobs to which they wished to return. Similarly, the intellectuals' Weimar culture, so often praised by literary critics and historians, only represented chaos and decadence to them. To counter the modernity they feared, Nazi women worked for a return to a largely mythical past in which they might win respect and feel secure.

Women Nazis did not, however, argue that patriotic, traditional German women ought to surrender to the masculine will and become the servants of men. Like the "emancipationists," they fervently believed women and men were equal. The path to achieving this equality, however, lay not in snatching away male occupations and professions but in restoring honor to traditional womanly responsibilities. Nazi women dreamed of a future in which men and women would be separate but equal. One Nazi woman leader claimed that women had been subjugated for centuries and declared the time had come for women to stop being "half-human beings." She urged women to return to the ancient Nordic traditions in which men and women were equal. Male historians, she continued, had deliberately obscured this truth for centuries. But now that she and other women historians had begun to rewrite history, the truth would be known. A Nazi woman who was interested in anthropology claimed that in ancient Germanic civilizations women were biologically equal to men. Recently discovered skeletons proved this conclusively, she said. The author did not, however, explain just how this biological equality would lead one to conclude that women ought to remain in their separate sphere. In the late 1920s a "racial scientist" concluded that women of "inferior" or "Mediterranean" races might well be inferior to the men of those races, but Germanic women and men had always been equal. Transferring this racial elitism to domestic politics, she declared that the Nazi state of the future would have to depend upon the skill of its very best qualified citizens, whether male or female. As society became more stratified along racial and class lines, talented members of both sexes would be recruited into the leadership. Elitism and racism, in the view of many Nazi women leaders, would replace sexism.

Many of these complaints about Weimar Germany emerged in other conservative writings as well as in Nazi works. It was their vehemence that differentiated Nazi women from other traditional and religious German women. While conservatives generally assumed that most problems would somehow be solved, Nazi women firmly believed that only a Nazi revolution could save the situation. Nowhere is this more obvious than in the speeches and autobiographical accounts of rank-and-file women who supported the party prior to the seizure of power.[1] These women—like their male counterparts—tended to be relatively young. Most joined in their twenties and thirties. Although their accounts abound in phrases like "we women," Nazi women viewed themselves as Nazis and Germans first and as women second. "We don't care about women's or men's rights—we are concerned solely with Germany's salvation!" wrote one woman. Not surprisingly, the family backgrounds of the women were character-

1 In 1934, Theodor Abel, a professor at Columbia University, posted announcements in all Nazi party meeting places to publicize an essay competition. He asked that the competitors describe their activities in the Nazi party before 1933 and emphasize "family life, economic condition, education, membership in other organizations, participation and important thoughts, experiences and feelings about events and ideas of the post-war period" (T. Abel, *Why Hitler Came to Power: An Answer Based on the Original Life Stories of 600 of His Followers,* Prentice-Hall, New York, 1938, pp. 1–4). Of the 683 answers, 48 were written by women. All of the essays are in the Manuscript Collection in the Hoover Institution at Stanford University, Stanford, California. Peter Merkl recently subjected these data to new analysis, and the results of his study appear in his book, *Political Violence under the Swastika: 581 Early Nazis,* Princeton University Press, Princeton, 1975.

For help in researching this material, I am greatly indebted to Mrs. Agnes F. Peterson of the Hoover Institution. Permission to quote was kindly granted by the Hoover Institution, from Hoover Institution on War, Revolution and Peace, Theodore F. Abel Collection.

A second source of information is a collection of local histories of pro-Nazi women's organizations assembled by the Nazi Party Archives in 1936. These essays are available on microfilm from the NSDAP Hauptarchiv, Hoover Institution.

ized by a religious childhood and a generally conservative education. The threat of socialism terrified them—as is indicated by their anxious and exaggerated accounts of the 1918 German revolution. One women had vivid memories of "street brawls, the mass graves, plundering, murder, and untold horrors of Bolshevik terror." Contrary to the assumptions of historians, women did not merely follow their husbands, fathers, or sons into the ranks of the Nazi party. One woman recalled, "Frequently it was the woman in a family who first understood the great ideas of Adolf Hitler and then—to her own personal misery—joined the Party against her family's wishes." In several cases women who joined the party noted that they created hardships for other members of their families—and sometimes husbands lost their jobs because of their wives' pro-Nazi activities.

Women in the early Nazi movement, like the men, were usually fanatic and dedicated. Frequently, these women expressed their scorn for passive, conservative, and traditional women. Nazi women viewed themselves as revolutionaries and proudly declared their "determination, joy at sacrifice [*Opferfreude*] and fanatical faith." But while autobiographical accounts by Nazi men emphasize violence, brawling, and paramilitary activities, the women's stories are characterized by an almost religious faith. Religious adjectives and metaphors color the narratives, and many women report joining the party as the result of a conversion experience. Said one woman,

> I had very little political experience [in the early 1920s] but then I heard Hitler speak and saw his pictures on so many posters. From then on I was converted into a fascist fighter and joined the German Freedom Movement [Nazi party].

Another "awaited the dawn of a new era," and believed that Hitler had been sent by God to usher in that new age. Some compared Hitler's life of hardship and faith to the life of Christ, and many early party members reported their impressions of Hitler in religious terms. "Quiet and sincere was his face, but a shining fire burned in his eyes!" wrote one woman. Another recalled, "I do not any longer remember how to describe it. When one had the great experience of looking the man in the eyes one simply became a fanatic!" This impression was confirmed repeatedly. "This simple man, with the true, steady, honest gaze that streamed like rays of the sun into the 22,000 enthusiastic people," renewed one woman's faith in her ideals. In the writings of these women Hitler appeared to be the messiah of a secular religion.

As dedicated followers of a messiah, women Nazis did not worry about whether they were respected as women. They were needed for the work at hand and participated enthusiastically in a variety of roles during those "glorious days of struggle." They "worked to the point of exhaustion" and frequently risked arrest or attack for putting up illegal posters after dark, caring for fugitive and wounded SA men, and smuggling illegal campaign literature throughout Germany. "We women could not merely stand aside and let the men do all the work. We wanted to call out in a feminine way, 'Germany awake!'' recalled a woman from a small town. One mother justified her frequent absences from home by saying, ''The Nation is in peril! I cannot remain happy and carefree at the supper table when Mother Germany weeps—and her children might die. Germany must live on—even if we must sacrifice our lives!'' These women may have been behaving like ''typical'' women in their adoring attitude toward Hitler, but in their day-to-day party activities they were courageous and spirited—and certainly did not behave like the stereotype of the passive, meek woman. Proudly they noted that their sex did not prevent them from being harassed by the enemies of National Socialism. A woman from Göttingen commented, ''We were so convinced of the righteousness of our cause, that we scarcely noticed the jeering and insults hurled at us.'' As Nazi women walked down the street, proudly wearing their armbands, they were met by calls of, ''Hitler whore!'' ''Nazi bloodhound!'' ''Brown pig!'' ''Nazi creep!'' and ''Nazi goose!'' One woman recalled an encounter in a park where she was leafletting:

> A proper citizen who felt I disturbed his peace, told me I was a bad person, and observed that I ought to go home and cook dinner for my family or else get myself elected to the Reichstag. But I told him, ''With so many people like you, we women can't afford to step back and cook . . . I don't want my children ever to be able to say to me 'Mother, where were you when disaster threatened Germany?' ''

Perhaps there was truth in one woman's comment, ''Harassment is the best teacher of political solidarity.'' Similarly, another early Nazi woman observed, ''The time of struggle forged a unity among us that no power on earth could have rent asunder!''

Although the early Nazi women recalled the splendid days of struggle, they were usually content to leave street violence, rallies, and anti-Bolshevik harassment to the men. Typically, women would address small political gatherings, conduct door-to-door campaigns, hand out leaflets, and organize women's clubs to support Nazi activities. In addition, they collected used clothing and food for the poorer party members, sewed clothing for unemployed SA men, organized children's parties, set up rest homes for the SA, and prepared food and refreshments for party rallies. The women were engaged primarily in the feminine activities for which they had been socialized, but they noted no feeling of inferiority on that account. Whether man or woman, it was victory that counted, they believed. Women's duties were not the same as those of the SA or SS, but they were equally important in the eyes of Nazi women. Moreover, the party leadership allowed women considerable organizational and ideological autonomy.

Naively, women anticipated that this relatively high degree of independence would persist after the victory of National Socialism. They failed to see that their autonomy resulted not so much from anyone's belief in the basic dignity or importance of women but from the Nazis' disregard for women altogether. Naturally, Nazi leaders would not refuse the women's contributions—whether those contributions were "comradeship or motherly love." But not for a moment did any Nazi leader seriously consider allowing women to pursue an independent policy or have a voice in policy making after the establishment of a Nazi state. As in so many other areas, the Nazi elite did not lay down a strict orthodoxy or establish a tight, centralized organization prior to 1933. Loyalty to Hitler alone constituted sufficient grounds for acceptance by the party. Thus, women who professed loyalty to Hitler were tolerated in the movement whether they wished to wear or to sew brown shirts. . . .

We may deplore the Nazi solution to Germany's problems, but it is clear that Hitler spoke to real needs. His promise to provide a husband for every woman, for example, had great appeal. Because of the staggering loss of life in World War I, about 2,000,000 German women would not be able to find husbands. Although the war had been begun by men and been fought by men, this shortage of men was commonly referred to as the "woman surplus." A bitter opponent of Nazism recalled that Hitler's promise of a husband and home "had an enormous effect, touching deeply as it did the innermost feelings and desires of millions of women for whom equal rights had 'til then meant merely the right to be exploited."[2]

In addition to the anxiety about marriage experienced by single women or widows, Hitler played on a more universal anxiety—the depression. He promised that all employed women with husbands or fathers who could support them would be removed from the labor market. This, declared the Nazis, would eliminate all families with double incomes and distribute jobs among male workers. With 6,000,000 women employed (10 percent of the total population, or nearly 20 percent of the labor force), it was understandable that there would be concern about this issue. The situation was exacerbated by the fact that while almost 30 percent of the male work force was unemployed, only about 10 percent of all employable women were out of work.[3] Women workers were blamed for stealing men's jobs because they would work for lower wages. A refugee from Nazi Germany looked back on those days and recalled that women became the breadwinners while their men sat idle. This, she said, created deep psychological depression in men, women, and children. In reality, however, women did not steal men's jobs. The sectors of the economy that both were better paid and employed mostly men (i.e., heavy industry and construction) were the hardest hit by the economic crisis. Still, pervasive antifeminism led the general public to make scapegoats of women workers for the conditions they could neither control nor comprehend.

2 Hilda Browning, *Women Under Fascism and Communism* (Lawrence, London, n.d.), pp. 1-2.

3 The Nazi statistical argument is best expressed in Richard Peikow, *Die soziale und wirtschaftliche Stellung der deutschen Frau in der Gegenwart,* Ph.D. dissertation, Humbolt University, Berlin, 1937. For the statistics on employment, see "Die Erwerbstätigkeit der Reichsbevölkerung," *Statistik des deutschen Reiches,* vol. 453, Heft II, Berlin, 1936.

Anxiety prevailed over analysis and people longed for "the good old days" when mothers stayed at home. The household for the German woman was like the small business, farm, or shop for the middle-class man. The home provided the wife with dignity, status, and security. Even when women had not yet been forced by economic necessity to take in washing, seek work in an office or store, or offer their services as housekeepers, they expressed great anxiety that such a fate might befall them. Middle-class women had been socialized to be wives. When this role appeared to be threatened, they fought to defend it rather than seeking new alternatives. Thus, Nazi women proselytized among their peers by using appeals to revive the traditional women's tasks.

It may be that the women who so adoringly worshiped Hitler did anticipate returning to a life centered on the home after the Nazi revolution. But the leaders of the Nazi women's movement had learned to speak in public, organize meetings, campaign, lobby, write political pamphlets, and direct welfare projects. They took great pride in their independence and accomplishments. Certainly, they considered themselves to be the equals of Nazi men. The women did not anticipate returning meekly to their homes after 1933. In Hitler's "second revolution" women would participate actively in the creation of a new society. They did not think this would necessitate their participation in politics. Political power, they believed, would remain in male hands while cultural power would fall under their jurisdiction. After 1933 women leaders did indeed make an important contribution to the new regime. But they contributed service to the Nazi state without gaining any influence over its basic policies. Early in 1933 Nazi policy became unmistakably clear:

> There is no place for the political woman in the ideological world of National Socialism. . . . The intellectual attitude of the movement on this score is opposed to the political woman. . . . The German resurrection is a male event.[4]

Although the Third Reich failed to endure for 1,000 years, as Hitler predicted it would, it did survive for twelve. An important factor in its survival was the Nazis' ability to manipulate traditional masculine and feminine role stereotypes. While storm troopers and soldiers brought terror first to Germany and later to all Europe, women were supposed cheerfully to make sacrifices and perform whatever functions the state required. Throughout, they were expected to remain idealistic, optimistic, and domestic. When the commandant at the Auschwitz concentration camp returned to his family after a day's work, he could assuage whatever conscience he had left with the secure knowledge that he was a decent family man. Except for the women in the resistance, German women made ideal collaborators. Naively anticipating that their womanly sphere would one day be elevated to prominence, they mistook propaganda for reality.

4 Engelbert Huber, *Das ist Nationalsozialismus,* quoted in George Mosse, *Nazi Culture,* New York, 1966, p. 47.

But cultural power without economic power is empty. Although women joined the vast array of women's organizations and heard themselves praised by hours of propaganda, they remained only privates in a civilian army commanded by Nazi men.

EDGAR MORIN

# THE MODERN WOMAN

The personality of the townswoman is changing along a broad front of generations that includes all women under fifty, some older, and all strata of the emergent bourgeoisie.

The townswoman, whether or not she has a job, is already a housewife. Since 1950, she has been the leading spirit of the domestic revolution, supported, not thwarted, by her husband. Young wives and the newly retired "suburbanized" wives are the vanguard of the movement which has accelerated since 1960. They complain impatiently when progress is held up: "Ah! If only I had a bathroom!" One necessity leads to another, and they all lead to a villa with every modern comfort.

The movement transforming the home is also transforming marriage itself, which remains the center of women's lives and aspirations. The old system of marriage, an arranged alliance between two families, was already disappearing in the country by 1950. An evolutionary process that had begun early in the twentieth century gradually opened up new possibilities of matrimonial self-determination to young people, and the social and economic transformations of the 1950's lifted the last prohibitions, the last of the family imperatives. Girls benefit more from the new freedom of choice. Whereas the boys want a good, pleasant, level-headed wife, the girls pose a wide range of qualifying conditions that include amorous considerations, good prospects, recognition of their authority in the home, and a suitable house. The demand for love is profound but domesticated. Of course, now as ever, couples are brought together by love

From Edgar Morin, *Plodémet: Report from a French Village,* trans. A. M. Sheridan-Smith (Allen Lane/The Penguin Press, 1971), pp. 153–157. 

at first sight, but even when passionate, love is not blind, which explains why parents are not unduly worried by their children's freedom. Mme. Goémon talked to us calmly about her daughters' freedom (one of them married a worker in Nantes). "Perhaps they'll go to work in Brest, Rennes, or Paris, and get married there. I wouldn't want one of them to marry a North African, but if they were really happy we'd be happy too."

The desire of young married couples to live away from their parents existed long before 1950, but it could be realized only by moving to one of the larger towns outside the commune. After 1950, with the women leading the domestic revolution, they succeeded in getting the house enlarged, making it possible to relegate the old people to their own quarters with a separate kitchen; meanwhile, they are pressing for a new house to be built that would definitely separate the generations.

The new mother, who now always has her baby in a hospital, follows the urban practice of devoting a great deal of attention to the hygiene and diet of her children. When they go to school, she takes an interest in their lessons and homework, takes pride in their successes, envies those of the neighbor's children, and sometimes even complains to the teachers. The mothers urge both boys and girls to go on to secondary school and do not take kindly to any objections. . . .

The use of make-up is spreading in various ways. Heavy make-up (lipstick, rouge, and eye shadow) is used mainly by the fashion-conscious women who have moved here from the cities. The old women say that make-up hastens the appearance of wrinkles, makes the face ugly, and wastes money, while the men believe that it is the mark of hidden eroticism. Make-up is used by bourgeois women over forty as a ceremonial mask for Sundays and feast days, younger women timidly apply a little lipstick, and teen-age girls use a little eye shadow—but only when they go dancing. Far more widespread and in daily use are the invisible cosmetics such as face cream, deodorants, and eau de cologne.

Women no longer restrict their visits to the hairdresser to the annual permanent at Easter but have a set once or even twice a week. The new habit has spread to the countryside, and in Menez-Ru where the men still cut each other's hair for a franc or a glass of red wine, the women now go to the hairdresser.

The two hairdressing salons in the town are expanding rapidly; according to one of the hairdressers, her clientele has increased by 50 percent each year since 1959. Both were modernized in 1966 and use the latest equipment. One of the salons even engaged the services of a beauty specialist in 1965, but the attempt was premature as only three women came in for advice. It is quite possible, however, that the specialist may have been visited by more women from Plodémet in the more discreet surroundings of Quimper. It is even said that one teen-age girl had her nose straightened!

The townswomen have varied wardrobes; some have dresses copied by a local dressmaker from fashion magazines. Young girls buy their sweaters, skirts, and slacks from stores in the larger towns. Fashion is triumphant even among country girls. Solange from Pors-en-Breval, who works in the fields, milks the cows, and consequently gets filthy at home, always arrives in the town impeccably dressed and never wears the same sweater or blouse two days running. "Here [Menez-Ru] you're supposed to wear everything out before you buy something new, but my sisters and I throw things away when they're out of fashion and buy something else" (Mimi, age 22).

The revolution in fashion and beauty care is following the urban norms. It is not confined to special occasions and holidays but is part of everyday life; women want to please not only others but themselves.

While developing their femininity, women do not hesitate to venture into masculine territory when they think it is to their advantage. Slacks, first worn by teen-age girls and later adopted by young married women, are the symbol of modernity, which casts off ancient proprieties for the sake of comfort. But slacks also express feminine rebelliousness; in appropriating the most masculine item of dress, women are attempting to abolish men's privileges by sharing them.

Young Mme. Le Bellec, twenty-one years old, from Lastronguy, works on the farm in slacks and a nylon blouse.

SHE. It's practical and warm.

HE. It's ugly.

HIS MOTHER. It's all right for everyday, but not for Sunday.

Smoking and drinking will soon be accepted publicly as feminine rights. For a long time and only at home, Bigouden women have been drinking "Catalunya," a sweet wine. More recently, smoking has been introduced, also in private, by women from the cities and young wives, but women are still not supposed to smoke or drink in public. Teen-age girls were the first to break the prohibition on their outings together. Cigarettes and drinks are now accepted accompaniments at teen-age get-togethers; in fact, smoking is a social activity before it becomes a private habit. Slacks, drinking, and cigarettes are stages toward the raising of the iron curtain that has long separated male and female society throughout the day, with the men reigning in the public forum—the *buvette*—and the women meeting for coffee in their homes. Women have now begun to broaden their world in the limitless areas outside the home.

The domestic revolution has increased women's mobility through the expansion of the range of acquisitions and by linking the home to the urban world—country to town, town to city. Both young women and old took to the motorbike as soon as it appeared. The car embodies the newly felt need for the outside world, a need as strong as that for the home. Women in their forties urge their husbands to buy a car, and younger women obtain their driver's license—the secret passport to freedom. Many women use the family car far more often than do their husbands, and almost all the wealthier women have cars of their own.

Women's slacks were symbolic of a desire for independence in the world; the car, another appropriation of male privilege, grants a spatial independence.

It opens up the streets, the shop windows, the cinemas, and the amenities of the city; it bestows a measure of urban citizenship. Moreover, it stimulates a need for mobility as an end in itself—for a change of air, a change of surroundings. It offers a foretaste of travel, the desire for which recurred in our conversations with women of all ages, almost like an obsession. At a meeting of the agricultural information group, one speaker suggested a study tour to England. The general response (from men of twenty-five to thirty-five) was, "Oh, that kind of thing is for women!" We learned that a number of women had joined a previous study tour to Holland as a means of satisfying their desire for travel. The first organized tours to Spain and Italy were initiated by young unmarried and retired women.

The desire to see the world is also a yearning to see another more beautiful, more interesting, more romantic world which is also a theatrical world of landscapes and monuments, a cinematic world of moving images. The desire to travel in the real world takes flight on the wings of the imagination.

It is in the context of such dual perspectives, sometimes disjointed, sometimes intermingled, that women pursue expanding horizons. Bourgeois women are being led to read books and novels; they feel their minds a mixture of the real and the imaginary. The sales figures of the Café des Sports indicate that women's magazines are bought in overwhelmingly greater numbers than any other periodicals sold in Plodémet. These magazines satisfy both practical (fashion) and imaginary (romantic fiction) yearnings; they are a link with Paris and provide instructive models not only for fashionable dress but for conduct and daily problems. Models and dreams are the stuff that great myths of the modern woman are made of.

CHAPTER 9

# THE CULT OF YOUTH

The demographic revolution of this century is such that more persons under twenty-five years of age are alive today than ever before. The renewal of the European population since the end of the Second World War has been an extraordinary phenomenon that has altered the entire composition of society. This is not a matter of sheer numbers. The attitudes and values of youth have become a political factor with which the ruling elders of every European nation must contend. To contain the energy and to harness the potential of young people has required that their ambitions be honored, not just guided. For this reason it seems appropriate to identify the cult of youth as one of the characteristic features of contemporary European society.

*Walter Z. Laqueur* probes the background of the German youth movement (*Wandervogel*), explaining why conditions in Germany were somewhat different from elsewhere and how the First World War came as an exhilarating shock to the young. The intensity of the war years was followed by a pervading sense of disillusionment in Germany and, along with it, a desire to change the "mechanistic society" that seemed so antithetical to the ideals of youth. In these terms Laqueur defines the origins of the Hitler Youth, which placed its trust in the Third Reich.

*Paul Wilkinson* explores the parallel in England, hoping thereby to show why it was that the youth organizations there remained relatively apolitical in orientation. He narrates how the English Scouts were "mobilized" in the First World War and how their learned skills were put to use in the war effort. But, as in Germany, a certain disillusionment was not long in coming. The English youth leader, Robert Baden-Powell, was nonetheless able to hold scouting securely within the political consensus and to maintain an idealistic and indeed chivalric ethic. Other youth groups came and went, each with its special appeal. Yet the Boy Scouts remained the quintessential English form of youth organization until the Second World War.

*John Ardagh* portrays the postwar change of climate in France, where there are now twice as many youths as in the final years of the Third Republic. After 1945 a whole new generation arrived, seemingly with their own dress, moral values, and life style. But Ardagh suggests that much of the innovating wind has gone out of their sails. Instead, France was swept in the 1960s by an emotional (and commercial) movement known as *Salut les Copains,* which generated at most a kind of subculture composed of rock, slang, and Coca-Cola. If Ardagh is correct, most young French radicals continued to be guided by a certain formalism taught in the schools and by basically bourgeois values inherited from the home. In his view the wild spectacle of student revolt in May 1968 was therefore largely episodic and did not signal a fundamental change.

It is more than a truism to say that the future of European society depends on its youth. At no other time in history has their number been so immense or their opinion so solicited. Nor have their possibilities ever seemed so bright. Europe has more to offer the young in terms of material prosperity and social mobility than at any time in the past. Whether the opportunity will be seized to create a more generous and more equitable society, no one can tell. The jury is still out, and Everyman must judge for himself.

—WALTER Z. LAQUEUR

# YOUNG GERMANY

## *ROMANTIC PRELUDE*

. . . Europe had made unprecedented economic and technical progress between 1860 and 1900. While standards of living rose faster than ever before, not all classes benefited equally and strong social tensions were generated. But in most European countries the working class could view with satisfaction and confidence the constant growth of its political influence, as well as its economic and social achievements. There had been no major war in Europe for several decades, and there was every reason to expect another long period of peace, progress, and general well-being.

But serious symptoms of cultural decline were not lacking in that world of growing plenty and rapid technical advance. It would be interesting to speculate about the psychological sources of the discontent, the sense of emptiness and general dissatisfaction that found its expression in a *fin de siècle* mood even in a country like Russia, which faced more urgent political and social problems than the West. Why did so many people throughout Europe welcome the outbreak of the First World War as a "liberation"? Such an investigation might show that man has often found it difficult to suffer serenely a prolonged period of tranquillity and well-being. When no major problems exist, minor problems tend to take their place.

We tend to look back on the world that ended in 1914 with a nostalgia mixed with a certain amusement. It is true that the great crisis of 1900 seems somewhat unreal, if not artificial, in comparison with the problems of the twenties and thirties. But for those who lived then, the cultural crisis was real enough; it turned some towards socialism, others towards an attitude of aristocratic disdain of the masses and hostility to bourgeois society and its culture or lack of culture. Politically, this rejection of society and its values could lead to either left- or right-wing extremist solutions. . . . The German youth movement was an unpolitical form of opposition to a civilization that had little to offer the young generation, a protest against its lack of vitality, warmth, emotion, and ideals.

From Walter Z. Laqueur, *Young Germany: A History of the German Youth Movement* (New York: Basic Books, 1962), pp. 3–4, 87–90, 133–35, 194–97, by permission of the publisher and C. A. Watts and Co., Ltd., London.

The angry young men of 1900 were found among the more articulate sections of the younger generation throughout Europe. Some developed a new cult of youth in an attempt to bring fresh air into the stale and musty atmosphere surrounding their elders. The writings of "Agathon" in France, and of the early Italian Futurists, are evidence of this trend. The *Wandervogel* was one of the specific German forms of protest. It was and remained unique in many respects, since Germany's situation in Europe was different from that of other countries. The triumph of liberalism in France, Britain, and the United States had never extended to Germany; the "bourgeois revolution" had never been completed; the middle classes were not fully emancipated. Capitalism had indeed prevailed in Germany and industrialization had made rapid strides, but in many sections of the population a medieval, antiliberal, and anticapitalist mentality survived because the people themselves had not taken a prominent and active part in these developments, which had frequently been initiated from above or from outside. . . .

## *THE FIRST WORLD WAR*

A prodigious wave of enthusiasm swept over German youth at the outbreak of the world war in 1914. "We had not known the reason of our existence . . . youth had seemed to us a burden and a curse," wrote Ina Seidel, in her poem ending: "O holy fortune, to be young today!"[1] Those who had previously found no dominant aim in life now felt that they knew the meaning of their destiny—total identification with the Fatherland in its hour of uttermost peril. "How stupid it is to ask what is our attitude to the war! Anyone who finds time to think about it shows that he does not know how to feel with his people, and is shutting himself up against the blessing that fate intended for him."[2] If any explanations were needed, they were to be found in the first appeal by the *Wandervogel* leader Neuendorff; the war had come "because the other peoples could no longer hold their own in peaceful competition with German power, German industry, and German honesty . . . they perfidiously sought to defeat Germany by brute force and weight of numbers."[3]

But German youth had been hearing for years past how jealous enemies and rivals begrudged the German people its rightful place in the sun. When the storm broke, it should not have found them altogether unprepared. Yet it struck them like a bolt from the blue, for despite all the warnings and the mounting tensions of the preceding months, (there had been a general, persistent belief that everything would somehow at the last moment be settled. )

1 *Führerzeitung,* November 1914, p. 205.

2 *Wandervogel,* I. Kriegsheft, p. 259.

3 *Ibid.,* p. 257.

To the members of the youth movement, war was so incredible as to seem unreal; their world had been one of carefree rambling, dreaming and singing—a joyful world of utter peace, in the greatest contrast imaginable to the ravages of war. To many, as to Rupert Brooke in England, the sense of liberation, of an awakening out of torpor, was the most memorable experience of those days of high patriotic emotion. But this was a reaction against spiritual emptiness and material frustrations that was perhaps more acutely felt by those outside the *Wandervogel* than by its members. For the youth movement was one of active idealism, in less need of an external moral stimulus; at any rate, it was so in the Reich, though conditions in Austria and the German regions of Bohemia were different. There, the possibility if not the desirability of a world war had been loudly discussed for years past.[4] The youth movement in those parts had also been much more involved in politics; more than once it had been said at their conventions that they were fighting a losing battle against Slavonic encroachment. Many of them seemed to think that the only way to stem this tide was a victorious war in alliance with Germany, leading to the eventual emergence of a *Grossdeutschland* in which foreign elements would be put in their place.

Many group leaders were called up in the very first days of the war, others volunteered, and the girls put themselves at the disposal of the Red Cross. Some of the younger ones feared that the war would be over before they saw any fighting, and a few even tried to reach the front line without having enlisted. Meanwhile groups of younger boys and girls went to the countryside to help with the harvest. Regular youth movement activities, needless to say, were disrupted for many months: some members, assuming that the war would soon be over, argued that no particular effort should be made to resume normal activities, that all energies should be directed towards the war effort. Others thought the time had come for a *rapprochement* with other youth organizations such as the Boy Scouts and the para-military *Jung Deutschland.*

As the months went by, however, and a certain wartime normality was established, the meetings and outings were resumed, albeit on a smaller scale. Girls frequently took over the leadership of groups, and after a few months were reinforced by soldiers who had been wounded and invalided out of the army.

In 1915 the youth movement resumed its longer expeditions despite the strict rationing of food and clothes; there were now enough prisoners of war to help with the harvest.[5]

One of the most important tasks was to maintain contact with those serving in the forces. The soldiers related their adventures and impressions in long letters that often were published, while the groups sent greetings and parcels to their leaders and members on the field of battle. Gradually an organizational network was established in the various army units; there were unofficial clearing

4 Luise Fick . . . [*Die deutsche Jugendbewegung* (Jena, 1939)], deals at considerable length with conditions in Austria before 1914.

5 *Wandervogel,* 5, 1916, p. 98.

houses, and eventually the *Wandervogel* soldiers even had their own circular letters and little newspapers on both the Western and Eastern fronts, and in other major theaters of war. Two hundred of them held a convention in Brussels at Whitsuntide 1917, and there were other, smaller meetings elsewhere.[6]

How did the individual *Wandervogel* soldier face up to the great patriotic challenge? In the first immense wave of national enthusiasm all petty quarrels were forgotten; all that was best in that generation was demonstrated: unselfishness, comradeship, the readiness to sacrifice. They had not the slightest doubt of the rightness of the cause they were fighting for, and the first great victories appeared to promise an early triumph. "We are chasing the enemy like a herd of sheep,"—Johannes Ilgen wrote on 2 September 1914 from Chalons-sur-Marne. But the German advance was soon halted, and the writer of the letter was killed the very same month; what then followed was grim-visaged war unrelieved by any great advances or triumphs, or by the hope of an early victory. At Langemarck in November 1914 thousands of German students, including many members of the youth movement, stormed the enemy lines and were mown down in swathes, singing "Deutschland, Deutschland über Alles"; the lists of "Fallen for their country" became longer and longer. Different undertones began to appear in letters from the front: "The war is not beautiful. I would thank God if it were over today, and if I could return home unscathed."[7] It was not only the war itself that was ugly; it soon transpired that the *Wandervogel* soldier had often to face serious difficulties within his own unit. After the first flush of excitement had ebbed away, there was not much left of the comradeship and understanding that he had expected. Max Sidow had been one of the most enthusiastic during the first weeks of war,[8] but five years later he wrote about the *Fronterlebnis* in a very different vein: "One was alone among the many. The uneducated hated every cultured soldier. Every conversation began and ended with obscenities."[9] Another wrote of the "sad days and the heavy nights among vulgar and mean people, the first terrible impressions, and the great ideas of fatherland and world history that made their impact only much later—and sometimes not at all."[10] What had caused the shock and disappointment? Rudolf Piper thought the assumption that the youth movement had really come to know "country and people" during its perambulations had been no more than an illusion. On such excursions they had seen only the best side of their people. Even the provincial inns, for instance, had been outside their experience; hence their "terrible disappointment in the army barracks."[11] Robert

6 There is a vast literature on the *Feldwandervogel.* See for instance *Rundbrief* on the Eastern front; R. F. Heiling, *Feldpachanten* (Glogau, 1918); *Zwiespruch,* the *Wandervogel* organ at the Western front; "Cölner"; "Der Feldwandervogel" in *Wandervogel,* 12, 1929; J.H. Mitgau, "Der Feldwandervogel," in Will Vesper (ed.) *Deutsche Jugend,* Berlin, 1934.

7 *Wandervogel,* 11/12, 1914, p. 284.

8 See his poem in *Wandervogel,* 9/10, 1914, p. 259.

9 *Krieg, Revolution und Friedeutsche Zukunft* (Hamburg, 1919), p. 27.

10 *Wandervogel,* 2, 1916, p. 35.

11 *Ibid.,* 10/11, 1916, p. 211.

Oelbermann, an army lieutenant and future leader of the *Nerothers,* said that "horror seized us. Were we human beings? Or animals? Duty alone upheld many of us until the end."[12]

In the early days of the war it had been commonly assumed that its moral effect would be that of a great purifying fire; it would destroy everything that was rotten and decaying. But gradually it became apparent that the war was bound also to destroy many real values and achievements; that it was bringing in its train a general brutalization which could be nothing less than an immense cultural and moral catastrophe.[13] . . .

## THE "WHITE KNIGHT"

For a long time the Boy Scouts had been regarded as the poor relations of the youth movement: led by adults, and specializing as they did in para-military education, they were somewhere on the periphery, outside the main stream of the movement. In contrast to the *Wandervogel,* the Scouts were not strictly selective in the recruitment of their members.

After the war the Scouts underwent a minor revolution analogous to that which occurred elsewhere in the movement; the adult leaders were deposed and younger members took over. But, unlike what happened in the *Wandervogel,* their revolution did not stop there. New forms of activity and new ideas were developed which were to have a decisive influence upon the whole German youth movement and, in effect, to shape the whole course of its development between 1919 and 1933.

At their first postwar meeting in Schloss Prunn there were discussions very much like those that went on among the *Freideutsche* and the *Wandervogel:* should the Scouts become the organization of an élite, or should they on the contrary try not to lose contact with the masses? Was a nationalist orientation to prevail, or should internationalist views be given wider currency? What about the place of religion in the life of the *Bund?*

Deliberations went on for some time, and in 1920 the reformers seceded and founded their own group, the *Neupfadfinder,* led by the so-called Regensburg circle (F. L. Habbel, Ludwig Voggenreiter and others) and a young parson from Berlin, Martin Voelkel. The Regensburg leaders were down to earth, mainly interested in education, and they provided some new ideas about "tribal education"—the tribe (Stamm) was to replace the group as the basic unit. Voelkel, the ideologist, provided the notions of the "Reich," the "knight," and the "holy grail," with their specific meaning for the young. But at the very center was the idea, and the reality, of the *Bund.* The former scouts found their way into the

12 *Ibid.,* 6, 1919, p. 156.

13 See for instance Johannes Müller in *Grüne Blätter,* quoted in *Freideutsche Jugend,* 7, 1917, pp. 223–4.

youth movement; it could be said that they took it over during an interregnum, and under their influence it was to change its character.

In its second, *bündische* phase the youth movement became much more ambitious. The very name suggested a new trend. Whereas rambling had been the central activity before the First World War, in the new era it became only one of several activities, and not necessarily the most important. The *Wandervogel* had been critical of society, but had never assumed that it had a mission to change the world. This was just what the *Bünde* tried to do; it was a romantic attempt to cope with realities. In the *Wandervogel* the group had been a comparatively loose association; the emphasis had been on the individual and his own development; there had been no specific plans for the future of its members, who were expected gradually to grow out of the youth movement. People belonged to a group because they liked it; there was little reflection and no sense of a purpose beyond this activity. But in the *Bund* created by Voelkel and his friends the collective mattered more than the individual; there was stricter discipline, and it was envisaged as an all-embracing bond making total demands upon the individual[14] for the rest of his life. One belonged to a group to serve a cause, and under the surface of all its activities there were magic formulas, or implied hints pointing to the cause itself. After an initial struggle girls had entered the *Wandervogel,* and although all its leading figures were male, it is impossible to think of the *Wandervogel* as exclusively a boys' movement. The *Bund,* on the other hand, had no mixed groups; it was a male society *par excellence.* Illogically enough, many of the *Bünde* included separate girls' groups, but these were merely subsidiaries and played no great part in the movement; there was too much talk about fighting, struggle, and battle, and it was difficult to imagine a female knight. Generally speaking the lyric romanticism of the *Wandervogel* had been replaced by something tougher—a romanticism that had been decisively affected by the First World War. Freedom and unrestraint had been sacrificed to duty and service in voluntary subjection to a greater whole. Whereas the ideal figure of the *Wandervogel* had been the itinerant scholar, an anarchist if not a democrat, the aristocratic tendencies of the *Bünde* were reflected, not only in the exemplary image of the knight who set himself a rule of conduct in deliberate contrast to that of the multitude, but also in a strict hierarchy within the *Bund.*[15] . . .

## *IN HITLER'S SHADOW*

The Hitler Youth adopted many of the outward trappings of the youth movement, but differed from the *Bünde* in essential respects. It adopted their uniform and organizational structure (group, tribe, and *gau*); it had its banners,

14 Including, according to their draft constitution, the duty to obtain the leadership's consent to marry. The constitution remained a dead letter.

15 These observations refer mainly to the first heralds of the *Bund,* the *Neupfadfinder.* There was a variety of form and content throughout the youth movement, and a more realistic approach generally prevailed in the late twenties, but there was hardly a single group that was not affected to some extent by early *bündische* ideology.

sang many of the movement's songs (as well as some of its own), and played war games. But whereas the primary concern of the *Bünde* was with group life and the education of individual character, the Hitler Youth was mainly a training center for future members of the S.A. or the S.S. While the *Bünde* retreated into the seclusion of woodlands, or went on long and adventurous journeys abroad, the principal task of the Hitler Youth was to impress the public by ostentatious parades through the streets of big cities. The youth movement engaged in mock fights and war games; a knife was part of the scout's equipment, but it was not to be used to wound or kill. The Hitler Youth, on the other hand, took part in frequent street fights in which weapons were freely used. Opponents were attacked and sometimes killed in these brawls, which occasioned some casualties among the Hitler Youth themselves, including the twenty-one "martyrs" of the "years of struggle." The overwhelming majority of *Bünde* members were high-school students, whereas, according to their own statistics, only twelve percent of the Hitler Youth were from secondary schools; the bulk of them were of working-class origin and many were unemployed.[16] Middle-class youth who joined Hitler's party were more likely to have belonged to the National Socialist *Schülerbund,* and some of them were group leaders in the *Jungvolk,* the junior section of the Hitler Youth for those between ten and fourteen years of age.

The leaders of the Hitler Youth were greatly irritated by what they regarded as a patronizing attitude in those circles of the *bündische* youth which professed *sympathy* with National Socialism. These sympathizers were always saying that the Hitler Youth were of course doing a useful and necessary work, but that it was "not our work."[17] Other *bündische* critics even deplored the Hitler Youth's total involvement in politics and its utter submission to the party, and one of them cast doubt upon the party's dogmatic omniscience, quoting Cromwell's remark that "he who knows not whither he goes, goes furthest."[18] They accused Gruber and von Schirach of trying to destroy the *Bünde,* and blamed them for the bodily violence practiced against their members.[19] But what infuriated the Hitler Youth most of all was the calm expectation of the right-wing *Bünde* that the key positions in the coming Third Reich would be theirs by right, for had they not paved the way and trained an élite for the new dispensation?

There were leaders of the *Bünde* who went over to the Hitler Youth in the twenties; but not all of them stayed the course, and some came to grief in the Third Reich.[20]

16 Günter Kaufmann, *Das kommende Deutschland* (Berlin, 1943), p. 19. There are no means of checking these figures, but there is good reason to believe that a fairly high proportion came from lower middle-class families who had been "proletarianized" during the years of inflation and economic crisis.

17 W. Fabricius in *Die Kommenden,* 13 December 1929.

18 G. Rebsch, *ibid.,* 28 March 1930.

19 W. Müller, *ibid.,* 19 July 1929.

20 According to a National Socialist source, 400 members of the *Bünde,* and 300 former members of the Socialist and Communist youth organizations (including the former secretary of the Communist youth), joined the Hitler Youth in 1929. *N. S. Monatshefte,* 5, 1930, p. 59. These figures cannot, of course, be checked.

The Hitler Youth undoubtedly had its share of misguided idealists, but the boys who were induced to join it (there were very few girls in it before 1933) had neither the makings nor the aspirations of the "ideal *bündisch* type"; it therefore attracted comparatively few of the members of the *bündisch* élite, who looked upon it as a collection of uncouth upstarts.[21] It appealed most of all to mass organizations on the fringe of the youth movement, such as the gymnasts and the Protestant youth groups. Leopold Cordier, one of the leading figures in the Protestant youth movement, estimated that in 1931 about seventy percent of the members of the "Bible Circles" were already under National Socialist influence, and an even higher figure was put forward by another Protestant observer. Many leaders of the Protestant *Bünde* attempted to resist the rising flood, but were soon swept aside, and the groups which tried to oppose it by declaring that membership of the Hitler movement and of their own confessional body were incompatible had as little success.[22]

It was National Socialism, not the Hitler Youth, that made such a powerful appeal to young Germans, above all by its activist character.[23] In vivid contrast to the interminable discussions of the *Bünde,* elaborating ideals that were to be realized in some indefinite future, Hitler affirmed that the hour had already struck; the day of national salvation had arrived. The *Bünde* had wanted their members to understand that all the different aspects and facets of the political problem had to be studied, each from its own angle, before a political judgment could be valid and comprehensive. Commendable in itself, this relativistic approach was also their weakness, and made them an easier prey to the fanaticism and one-sidedness of National Socialism. While the *Bünde* were talking about sacrifice, their rivals were demanding, and getting, immediate action.[24] Facing the rising tide of National Socialism, more and more of the *bündische* youth feared that history would pass them by, and felt incapable of remaining inactive. The cry for political engagement awakened a profound response in such a period of disarray and desperation. It must be remembered that the middle classes were hardly less seriously hit by unemployment than the working class; everything seemed undermined by the general economic decline and the specter of academic and white-collared poverty was becoming a grim reality. Choosing Hitler was not an act of political decision, not the choice of a known program or ideology; it was simply joining a quasi-religious mass-movement as an act of

21 The chief exception was the *Junabu,* some sections of which went over to Hitler in 1930.

22 Leopold Cordier in the *Evangelische Jugendführung,* 3, 1931, p. 70; Manfred Müller, quoted in M. Priepke . . . [*Die evangelische Jugend im Widerstand gegen das Dritte Reich von 1933 bis 1936* (Frankford, 1960)], p. 17.

23 The *Jungmannschaft* of almost all the *Bünde* and the Protestant youth are in their majority either members of the NSDAP or its storm troops and youth sections, or about to join the party" (Werner Kindt in *Das junge Deutschland,* 12, 1932, p. 397).

24 For a critique of the relativism of the *Bünde*'s thinking as the source of their weakness in confrontation with National Socialism, see G. Rebsch, quoted in *Wille und Werk,* 1, 1930, pp. 6–7.

faith. Rational misgivings about the relevance of Hitler's professions to the solution of Germany's real problems cannot have been entirely absent from the minds of many, but they were perfectly willing to surrender their own critical judgement. It meant abandoning democracy and freedom as impotent and discredited ideas and trusting the Führer, who would know best what to do.[25]

25 A leading member of the *Bünde* complained bitterly about the "shocking lack of independence among our older members" who preferred to be fellow travelers rather than to think for themselves. "They trust one man who is to be in charge of everything" (*Der Bund,* 12, 1932, p. 169). Erik H. Erikson, an American psychoanalyst of German origin, touched the very kernel of the problem, observing several years later that Hitler had replaced the complicated conflict of adolescence with a simple pattern of hypnotic action.

PAUL WILKINSON

# ENGLISH YOUTH MOVEMENTS

A recent survey[1] using a national sample has shown that 34 percent of males born between 1901 and 1920 claimed to have belonged to the Boy Scouts, and that a further 14 percent claimed membership in the Boys Brigade. Even allowing for a small amount of dual membership, it is reasonable to assume that around 40 percent of all men in this age group have, at some stage in their lives, been brought into touch with one of the two predominant youths movements in Britain. The popular impact of these movements has been enormous, yet they have received scant attention in historical writing, which is all the more surprising given the abundance of colorful material on their early history available at their national headquarters.[2] Still more colorful, often bizarre, are the histories

From Paul Wilkinson, "English Youth Movements, 1908–30," *Journal of Contemporary History,* vol. IV, no 2, pp. 3–4, 14–17, 22, by permission of George Weidenfeld and Nicolson, London.

1 The survey was carried out by Mass Observation in Spring 1966, using a sample of 2000 adults. 59 percent of all men interviewed and 52 percent of all women said that at some time they had belonged to one or more of the uniformed youth movements.

2 Archives of a fairly comprehensive nature (minute books, administrative memoranda, complete sets of early publications, etc.) are held at the headquarters of The Scout Association, The Boys Brigade, and The Church Lads Brigade. It is from their reports and files that the figures in this essay have been taken.

of the small woodcraft movements, the Order or Woodcraft Chivalry, the Kibbo Kift Kindred and the Woodcraft Folk, that attempted to create a new kind of youth movement in England in the 1920s. One is forced to conclude that they have been ignored because of their essentially Fabian and pacific role, because they eschewed involvement in extremist political movements, and because of the very success and social acceptance of the established movements, the Scouts and the Brigades.

The interesting thing about the English movements, in contrast to the continental, is why they did *not* become vehicles of overt political protest or instruments of party political manipulation. It is temptingly simple, but misleading, to suggest as the reason the relatively stable conditions in English society: even in the midst of depression the degree of economic or social dislocation was not intolerable; in war the country was neither defeated nor humiliated; the general willingness of successive governments to introduce piecemeal social reforms. One would then have to explain the reasons for this stability. Young and adult alike clearly experienced the tensions and pressures that crowded in on their everyday lives, whether in sustaining an exhausting and costly war, or fighting for their personal or national economic survival.

What then were the moral and psychological resources within English society, and in particular within the young generation, which helped them to take these strains? I suggest that the mass youth movements were themselves important agencies in the creation of these resources. They fulfilled this role by a series of imaginative and original responses to the demands and pressures on the young generation. The simple model of a rebellious, nihilistic youth standing against adult values and institutions does not fit the English case. There was a far more complex and subtle intergenerational dialectic of pressure, response, leadership, and collaboration. The ambiguities and inner contradictions of the movements are illustrated in their history and in that of some of their less well known competitors. . . .

The outbreak of war in 1914 gave the Scouts and their leaders an opportunity to show their value as a patriotic and enthusiastic auxiliary national service. Baden-Powell, keen for his boys to show their worth Mafeking style, issued a Mobilization Order and listed the tasks they could undertake under the direction of Chief Constables; these included guarding against sabotage, messenger duties, organizing relief measures, and establishing first aid, dressing or nursing stations, refuges and soup kitchens.[3] Some of their duties on the home front, such as giving air raid warnings and sounding the all clear on their bugles, could often expose them to danger. In other roles, such as working as bellboys on Birmingham's trams and helping with the flax harvest, they released large numbers of men for more urgent tasks and for military service.[4]

3 See *B-P's Scouts,* 73, and circular letter in Scout Association archives, Vol. 3, Ref. 68.

4 Cf. Asa Briggs, *History of Birmingham,* II (London, 1952), 209; Scout Association archives, Vol. 3A, Ref. 29.

Many ex-Scouts and Brigade members, of course, volunteered or were conscripted into the armed forces. Many, like Jack Travers Cornwell, the ex-Scout who won the V.C. at Jutland, were entered on the agonizingly lengthening roll of honor. Many more, like John Hargrave (who has described how he had to teach his own officer how to orient a map[5]), proved the value of Boy Scout resourcefulness and practical training, loyalty and dependability. They formed the backbone of the citizen armies.

While some of the boys were held spellbound by accounts of the fighting and worshipped the young officers as heroes,[6] many of the soldiers at the front were experiencing a change in attitude. The frustration, disgust, and anger expressed in Graves's *Goodbye to All That* and Sassoon's *Memoirs of an Infantry Officer* reflected the feelings of legions of less articulate cannon-fodder. Baden-Powell was sufficiently imaginative and responsive to grasp the change in the national mood, the revulsion against the war, against the sacrifices it had exacted, and against a social system that, it was widely felt, had somehow been responsible both for Britain's involvement in the war and for the disastrous losses. As early as September 1914 he had written: "the lessons of this war . . . should not then be thrown away and forgotten; they should give urgent reason for a more effective education in the brotherhood of man . . . with the dawn of peace . . . our Scout brotherhood may take a big place in the scheme of uniting the nations."[7]

Imperialism was cast aside in favor of the League of Nations idea, and in the 1920s and 1930s Scouting was notable for its well publicized international jamborees, and its phenomenal growth into the largest youth movement in the world. At the same time Baden-Powell stressed that peaceful reconstruction and advance at home could be achieved only by preserving class unity and avoiding the infection of bolshevism:

> Reconstruction after the war may bring about the best democratic government with ultimate prosperity—and peace for all: at the same time it may not, unless we are very careful. . . . There are men who, through their orators and their literature, preach class hatred and down with everything. . . . It is simple mad Bolshevism such as might bring about not merely the downfall of capitalists but the ruin of the great mass of quiet steady-going citizens and wage-earners.[8]

Baden-Powell knew that he was expressing the views of the great mass of steady-going citizens; they followed him in his League of Nations internationalism and

5 John Hargrave, *Suvla Bay Landing* (London, 1965), Chapter 2.

6 See, for example, The Earl of Lytton, *Antony: A Record of Youth* (London, 1935), 20–21, for an account of Antony Knebworth's experience as a schoolboy scout. An ex-Scout Commissioner, Captain Roland Phillips, visited the school and told "lovely yarns about the front." Antony (aged 13) wrote: "We have got a God in the room. . . . He is talking so well that he makes you think you are in the trenches."

7 "The War," in *The Scouter* (September 1914), reprinted in *B-P's Outlook* (London, 1941).

8 Baden-Powell, *Scouting towards Reconstruction* (London, 1918), 12.

his firm antibolshevism. Scouting had placed itself shrewdly and securely at the liberal center of the British ideological spectrum. Only the minority on the extreme left showed real hostility to Scouting in the interwar period—the Young Communist League described it as an "anti-working-class organization."[9] Such denunciations were not taken seriously by the general public. For them Scouting had proved itself politically safe and reasonably adaptable; one of the mistakes its rivals made in the 1920s was to underestimate the extent to which Scouting could adapt its image to meet new conditions. The climax of Scouting's interwar internationalism was reached at its coming-of-age Jamboree in 1929 held at Birkenhead. At this vast tented camp of over thirty thousand scouts, contingents from forty-two nations represented a two-million-strong movement. In his address to the Jamboree Baden-Powell proudly proclaimed: "We alone have the universal ear of the young. Let us set about teaching that the highest virtues are friendliness and good-will. And there will be no more war."[10]

In the United Kingdom Scouting also expanded its appeal by catering for a wider age range. The original scheme was aimed primarily at boys between eleven and fifteen. The Wolf Cub sections for the younger boys were started in 1914. The problem of the older boy remained. When he reached the age of fifteen, the average boy scout had left full time schooling and was anxious to leave the world of smaller boys and short trousers behind him: it was difficult to retain any but the keenest among them. To meet this need, Rover sections were developed in the 1920s and in 1923 Rover Regulations, stipulating a minimum age limit of seventeen, and laying down the procedure for Rover scout tests, were issued by Headquarters.[11] Baden-Powell wrote *Rovering to Success* (1922), prescribing a chivalric code of service to the community, patriotism, and "clean living" for the Rover. Despite these efforts, Rover sections had only a minor share in the enormous expansion of Scouting in Britain in the 1920s. Although total membership almost doubled between 1920 and 1930, from 232,758 to 422,662, in the latter year Rovers were still outnumbered by scout leaders.

By the mid-twenties the predominant position of Scouting as a British mass youth movement was apparently unshakable. Attempts to form a new type of youth movement had no chance of displacing it. . . .

The successful English youth movements were not simply movements of protest by the young. Rather they were carefully designed attempts to respond to their needs and demands, to harness their energies for great causes approved by their adult leaders—imperial defense, national defense, international cooperation, national efficiency, and so on. As educational movements they had no need to challenge the political status quo. They brought about improvements in training and recreational facilities, physical fitness (and incidentally increased oppor-

9 Young Communist League circular dated 19 October 1927, signed by William Rust, then national secretary.

10 Scout Association archives, Vol. 13. Ref. 17.

11 *Policy, Organization & Rules,* Boy Scouts Association (1923).

tunities for social advancement) on behalf of the less privileged. Tactically they were restricted to the pace permitted by their patrons among the political, ecclesiastic, and military elites. They should therefore be regarded as movements not of protest, but of peaceful reconstruction and reform. Through their agency many demands of the young were contained, absorbed, and redirected, with astonishing success. . . .

—JOHN ARDAGH

# FRENCH YOUTH WITH A DUSTY ANSWER

It was in the corridors of the new Préfecture building near the Bastille, one day in 1965, that I had my own Gibbonian moment of awareness of the rise of a huge new generation in France. Usually one expects French public offices to be filled with shuffling, elderly bureaucrats and messengers, spun about with the cobwebs of the Third Republic, and nothing is more typical of this than the old Préfecture in the Hôtel de Ville. Suddenly in this new annex, as the clock struck noon for lunch, I was besieged by hundreds of chattering clerks and typists, few of them over thirty. Visibly I saw confirmation of the statistics: there are more than twice as many people under twenty-five in France today as in 1939, although the population has risen only 15 percent. In many offices the old *huissiers* with their stained suits and sad faces are being replaced by sleek young *hôtesses* with public-relations smiles; and it is easy to find scores of other symptoms, too, of France's demographic facelift and of the new national emphasis on youth.

Every Frenchman today professes his faith in *la jeunesse. Une France jeune—soyez jeune—il faut l'esprit jeune*—the phrases tumble daily from the mouths of politicians and the pages of glossy magazines, as though youth were synonymous with virtue. In a country previously dominated by the prerogatives of age and hierarchy, this marks a striking change of heart. "*We* may have failed—but *les jeunes,* they are serious, they are made of good stuff, they will do better than us": this a comment you sometimes hear from older people still ashamed of the defeats of recent decades. Often this kind of sentiment seems to be based more on hopeful thinking than on reason: few older people, even parents and teachers, claim to know what this reticent and elusive new generation is really like. But at least they are given more public attention than ever before. In their name a great national debate on education is now raging, and the highly traditional structure of French schools and universities is being remodeled to an extent unparalleled since Napoleon. . . .

## *LA JEUNESSE:* NOT SO MUCH REBELS, MERELY CHUMS

"*Mais que pensent les jeunes?*" ask the headlines in a constant stream of magazine articles: "*Nos jeunes, qui sont-ils?*" And few of them can find an easy answer. What are they like, this mysterious new generation, for whom all the educational crusades are being fought? Ostensibly, they are following much the same paths as modern youth in other Western countries, though less aggressively than in Britain. They have their own powerful new consumer market for music, clothes, and cars; their own world of young singing idols like Johnny Hallyday and Françoise Hardy, their own fringe minorities of delinquents and beatniks with hair-styles imported from London. All, or nearly all, have far more freedom from parents than cloistered French youth had before the war. Many are conscious of the gulf between their own morality and that of the older generation.

And that older generation in turn has become aware of youth as never before. *La Jeunesse* is now a slogan, a doctrine of faith in the future, a symbol of France's recovered vitality. For more than a century this used to be an adult-dominated country, where teenagers were treated as small-scale adults and were not expected to exist as a national group in their own right. Now the grown-up world has woken up, as it were, to the existence of a neglected minority in its midst, with its separate values and needs. Youth is solicited, analyzed, indulged (except by its teachers). But this parental lip-service to the new cult of youth is not always accompanied by actual understanding of individuals. And in some ways the youthful revolution *à l'anglaise* is more apparent than real in France; or at least, it has not yet found proper expression.

In the first decade or so after the war, many of the most important changes in France were due to a new generation rising against the standards of its elders—from the young farmers of the JAC to the cinema's *nouvelle vague.* And other phenomena (St. Tropez, Françoise Sagan, the early existentialists) gave the world a popular image of French youth in open revolt. Today, in the late

'60s, that image has become strangely deceptive. As often as not, older people nowadays complain, "But the young, they're so docile, so conformist." While Britain's youth have now leapt ahead in precocious emancipation, the French are still, relatively, under the shadow of school and parents. Seduced by prosperity and placated by adult acceptance, many of them seem to be tamed into a listless submissiveness, or else into a feeling of impotence.

The climate of 1945 was very different from today's: more austere, but also more adventurous. The upheavals of wartime had broken down some of the barriers that previously kept youth in its place, and an idealistic new generation was able gradually to make lasting inroads into the *positions acquises* of the age-hierarchy. It happened most strikingly in agriculture, and in the civil service and industry where some older men emerged discredited from the Occupation and young ones took their place. It is remarkable how youthful many of the postwar pioneers were at the outset: Leclerc was twenty-three when he began his cut-price campaign in Brittany, and Planchon founded his Villeurbanne theatre at twenty-one. Today the impetus of this generation is still driving forward, in nearly every field; and many of its leaders, now around forty, are in key national positions. But their successors, now around forty, born into an age of greater ease and acceptance, have seldom shown the same innovating spirit. This has been even more apparent in the intellectual world. After the Liberation, many young people flocked excitedly around Sartre and Camus at St.-Germain-des-Prés, eager to revolt against their bourgeois backgrounds and help to forge a better world. This existentialist climate has since gradually dissipated. The Sartrian disciples of those days have mostly settled down and become prosperous, and many are now leading the bourgeois lives they once denounced. Their young successors either find money-making, fast cars and hi-fi more appealing than philosophy; or else they are cynical and dispirited at the antibourgeois rebellion's failure to create a new society.

In the mid 1950s a few isolated and much-publicized events, vaguely influenced by existentialism, managed to sustain the impression of a generalized youthful revolt. In 1954 the eighteen-year-old Françoise Sagan, daughter of an industrialist, published her first novel, *Bonjour Tristesse.* Her sophisticated world of whisky and wealth was some steps away from the severe, intellectual *milieu* of the true existentialists; but her heroine's cool disillusion and rejection of social morality sounded a note that seemed to borrow something, however ill digested, from the ideas of Sartre. Two years later the young director Roger Vadim took a little-known actress to a modest Riviera fishing-port and there made on location *Et Dieu créa la femme.* And God-knows-who created Bardot and St. Tropez. Thousands from *une certaine jeunesse* rushed there at once. France and the world were amazed. Was this what French youth was like? Was Sagan's free-living heroine typical of French girls of eighteen? The next year, in 1958, the veteran director Marcel Carné made a film, *Les Tricheurs,* that seemed to confirm the picture. He described a *milieu* of young Parisians, bohemian "intellectuals" and idle bourgeois students from good homes, united in the same anarchic dissipation, breaking up their parents' smart flats with wild parties, stealing and cheating and casually fornicating. According to Carné, everyone in this *milieu* is a *tricheur* (cheat) and honest feelings are taboo: in the climax of the film, bohemian slut and weak rich *fils-à-papa* do genuinely fall in love, but dare not admit it to each other and this leads to tragedy. The girl, trapped in her own depravity, cannot take the strain any more, drives off into the night in a stolen car, and crashes to her death. Another character (a nice one, a sort of Greek chorus) then blames it all on society. As you can see, a sensational and contrived film, hardly a great work of art; but it did carry a certain veracity, and Carné claimed that he knew this world intimately and had drawn his portraits from life. The film caused more of a stir than any other in France for years: many pressure-groups tried to ban it, and *l'Exprèss* gleefully published a twelve-page supplement, "Qui sont les tricheurs?" Some people thought that the film's portrait was out of date and related to a St.-Germain-des-Prés of the late '40s, to the phony existentialists who mistook liberty for license. Others felt it was still true, of a minority. There are still some *tricheurs,* even today, just as the early Sagan novels were clearly based on experience and the crowds around the bars and beaches of St. Tropez are patently no fiction. The *tricheurs* borrowed from existentialism its permissiveness without its responsibility and took it as a cue to do just what they liked: when the young bohemian Mephistopheles of Carné's film goes into a shop to steal a record that he does not want, he claims he is performing the perfect Gidean or Sartrian *acte gratuit.* This muddled intellectual self-justification has underlain a good part of the fringe rebellions among postwar French youth—though one can hardly claim that every St. Tropez lay-about is motivated by such philosophical principles.

The St. Tropez phenomenon has had plenty of postwar counterparts in Chelsea, California, and elsewhere. What is remarkable here is its intensity in one small, picturesque seaside location. The whole affair was hardly Vadim's fault, or Bardot's: the publicists of *Paris-Match* and other such papers pounced on them while they were filming, and somehow managed to inspire a popular cult that answered a youthful need. Bardot was built into a symbol of sensualist emancipation—and the young crowds came, some innocently and some less so, to find and to worship their goddess. Of course they simply drove her away: she had bought a villa just outside St. Tropez, where she still spends part of each year, but she was soon forced to build a high wall around it, and neither she nor any other star today dares to be seen in the streets or cafés of the town, through fear of being mobbed by adoring fans. Yet the crowds still come, from every part of the world, impelled by the new religion of glamour and stardom, or simply by curiosity. I met a Dominican priest in St. Tropez who told me, "This place is a kind of Lourdes. Young people feel a lack in their lives today, they want to be cured of their desolate yearnings, so they come here to be touched by magic and reborn. But they go away disappointed. All they find is each other." Many of the most vicious elements in St. Tropez today are foreign, not French—the hordes of young German thugs and paederasts, the Chelseaites, the Swedes, the American beats. But the French are still there too in plenty; the girls of little more than sixteen who arrive from Paris without a penny and see how far their charms can carry them. Any summer night you can see them by the score, wide-eyed popsies with gaudy jeans, bare midriffs, and Bardot hair-styles, hanging around the modish bars like l'Escale, waiting for the next well-heeled pick-up who will let them sponge and stay a few more days.

Many of the boys and girls of this kind of milieu, in Paris or St. Tropez, come from cultured, conventional homes and have broken with their families. But they are not typical, totalling perhaps a few thousand. Many other young people today, especially students, seem to have managed to extricate themselves from old-style bourgeois morality in a less irresponsible manner; and if they are discreet, even while still living at home they can practice a good deal of Sartrian "sincerity" in their private lives. Girls have become readier to undertake affairs before marriage, but without ceasing to be *sérieuses.* As one Parisian student told me, "It's not that we're trying to set up counter-conventions like the *tricheurs.* We're not against our parents' morality, we ignore it. The basis of our behavior is rejection of constraint, and within this framework we are very moral."

Among the less intellectual teenagers, the archetype today is not a *tricheur* but a *copain*—the word means "chum" or "pal." And in the 1960s it is the extraordinary pop movement of the *copains,* innocent and mildly charming but vapid, that has given a new brand-image to the whole of French youth and pushed the precocious cynicism of Sagan firmly on to the sidelines. A new generation, sipping its Coca-Colas, looks less to Bardot the sex-kitten than to Sylvie Vartan, chirpy little chum and elder sister, or to Françoise Hardy huskily leading all-the-boys-and-girls-of-her-age-hand-in-hand.

This movement began in 1959 when Daniel Filipacchi, a young disc-jockey and former *Paris-Match* photographer, launched a jazz program on Europe Number One radio and borrowed the title of a song by Gilbert Bécaud to call it *Salut les Copains.* Instantly it was a smash-hit with teenagers, who were tired of sharing Brassens and Trenet with their elders and wanted something swinging and modern of their own, like the Americans had. Soon the program was running for two hours nightly, using mainly American material.

Around the same period an obscure bar near the Opéra, the Golf Drouot, turned itself into a kind of teenagers' cabaret and so provided a breeding-ground for the first of France's own young pop singers. There a boy of sixteen with fair curly hair and an ugly mouth made his hesitant *début* under the name of Johnny Hallyday, singing American rock 'n' roll tunes in French. Filipacchi took him up—and a whole generation chose Johnny as their idol and self-image. French pop was born. He was followed by scores of others—besides Sylvie and Françoise (surnames are taboo among *copains*), the best known have been

Richard Anthony, Claude François, Adamo, Sheila, France Gall. And in 1962 Filipacchi astutely complemented his radio show with a glossy magazine also called *Salut les Copains,* which reached and has held a sale of a million copies a month and gets 10,000 fan letters a week. Its rather similar sister monthly for girls, *Mademoiselle Age Tendre,* sells 800,000—both of them astoundingly high circulations for France.

At first the movement was highly derivative, much more so than its Liverpool equivalent. Not only did the stars borrow American tunes; many of them found it smart to adopt Anglo-Saxon names like Dick Rivers and Eddy Mitchell; Hallyday's real name is Jean-Philippe Smet. Gradually, however, the *copains* have acquired a certain French style of their own, less virile and inventive, more romantic and sentimental, than either Beatledom or American folk and rock. Some of them, including Johnny and Françoise, composed and write many of their own songs, and today probably about half the *copains'* material is home-grown and the rest imported and translated. The whole affair is basically a shrewd commercial operation by Filipacchi, who by now is one of the richest men in France. But he and his young stars can afford their mink and Ferraris just because they have managed to provide millions with an outlet of self-identification they were looking for. The tradition of modern popular songs is much older and stronger in France than in Britain, but it has, therefore, belonged to an older generation, from Piaf through to Aznavour. Teenagers resented these as their parents' idols. But their own Johnny, singing ingenuously about being sixteen and its problems, was themselves and the boy next door. At his concerts, children wave and shout hallo: "He's young, he's gay, he's just like us," said one girl of fourteen, "and not at all like a real music-hall star. So we love him." Idols and fans are all equally *copains* together, and all are *tu:* this is the carefully fostered principle of their success, and if any idol breaks the code and behaves like an aloof Hollywood star, he is finished.

Parents at first were a little anxious, as gramophone-record sales shot into scores of millions and Hallyday became the most-photographed male in France after de Gaulle. Their concern reached its height after the night of 22 June 1963, when Filipacchi staged a "live" open-air broadcast from the Place de la Nation in Paris, and 150,000 boys and girls, twisting and rocking, surged into the square and brushed aside the police. It was the first time in French history that teenagers had displayed their solidarity in public, on this scale. Some observers saw it as a political portent, comparing it with the mass-hysteria of the Nazi rallies. A few arrests were made and an enquiry was ordered. A little damage had been done to cars and windows, but this was due simply to the weight of the crowds, and to the presence among them of a handful of hooligans. Once the fuss had blown over, it became clear that the famous *Nuit de la Nation* was really quite innocent: the kids had simply wanted to dance, and to have a look at their heroes.

Parents soon came to see there was nothing much to worry about. Filipacchi, in fact, has always been shrewd enough to steer the *copains* away from rebellious paths that might have got him into trouble. Their revolt has been purely one of music and rhythm, not of morals. The very phrase *Salut les Copains* ("Hello, Chums!") gives some idea of the *Boys' Own Paper* or *True Romance* spirit of the thing; and so harmless is the magazine that the Catholic Church has felt safely able to copy it with its own rival monthly for the teenage faithful, *Formidable,* a bit more varied and a bit less artfully glossy but otherwise much the same. Filipacchi's editor-in-chief, Raymond Mouly, a young man in black leather jacket and side-whiskers, told me: "I suppose we've simply created a new conformism, inevitably. But there's still something zippy and fresh about us—and we needed a change from Yves Montand. What we're really doing is to prolong the age of innocence, the *âge tendre.* Life is easier than in 1945, and people have more time to live their youth."

This belongs to a typically French romantic tradition that seems to hark straight back to Gérard de Nérval and *Le Grand Meaulnes:* adolescents playing at love, sometimes touched by melancholy and *ennui* but not by cynicism or social indignation. Browse through the brilliantly edited pages of *Salut les Copains* and you will see what these idols are like, or at least how they are presented to be. Huge snazzy color photos in the manner of *Un homme et une femme* show the various stars wandering hand in hand through autumn woodlands or lazing on Mediterranean beaches. Photo-articles forty pages long proclaim *Tout tout tout sur Sylvie* and *Tout tout tout sur Johnny:* that Sylvie dislikes celery and likes colored candles, that Johnny likes hot-dogs and dislikes umbrellas. Johnny, philistine and petit-bourgeois, mad about cars and motor-bikes, is in reality much as he is made to seem; he is the perfect modern folk-hero and looks exactly like any French youth you see hanging around the streets with his *vélo* on a Sunday. Sylvie, Bulgarian by birth, is more intellectual: she used to read philosophy on the Métro before she became famous, and is known as *la collégienne du twist.* But with her tulip-mouth, her long ash-blonde curls and sturdy little figure, she projects the perfect image of the jolly bobby-soxer who's become a star by mistake; and when she bounces on to the stage of the Olympia music-hall as if it were an end-of-term concert, to trill *Ce soir, je serai la plus belle pour aller danser,* every *midinette* in the audience identifies with her. In 1965, after a long engagement, Johnny and Sylvie became Mr. and Mrs. Smet: two hundred photographers were present, yet it seemed much closer in spirit to a typical middle-class wedding than, say, to aloof Bardot marrying some foreigner in Las Vegas.

Not all the *copains* conform quite so closely to this tame bourgeois ideal. Françoise Hardy, ex-student of German at the Sorbonne, tall and languid with a spoilt, sulky temperament, has even brought a note of Grecoesque sorrow and self-doubt into some of her recent songs; there is more than a touch of Garbo about her, and she is one of the very few *copains* to have much following among maturer people as well as teenagers. But she does keep roughly in line with the Filipacchi ethic, and her *mystère* does not simmer into actual revolt. However, an intruder of a much more violent sort, calling himself Antoine, did manage to burst into the *copain* world briefly in 1966: his hair was far longer than Lennon's or Jagger's (shocking by most *copain* standards), and, instead of sweet love-lyrics, the songs he wrote and then growled at the audience were full of bitter, socially-conscious nihilism that any intellectual beatnik might have envied. His clamorous success indicated that some French youth, at least, hankered for a stronger diet than chummery. But Filipacchi was against him, so was French adulthood; and he fizzled out.

And what will happen to the *copains*? After tiffs and reconciliations that filled all the headlines, the Smets are now parents in their twenties, growing away fast from their teenage equals. *"Adieu les copains!"* wrote *l'Exprèss* after their wedding; "Johnny and Sylvie are *copains*. Mr. and Mrs. Smet will try to remain stars. And they will have lots more little Ferraris!" Others no doubt will take their place, but the movement may well change or fade. The *copains'* appeal has always been mainly to the less sophisticated middle teens; older or more alert ones have often preferred a more robust nourishment such as Bob Dylan or English pop. A youth in Filipacchi's office who had spent some time in London told me, "I admit your young singers are more mature and original than ours; a group like The Animals, for instance, seem to have firm ideas about modern society. Your youth as a whole is more aggressive, creative, and nonconformist than ours. But they get more freedom."

On its credit side, the *copain* cult may have fostered a kind of sweet romantic comradeship among French youth. Like British pop it has certainly helped in the struggle against delinquency; and unlike British pop it is seldom crudely hostile to real culture. Its idols have undeniable puppy-charm; and, for all the commercial wire-pulling, there has been something spontaneous and infectious about their appeal to French youth in a voice it could recognize as its own. But that voice has not proved a very inspiring one: insipid, somewhat effeminate, content to idolize a safe world of glamour and niceness. Even the melodies are not very exciting. Parents, in fact, can safely look on the *copains* as a harmless way of keeping the children out of mischief. The young things are now being allowed to throw a party on their own; but Mummy and Daddy are on the *qui-vive* upstairs. . . .

In Parisian upper-class society, parents in recent years have resorted to various ingenious devices to keep their teenage children in check. One of the most remakable of these is the *rallye,* a kind of exclusive dancing-club for girls of fifteen to nineteen and their carefully chosen escorts. There are some dozen of these *rallyes* in Paris today; and a boy or girl who is entered for one by his or her mother must expect to spend from four or five years in a steady round of formal parties and dances, under close parental supervision. It helps to steer the young things towards suitable marriages, and to keep them out of mischief. And astonishingly, most of the young things appear to accept this discipline, as teenagers rarely would in London.

Another reason for the French teenager's submissiveness is purely practical: the housing shortage. Emancipation from parents is not so easy when cheap furnished flats or rooms are still such a rarity: three in four of sixteen-to-twenty-four-year-olds live at home until marriage, including 54 percent of young men of twenty-two to twenty-four. Yet even if there were no housing shortage, the picture might not change so radically. It is still considered the "norm" to live with your parents; and very many young people, even when they do have the means to move away, prefer not to do so. This is changing, but not fast. A rich young girl I knew in Paris, who could easily have found and afforded a small flat of her own or with girl-friends, told me just before her wedding at twenty-six: "Now at last I can get away from my mother." In such cases, children are suffering from parents' emotional blackmail; but in millions of other cases it is simply that young French, far more than young Anglo-Saxons or Nordics, seem to remain tied to their parents by psychological cords that they find hard to cut, even when there is no parental pressure. They are still often in the grip of the kind of obsessive child-parent relationships that are such a recurring theme of modern French literature. Perhaps this is why, when they do revolt—against parents or against society more generally—the gesture is all the more extreme, just because it has cost them so much of their inner selves.

Young people will often profess unconventional or progressive ideas in abstract, but in practice when faced with concrete situations will defer to the lead and authority of their elders. I met a twenty-year-old Sorbonne philosophy student, living with his parents in Paris, who delighted me with his mature and profound ideas about modern society and his own destiny, then surprised me by saying, "A few young friends of mine and I have formed a local dramatic club. Luckily, my father runs it for us. You see, without him, none of us would have the right authority, we'd just quarrel." I refrained from replying that, in England, boys much younger and stupider than he were often in charge of the discipline of large schools. But it is plain as daylight that the French school system has a large influence here. It fails to provide any training in group initiative or responsibility, and so throws the child back on parental discipline. It presses him towards an intellectual precocity that is basically conformist. And the severe and formal approach of teachers outwardly inculcates docility, while inwardly producing a kind of frustrated resentment. Perhaps it is reaction against the severity of school, or against the shadow of parents, that makes so many French teenagers behave so very badly when they escape to a different setting. In English towns such as Brighton, where they come *au pair* in the summer, they have a worse reputation for trouble-making than any other nationality. It is often hard to decide whether they are spoilt little brats or sadly deprived. . . .

## *POSTSCRIPT, JULY 1968*

For a few weeks in spring, half of France went joyfully and creatively mad. There were many diverse elements in that madness, and it is still too soon to assess their real significance. On the one hand, I think one should not overlook the purely theatrical element. Although with a part of themselves the French are conservative and attached to security, they also enjoy drama and action and a relief from the boredom of papa-knows-best government; and although the students and *lycéens* were certainly in earnest about their frustrations and injustices, they would not have been human had they not also relished the dramatic break from routine. One American observer has sceptically dismissed the euphoria of May as ''the Club Méditerranée on a nation-wide scale,'' a kind of irresponsible holiday. I would not go nearly as far as that; but I think it is important for foreigners to remember that the ideal of ''revolution' has a very special and romantic appeal in France. And during the crisis many a Frenchman's instincts was to rally emotionally to the challenge of Cohn-Bendit without necessarily sharing his views or his aims. . . .

## EDUCATION

The most astonishing aspect of the May crisis is the new visage it has uncovered of French youth. We thought them docile and conformist, or frivolously *yé-yé;* we knew that a number were serious and idealistic, but most of these were frustrated by a sense of impotence and felt isolated not only from society but from each other. Among those who felt this isolation, and this impotence, were the little group that met around Cohn-Bendit at Nanterre on March 22. Two months later, half the nation was at their side. It needed only this detonator, the Sorbonne revolt of May 3, for French youth to come out of its reserve and discover a solidarity and a force that were always latent but never before expressed. Across France, young people who for years had been nourishing certain hopes, certain feelings, became aware of each other for the first time. This was genuinely a kind of revolution, and French youth and French society will never be quite the same again.

But this is not to say that all French youth, or even a majority of it, shares the views of Cohn-Bendit and Jacques Sauvageot. The small extremist element in the revolt rallied wide sympathy for a while because of its daring and because of the stupid police repression against it; but in itself, it contained many unpleasant and negative aspects of nihilism, violence and irresponsibility. I met many serious students in Paris who at first were delighted by the seizure of the Sorbonne and the outburst of free debate, but later felt that the whole thing had turned sour. This is not very surprising; but if some of the revolutionaries went too far and spoilt their own cause, it does not invalidate the importance of the nationwide movement as a whole. Youth rose up not only against the archaic and muddled education system but also against its own parents, their paternalism, and their strange mixture of over-indulgence and sheer lack of understanding. Family crises broke out ''on a scale the nation has not seen since Dreyfus,'' as one paterfamilias put it. This breach in traditional French parent-child relations carries many dangers, as does any new vacuum; it also carries hope. Exactly as in industry, much will depend on how "les chefs de famille" react.

. . . But *now or never* is the opportunity to tear French education once and for all from its encrusted feudal encasements and reshape it to the needs of a modern society, a technological society but also a human and a just one. Something *will* happen. In education, more than anywhere, people are saying, "I am deeply pessimistic about the short term, but for the longer term I now have new hope."

# SUGGESTED READINGS

## *THE AGONY OF INDUSTRIALIZING (1750–1850)*


ACOMB, EVELYN, and MARVIN BROWN, eds. *French Society and Culture Since the Old Regime* (New York: Holt, Rinehart and Winston, 1966)

COBB, R. C., *The Police and the People: French Popular Protest, 1789–1820* (Oxford: Clarendon Press, 1970)

COBBAN, ALFRED, *The Social Interpretation of the French Revolution* (Cambridge: Cambridge University Press, 1964)

DEANE, PHYLLIS, *The First Industrial Revolution* (Cambridge: Cambridge University Press, 1965)

INGLIS, BRIAN, *Poverty and the Industrial Revolution* (London: Hodder and Stoughton, 1971)

LEFEBVRE, GEORGES, *The Great Fear of 1789: Rural Panic in Revolutionary France* (New York: Pantheon Books, 1973)

MOORE, BARRINGTON, JR., *The Social Origins of Dictatorship and Democracy: Lord and Peasant in the Making of the Modern World* (Boston: Beacon Press, 1966)

OSBORNE, JOHN W., *The Silent Revolution: The Industrial Revolution in England as a Source of Cultural Change* (New York: Scribner's, 1970)

PALMER, R. R., *The Age of the Democratic Revolution,* 2 vols. (Princeton, N.J.: Princeton University Press, 1959–1964)

RANUM, OREST, and PATRICIA RANUM, eds. *Popular Attitudes toward Birth Control in Pre-Industrial France and England* (New York: Harper & Row, 1970)

ROBERTSON, PRISCILLA, *Revolutions of 1848: A Social History* (Princeton, N.J.: Princeton University Press, 1952)

ROBIQUET, JEAN, *Daily Life in the French Revolution* (New York: Macmillan, 1965)

———. *Daily Life in France under Napoleon,* trans. Violet M. MacDonald (New York: Macmillan, 1963)

RUDÉ, GEORGE, *The Crowd in the French Revolution* (New York: Oxford University Press, 1973)

SOBOUL, ALBERT, *The Sans-Culottes* (New York: Doubleday, Anchor Books, 1972)

VUCINICH, WAYNE S., ed. *The Peasant in Nineteenth Century Russia* (Stanford, Calif.: Stanford University Press, 1968)

## ACCELERATION AND SOCIAL CONFLICT (1850–1914)

EVANS, RICHARD J., ed. *Society and Politics in Wilhelmine Germany* (London: Croom Helm, 1978)

GREGG, PAULINE, *A Social and Economic History of Britain, 1760–1970,* 6th ed. (London: George G. Harrap, 1970)

HAMEROW, THEODORE S., *The Social Foundations of German Unification, 1858–1871,* 2 vols. (Princeton, N.J.: Princeton University Press, 1969–1972)

HOBSBAWM, E. J., *Bandits* (New York: Delacorte Press, 1969)

———. *Labouring Men* (London: Weidenfeld and Nicolson, 1964)

———. *The Age of Capital* (New York: Scribner's, 1975)

HOBSBAWM, E. J. and GEORGE RUDÉ, *Captain Swing* (London: Lawrence & Wishart, 1969)

HOM, PAMELA, *Labouring Life in the Victorian Countryside* (Dublin: Gill and Macmillan, 1976)

JUDT, TONY, *Socialism in Provence, 1871–1914: A Study in the Origins of the Modern French Left,* (New York: Cambridge University Press, 1979)

MORAZE, CHARLES M., *The Triumph of the Middle Classes: A Study of European Values in the Nineteenth Century,* trans. Peter Wait and Barbara Ferryan (London: Weidenfeld and Nicolson, 1966)

PRICE, ROGER, *The French Second Republic: A Social History* (Ithaca, N.Y.: Cornell University Press, 1972)

SEABROOK, JEREMY, *The Unprivileged* (London: Longmans, Green, 1967)

SHEENAN, JAMES J., ed. *Industrialization and Industrial Labor in Nineteenth-Century Europe* (New York: John Wiley, 1973)

STEARNS, PETER N., *European Society in Upheaval: Social History since 1800* (New York: Macmillan, 1967)

STEDMAN-JONES, GARETH, *Outcast London* (Oxford: Clarendon Press, 1971)

TOBIAS, J. J., *Crime and Industrial Society in the Nineteenth Century* (New York: Schocken Books, 1968)

WEBER, EUGEN, *Peasants Into Frenchmen* (Stanford, Calif.: Stanford University Press, 1976)

WUNDERLICH, FRIEDA, *Farm Labor in Germany, 1810–1945* (Princeton, N.J.: Princeton University Press, 1961)

ZELDIN, THEODORE, *France 1848–1945,* Vol. I: *Ambition, Love and Politics;* Vol II: *Intellect, Taste and Anxiety* (Oxford: Clarenden Press, 1973, 1977)

## *BRAVE NEW EUROPE: 1914 TO THE PRESENT*

ALLEN, WILLIAM S., *The Nazi Seizure of Power: The Experience of a Single German Town, 1930–1935* (Chicago: Quadrangle, 1965)

BLYTHE, RONALD, *Akenfield: Portrait of an English Village* (New York: Pantheon, 1969)

CRITCHLEY, T. A., *The Conquest of Violence: Order and Liberty in Britain* (New York: Schocken Books, 1970)

DAHRENDORF, RALF, *Society and Democracy in Germany* (Garden City, N.Y.: Doubleday, 1967)

DUPEAUX, GEORGES, *French Society, 1789–1970* (London: Methuen, 1976)

EVANS, RICHARD. *The Feminist Movement in Germany 1894–1933* (London: Sage Publications, 1976)

FUSSEL, PAUL, *The Great War in Modern Memory* (New York: Oxford University Press, 1975)

MARWICK, ARTHUR, *The Deluge: British Society and the First World War* (New York: Norton, 1965)

MAYS, JOHN B., *The Introspective Society* (London: Sheed & Ward, 1968)

MEISSNER, BORIS, ed. *Social Change in the Soviet Union* (Notre Dame, Ind.: University of Notre Dame Press, 1972)

MILLAR, JAMES R., ed. *The Soviet Rural Community* (Urbana: University of Illinois Press, 1971)

MOSSE, GEORGE L., *Nazi Culture* (New York: Grosset and Dunlap, 1966)

SAMPSON, ANTHONY, *Anatomy of Europe* (New York: Harper & Row, 1968)

SCHOENBAUM, DAVID, *Hitler's Social Revolution: Class and Status in Nazi Germany 1933–1939* (New York: Doubleday, 1967)

SONTAG, RAYMOND, *A Broken World, 1919–1939* (New York: Harper & Row, 1971)

STEPHENSON, JILL, *Women in Nazi Society* (New York: Harper & Row, 1975)

STRACHVERA, PETER D., *Nazi Youth in the Weimar Republic* (Santa Barbara, Calif.: Clio Press, 1975)

WRIGHT, GORDON, *Rural Revolution in France* (Stanford, Calif.: Stanford University Press, 1964)